ESSENTIALS OF SUBFILE PROGRAMMING

AND ADVANCED TOPICS IN RPG

PHIL LEVINSON

DUKE PRESS

A Division of
DUKE COMMUNICATIONS INTERNATIONAL
221 E. 29th Street • Loveland, CO 80538
(800) 621-1544 • (970) 663-4700
www.dukepress.com

Library of Congress Cataloging-in-Publication Data

Levinson, Phil, 1947–
    Essentials of subfile programming and advanced topics in RPG /
by Phil Levinson.
    p. cm.
    Includes index.
    ISBN 1-882419-64-2
    1. IBM AS/400 (Computer)—Programming. 2. RPG (Computer program
language) I. Title.
    QA76.8.I25919 L48 1998
    005.74—ddc21

                                                                    98-8863
                                                                    CIP

Published by DUKE PRESS
DUKE COMMUNICATIONS INTERNATIONAL
Loveland, Colorado

Copyright © 1998 by Phil Levinson

This book was printed and bound in Canada.

ISBN 1-882419-64-2

1 2 3 4 5 6 7 WL 0 9 8

To my loving bride, Janice,
and our two bundles of joy,
Jeremy and Joshua.

Acknowledgments

Many people made this textbook possible, among them Bryon Escobar and the Cooper Bussman IT team, who provided me with resources and real-world experiences; Dean Frank Thoendal and Vice President Dan Steadman of Jefferson College, who provided confidence and support; my students, who inspired me to continue to develop this material and identified where improvements were needed; my fellow faculty members, who carried an extra load to allow me the time to complete the manuscript; and my family, who made time whenever it was needed. This textbook also would not exist without the guidance and assistance of Veronica Patterson and the other editors and staff of Duke Press.

Table of Contents at a Glance

Table of Contents

Welcome to the World of Subfiles

Many courses for AS/400 programmers stop short of teaching you subfile programming. Subfiles are the AS/400 tool that supports displaying lists of data on the screen, and in today's increasingly screen-based world, you must understand and be able to use them. In fact, every list that you have seen the AS/400 display has been created using the same programming techniques that you will learn in these chapters.

This text introduces you to subfiles and leads you through the process of creating and debugging subfile programs. As new subfile concepts are presented, you will develop and expand the same programs to meet expanded specifications. This approach mirrors the real world in which new specifications continually add to the complexity of interactive programs. You will program interactive displays that help users find the data they need and update records as required. You will learn several techniques for designing screens that help make user displays intuitive and easy to use. In a later chapter, you'll learn to use two tools—journaling and commitment control—that will protect your database's integrity when programs let records be changed.

The two ongoing sets of exercises in this text take you through the process of developing an inventory display screen and a purchase order line display screen with data maintenance capabilities. To get the most from this book, work through all segments of the continued exercises, as well as through the additional bookstore order system project that follows Chapters 5 and 7.

Other advanced topics include using such file-oriented elements as record format level identifiers, the OVRDBF (Override with Database File) and OPNQRYF (Open Query File) CL commands, file and record locks, and file security; mining the file-information and program-status data structures for information; handling errors via the *PSSR subroutine, the INFSR keyword, and the Input/Output operation error indicator; and using data queues for program-to-program communication.

Don't neglect the appendices! Appendix A explores the programming standards you'll meet in most IS departments and takes you beyond them into issues of programming style. Appendix B introduces debugging tools and techniques to support your programming skills. Finally, Appendix C gives you invaluable training in using Screen Design Aid (SDA).

When you interview for a job as an AS/400 programmer, you will be asked about your knowledge of subfiles and other advanced RPG topics. Once you complete this text, its exercises, and the additional bookstore order system project, you'll have a head start on your first programming position or—if you're already a programmer, additional professional development that will count in your department and your company.

Section 1

Essentials of Subfile Programming

Today more than ever, programs and systems are screen-based. Section 1 (Chapters 1 through 7) of *Essentials of Subfile Programming and Advanced Topics in RPG* focuses on screen-based, interactive programs, especially on the use of subfiles. Subfiles are an AS/400 tool used to display lists of data on the screen. In fact, every list that you've seen the AS/400 display can be created with the programming techniques presented in Section 1.

As an AS/400 programmer, you must understand and be able to use subfiles. Chapter 1 introduces subfiles by taking you through the development of simple subfile display screens. You learn to create subfile records, subfile control records, and footer records, as well as to write the RPG code to load, display, and clear a subfile, and to manage the no-records case.

Chapter 2 shows you how to modify programs to accept user options for deleting and changing records. You'll learn to use the READC (Read the Next Changed Record) operation, create pop-up windows, and write display-file and RPG code for interactive file maintenance (Add, Delete, and Change options).

Chapter 3 introduces three methods for loading subfiles with multipage lists. You will learn one method that loads all records, one that lets a subfile grow, and one that loads a single page at a time.

Chapter 4 examines the issues of programming subfiles for which the amount of display data requires multiple lines per record. When you finish Chapter 4, you will be able to describe and use the SFLDROP (Subfile Drop) and SFLFOLD (Subfile Fold) keywords, the SFLPAG (Subfile Page) keyword, and the SFLCSRRRN (Subfile Cursor Relative Record Number) keyword. You will also learn to place a blank row between records and to add Input, Output, or Both fields to the header records.

Chapter 5 explores ways to locate records and load the desired data into the subfile. You will learn programming techniques to load records from the correct position in a physical file via a selection screen and also via a selection field in the header record. You will also learn techniques for locating records based on various fields, loading the subfile from different logical files, creating a display file, and writing a program with more than one subfile.

Chapter 6 presents ways to make the system more user friendly, including changing data in list mode, adding user prompts, and including Help screens. This chapter helps you develop subfiles that let users change the data on the screen. You learn to use hidden fields, create prompts for fields, and add Help at field and screen levels.

Finally, Chapter 7 explores using subfiles in windows to provide advanced prompting features for users. You will learn to create subfiles in windows from which users can make selections using the prompt option and using the point-and-shoot feature.

In addition to the inventory maintenance and purchase order exercises that run throughout the chapters, a subfile project for a bookstore system is presented in two parts, following Chapters 5 and 7.

One of the first questions that you can expect when you interview for a job as an AS/400 programmer will be about your knowledge of subfiles. Completing Section 1's carefully developed coverage of subfiles will let you answer with confidence that you have a good working knowledge of this essential AS/400 tool.

Chapter 1

Introduction to Subfiles

Chapter Overview

Chapter 1 introduces you to the basic concept of a subfile, including

✓ the purpose, design, and creation of a subfile record

✓ the purpose, design, and creation of a subfile control record

✓ the purpose, design, and creation of a footer record

✓ the RPG code to

  ✓ clear a subfile

  ✓ load a subfile

  ✓ display a subfile

  ✓ manage the no-records case

What Is a Subfile?

A **subfile** is a special type of AS/400 display-file record. It is designed to hold a column-based list of data and to display that list in a column format. A subfile is a data file, with data-file attributes, such as

- a record name and record structure
- fields with field structures and other field attributes
- records that contain data, much like records in a physical file (You can add, update, and use these records for input to an RPG program in ways that are similar to the same processes on a physical file.)

A subfile differs from other physical files in the following ways:

- It is temporary, existing only until the RPG program that creates and owns it ends.
- Within a subfile, each field's description also identifies its screen location and its display attributes, much like the description of a field in a simple interactive screen.

Subfile is an appropriate term in that we often load a subset of the records from a physical file into it. Subfiles' real use is in user screens that show multiple records at one time (in a list or spreadsheet-like layout of data).

Although AS/400 screens are actually built with a different technology, AS/400 "Work with" screens provide examples of the look and feel of subfile-based screens.

For example, the WRKOBJPDM (Work with Objects Using PDM) screen shown in Figure 1.1 presents several elements:

- The header area at the top of the screen contains general information, options, column headings, and some input/output fields that let the user control the displayed data, such as which library is displayed and where in the library the listing is positioned.
- An area in the center of the screen lists a set of objects — in this case, eight at a time.
- Just above the list of objects, the user is offered a selection of options via which the user can act upon one or more of the listed objects.
- Function keys, defined on lines 22 and 23, provide control of global functions
- The Page down key displays the next eight objects, and the Page up key displays the previous eight objects.

Figure 1.1
Work with Objects
Using PDM Screen

```
                          Work with Objects Using PDM

Library . . . . .   A300C1_STD        Position to . . . . . . . . _____
                                      Position to type  . . . . . _____

Type options, press Enter.
  2=Change        3=Copy        4=Delete      5=Display      7=Rename
  8=Display description         9=Save        10=Restore     11=Move ...

Opt  Object       Type      Attribute   Text
 _   OPB140ABAK   *FILE     PF-DTA      CONTRACT COPY REQUEST FILE
 _   OPB524P      *FILE     PF-DTA
 _   QCLSRC       *FILE     PF-SRC
 _   QCMDSRC      *FILE     PF-SRC
 _   QDDSSRC      *FILE     PF-SRC
 _   QRPGSRC      *FILE     PF-SRC
 _   SEPTFILL     *FILE     PF-DTA      September fill rates
 _   STD          *FILE     PF-SRC      ORIGINAL COPIES OF STD SOURCE
                                                                   More...
Parameters or command
===> _____
F3=Exit          F4=Prompt           F5=Refresh         F6=Create
F9=Retrieve      F10=Command entry   F23=More options   F24=More Keys
```

In subfile processing, the data to be displayed is loaded into records in the subfile and displayed on the screen. An RPG program loads the records, turns over control to the display screen with an EXFMT (Execute Format) operation, receives user input via the function keys — the Enter key and the Page up and Page down keys — and then responds appropriately.

The source code that describes the display file can contain a large number of records — each describing a different screen, overlay, or window. A simple subfile screen, such as the WRKOBJPDM screen, would actually require the following three separate records in the source code that defines the display file.

The **subfile record** describes the subfile record layout. The subfile record declares

- each field's name
- each field's definition

  - Field width, type, number of decimals, and other attributes can be explicitly included in the specification.
  - Field definitions can be adopted by reference to a field definition in a physical file.

- the location of the first record of the file on the screen (The area above this line can be used for the screen header data, which is usually included in the subfile control record definition.)

The **subfile control record** contains

- control data for the subfile record, including

  - the number of records the subfile can contain (SFLSIZ)
  - the number of rows that can be displayed on the screen at one time (SFLPAG)
  - a control to display the subfile (SFLDSP)
  - a control to display the control record itself, which may contain the header information (SFLDSPCTL)
  - a control to clear (remove) all records from the subfile (SFLCLR)
  - other special subfile controls that we explore in later chapters (e.g., OVERLAY)

- the screen heading display, which defines what is to be displayed at the top of the screen above the subfile's columnar list area (Like a typical display, it can include text and variables with their locations and edit codes. This area would include the screen heading, user identification, date and time identification of user options (e.g., 4=Delete), and headings for the columns.)

The **footer record** is not necessary to create a subfile display. However, standard screen designs typically provide the definition of the function keys at the bottom of the screen.

- Everything that is displayed below the subfile on the screen must be defined in this record.
- Do not include any part of the footer on line 24, which is reserved as the default message line.

The Computers Are US Inventory Project

To demonstrate subfile programming, let's develop a simple inventory system for the fictional company Computers Are US to store and display inventory data.

- The system will store inventory data in the physical file INVPF.
- The data in the file identifies inventory currently in stock.
- Each record in the file represents a specific product, including product number, product description, quantity on hand (the number of items in stock), cost (the purchase cost for a single item), the specific warehouse in which the product is stored, and the product's physical location in the warehouse.

- The system will display the data on the screen shown in Figure 1.2.
- Inventory data is shown on a multirecord (subfile) screen.
- The first eight records appear on the screen.
- The extended cost (computed as quantity times cost) is computed and displayed.

Figure 1.2
Computers Are US
Inventory List Screen

```
USERID                    COMPUTERS ARE US INV SYS            12/18/98
                          WORK WITH  INVENTORY LISTS

PART NUMBER  DESCRIPTION                      QNTY       COST    EXTENDED

A123         Computer x486                      21   1,301.15   27,324.15
A124         Computer Pent                     215   2,100.16  451,534.40
A125         Printer - Laser                    81     974.21   78,911.01
A213         Printer - Ink Jet                  15     457.15    6,857.25
A214         Printer - Dot Matrix               21     251.14    5,273.94
A215         Scanner - Hand                     15     127.19    1,907.85
A216         Scanner - Flat Bed                  5     421.15    2,105.75
A319         CD-ROM                              6     115.96      695.76


==============================================================================
F3=Exit Subsystem
```

In later chapters, we will expand this system to maintain as well as display the data in this file.

Figure 1.3
File INVPF

```
*...1....+....2....+....3....+....4....+....5....+....6
A                        Unique
A          R INVPFR
A            INPN        11A         TEXT('PART NUMBER')
A            INDESC      30A         TEXT('DESCRIPTION')
A            INQOH       5S 0        TEXT('QUANTITY ON HAND')
A            INUCST      6S 2        TEXT('UNIT COST')
A            INWH        3A          TEXT('WAREHOUSE STORED IN')
A            INWHL       5A          TEXT('WAREHOUSE LOCATION')
A          K INPN
```

We will load this data from the first eight records of INVPF. The file definition is shown in Figure 1.3.

And, of course, we have some data in our physical file, as is shown in Table 1.1.

Table 1.1
Physical File Data

INPN	INDESC	INQOH	INUCST	INWH	INWHL
A123	Computer x486	21	1301.15	DLS	15A
A124	Computer Pent	215	2100.16	FTW	219
A125	Printer — Laser	81	974.21	DLS	X19
A213	Printer — Ink Jet	15	457.15	FTW	319
A214	Printer — Dot Matrix	21	251.14	FTW	320
A215	Scanner — Hand	15	127.19	DLS	X21
A216	Scanner — Flat Bed	5	421.15	DLS	X22
A319	CD-ROM	6	115.96	FTW	315
A320	4x CD-ROM	6	215.96	FTW	316

Creating the Subfile Record Description for the Computers Are US Inventory System

The subfile record must define the fields for the five columns shown in Figure 1.2. The subfile record is shown in Figure 1.4. It defines the fields of a single row: row 8. This is the first row of the subfile.

```
*...1....+....2....+....3....+....4....+....5....+....6

A* Subfile example DDS
A* Member Name: INVD011C
A* Member Type: DSPF
A* By PHIL LEVINSON 9/3/98
A*******************************************
A                                     PRINT
A                                     CF03(03)
A*******************************************
A**    subfile record - DSP01
A
A           R DSP01                   SFL
A             D1PN        11A  0  8  2
A             D1DESC      30A  0  8 15
A             D1QOH        5Y 00  8 47EDTCDE(1)
A             D1UCST       6Y 20  8 55EDTCDE(1)
A             D1LTOT       8Y 20  8 65EDTCDE(1)
A*******************************************
```

Figure 1.4
Subfile Record Definition for Computers Are US Inventory System

The example in Figure 1.4 contains definitions at the file and record level. Keywords used before the first record begins are called file-level keywords. File-level keywords are in effect for all of the records in the file. In this example, both **PRINT** (Print) and **CF03(03)** are file-level keywords.

Keywords used within a record but before the first field definition are called record-level keywords; they apply to that record and all the fields of that record, but not to other records (unless also declared in the other records). In the example in Figure 1.4, **SFL** (Subfile) is a record-level keyword.

Using SDA with Subfiles

Screen Design Aid (SDA) is a great tool for creating, editing, and testing screen designs. It can be used effectively on subfile records, subfile control records, and simple records, such as our footer record.

To change the header layout or controls, work with the control record (DSP02). When you are working with a subfile control record, SDA displays that record and a layout of the subfile itself so that you can get an idea about how the entire screen will look.

To change the column layouts or attributes of a field in the subfile, work with the subfile record (DSP01). The header record is also displayed.

For more about SDA, see Appendix C.

Keywords used in a field definition, either on the same line as the field or on subsequent lines (but before the definition of the next field), apply to that single field only and are called field-level keywords. In the example in Figure 1.4, **EDTCDE** (Edit Code) is a field-level keyword.

Record DSP01 describes the subfile. The record-level keyword SFL indicates that this record describes a subfile. In many ways, this record resembles a physical-file description because it describes fields and their definitions. However, it also describes the location of the fields on the screen display (e.g., row 8, column 2).

The subfile record also describes each field's usage. In our example, all the fields are output only (O), which means that the program can load the data and display it on the screen, but the user cannot alter the screen value. Fields that are input (I) only, let users make entries, but they cannot display data the program loads. Fields capable of both input and output (B) let the program load data that can then be displayed and updated on the screen.

This subfile contains five fields, and columns are displayed beginning on row 8 (note the 8 in every field's row position). The designated usage of all fields is currently output (O), but later we introduce subfile fields with input (I) and with both (B) capabilities.

Creating the Subfile Control Record Description for Computers Are US

The subfile DSP01 described in Figure 1.4 requires a control record in the same display file. The control record DSP02 (shown in Figure 1.5) contains the necessary keywords to define and control the subfile, as well as screen-heading information. The subfile control record (DSP02) must be entered into the same member as the subfile record that it controls (DSP01). The subfile control record description always immediately follows the subfile record description. The subfile control record controls the processing of the subfile DSP01 as indicated by the record-level keyword SFLCTL (Subfile Control), which must be followed by the name of the subfile record that it controls, in our case, SFLCTL(DSP01).

```
*...1....+....2....+....3....+....4....+....5....+....6

A*******************************************
A*** SUBFILE CONTROL RECORD DSP02   ***
A
A          R DSP02                   SFLCTL(DSP01)
A
A*** S U B F I L E   C O N T R O L S ***
A
A                                    SFLSIZ(08)
A                                    SFLPAG(08)
A                                    OVERLAY
A  50                                SFLDSP
A  50                                SFLDSPCTL
A N50                                SFLCLR
A
A*** S C R E E N   H E A D E R *****
A
A                                    1 31'COMPUTERS ARE US INV SYS'
A                                    2 31'Work with Inventory lists'
A                                    1  2USER
A                                    1 71DATE
A                                      EDTCDE(Y)
A                                    6  2'Part Number'
A                                    6 15'Description'
A                                    6 47'Qnty'
A                                    6 55'Cost'
A                                    6 65'Extended'
A*********************************************
```

Figure 1.5
Subfile Control Record
for Computers Are US

Although this is a single record, I've inserted comments to divide the record into two sections:

1. The subfile control section contains the subfile control commands.
2. The screen-header section contains the screen heading definition of the first six rows of the screen.

Subfile Control Keywords

Let's examine each of the subfile control keywords introduced in Figure 1.5.

```
*...1....+....2....+....3....+....4....+....5....+....6

A                                    SFLSIZ(08)
A                                    SFLPAG(08)
A                                    OVERLAY
```

SFLSIZ (Subfile Size) declares the number of records the subfile can contain. This number cannot exceed 9999. For the moment, we will keep the number of records low enough for all records to be displayed on a single screen.

SFLPAG (Subfile Page) declares the number of records to be displayed on the screen at one time. The number cannot exceed SFLSIZ.

OVERLAY (Overlay) lets the header and subfile be displayed on a screen that already contains other records — as long as the other records are on different areas of the display. This applies to our design because we want to display the function key definitions at the bottom of the screen, on rows 22 and 23. The OVERLAY keyword on this subfile control record lets us write the footer record with the function key definitions to the bottom of the display screen and then write the header and subfile display to the top and middle of the screen, "overlaying" and replacing any previous records in that geographic area.

To compute the area overlayed, we must consider that the header occupies rows 1 through 6 and that the subfile occupies up to eight rows, starting at row 8 and ending at row 15. Therefore, when we overlay the subfile control and subfile records onto the screen, they replace any records with geography overlapping any of the rows between 1 and 15.

Our RPG program uses indicator 50 (any number from 1 to 99 can be used) to turn on/off three subfile controls. These three keywords used in these subfile controls nearly always appear together, and SFLCLR (Subfile Clear) must have the opposite indicator value (N50 vs 50), as shown below.

```
*...1....+....2....+....3....+....4....+....5....+....6

A  50                              SFLDSP
A  50                              SFLDSPCTL
A  N50                             SFLCLR
```

When indicator 50 is *ON and the RPG program WRITES the control record or does an EXFMT on the control record, the following occurs:

1. SFLDSP (Subfile Display) is on and the subfile will be displayed.
2. SFLDSPCTL (Subfile Display Control) is on and the header section of the control record will be displayed.
3. SFLCLR (Subfile Clear) is off and has no effect.

When indicator 50 is *OFF and the RPG program WRITES the control record, the following occurs:

1. SFLDSP is off and the subfile will not be displayed.
2. SFLDSPCTL is off and the header section of the control record will not be displayed.
3. SFLCLR is on and removes all records from the subfile.

Creating the Footer Record Description for Computers Are US

AS/400 standards that IBM developed and many organizations use require that we display the function key definitions at the bottom of the screen. To do so requires a third record definition for the footer record (see Figure 1.6). In the RPG program, this record is written to the screen first. It may seem a little odd to build the bottom of the screen first, but because this record does not require user input, it can be put on the screen (with a WRITE statement) before the other records are put on with a command that requires a response (EXFMT). Because DSP02 contains the OVERLAY keyword, the FOOTER record is displayed while the subfile is displayed. Remember: this approach requires that the rows used for the function key record (22 and 23) are not used by the record that is subsequently OVERLAYed. (Also remember that row 24 is reserved for error messages.)

```
*...1....+....2....+....3....+....4....+....5....+....6
A           R FOOTER1
A                                   OVERLAY
A                           22  2'===================================-
A                               ===================================-
A                               ======='
A                           23  4'F3=Exit Subsystem'
```

Figure 1.6
Footer Record

Some Notes on Using SEU

I usually begin my design with a rough layout that I create with the Source Entry Utility (SEU) editor. One of the reasons for this is that I typically copy an earlier example of a subfile's DDS (that's right, copy — many programming activities include copying earlier code). To copy in SEU, enter **SEU** with the name of your new DDS file and then press F15 (Shift F3). Notice the 1 that means view a member. Move down to the member definition and type in the Member name, Library, and File of the member that you want to copy from, and then press Enter.

Your SEU screen is now split horizontally. On top is your new work in Edit mode; below is the member that you copy from in Browse mode. You can quickly copy code by putting copy codes such as CC ... CC or C9999 in the sequence number area of the Browse member and in the destination location for the lines — using A(fter) or B(efore) in the edit member.

This split-screen capability is also useful for editing your program because you can view the display member, the physical file member, or RPG code without exiting the editor.

F12 returns SEU to full-screen capabilities.

The Browse/Copy options (invoked by F15) are also extremely useful when you debug code. Option 2 displays the latest compile listing for the member that you are editing on the bottom of the screen. Move to the BROWSE session and page down to scan the listing.

When you use SEU in browse or edit mode, you can use the following controls on the command line:

- B — go to bottom
- T — go to top
- xxx F16 (shift F4) — search for xxx, or any other entry
- QRG F16 (shift F4) — search for RPG error messages
- *ERR F16 (shift F4) — search for next error in source listing

As you find each error, simply move to the top and use the search capability to find the code to be corrected and make the change. Return to the bottom and locate the next error. Once you are familiar with the diagnostic messages and how to use SEU, it is rarely necessary to print out the compile listing.

Exercise 1.1A Computers Are US Inventory Project

Purpose
To test your understanding of the information and examples provided. In the first section of this book — Chapters 1 through 7 — Exercise 1 (called Exercise 1.1 in Chapter 1, Exercise 2.1 in Chapter 2, Exercise 3.1 in Chapter 3, etc.) is based on the code samples provided and follows the development of the Computers Are US Inventory Project. You should do all of the segments of Exercise 1 as they occur throughout each chapter and this section of the book because each set of steps is used to build the concepts and code developed in subsequent sets.

General Program Specifications
Create the physical file, load sample data, and create the display file with all three records for the Computers Are US Inventory screen, as outlined below.

1. Create the physical file INVPF (Figure 1.3) and compile it.
2. Use Data File Utility (DFU) to enter the records shown in Table 1.1. An easy way to start DFU is with the Update command UPDDTA INVPF.
3. Create the DDS INVD011C with the three records DSP01, DSP02, and FOOTER1.
4. View and enhance the layout using Screen Design Aid (SDA).

Exercise 1.2A Purchase Order Line Project

Purpose

In the first section of this book, Exercise 2 (called Exercise 1.2 in Chapter 1, Exercise 2.2 in Chapter 2, Exercise 3.2 in Chapter 3, etc.) follows the development of the Purchase Order Line Project and requires that you draw from the concepts and applications presented to create a solution to a new problem. You should do all of the segments of Exercise 2 as they occur throughout each chapter and this section of the book because each set of steps builds upon the concepts and code developed in previous steps.

General Program Specifications

Computers Are US buys computers wholesale and resells them. The company needs to keep a record of the items that it has on order. Figure 1.7 contains a sample purchase order (PO) issued by Computers Are US.

The top section of the PO provides information specific to that order, such as

- the order number and date of order
- from whom the items are being ordered
- where and how to ship the items
- where to send the bill

This information is often referred to as the order header information and is stored in the Purchase Order Header File. Our current project is not concerned with the header information.

In the middle of the PO form is a table of items ordered. We can have multiple items ordered (sometimes referred to as lines) on the same PO. The data that relates to a single line from a PO is stored in a second file called the PO Line File. Our project is to create the physical file and display file to show the data in the PO Line File (ORDLNP).

1. Create the Physical File ORDLNP and compile it. This file will have a UNIQUE KEY and the following fields:

OLNUM	6A	-	Order Number	Key 1
OLSEQ	3S 0	-	Sequence or Line Number	Key 2
OLPN	11A	-	Part Number	
OLPRC	7S 2	-	Unit Price	
OLOQN	5S 0	-	Quantity Ordered	
OLEDT	8S 0	-	Expected Date	
OLADT	8S 0	-	Actual Delivery Date	
OLAQN	5S 0	-	Actual Delivery Quantity	

continued

Exercise 1.2A *Continued*

Figure 1.7
Purchase Order
Form for
Computers
Are US

Computers Are US

Purchase Order

PO #: 000015   **Date:** 09/21/98

TO: Fast Eddie's Computer Company
          21 Fleet Street
          Westmoreland, VA 53071

SHIP TO: Computers Are US   **BILL TO:**   Computers Are US
               100 Broadway   PO Box 175100
               St Louis, MO 63105   St Louis, MO 63100

SHIP VIA: Fastest Way

PART #	DESCRIPTION	QUANTITY	PRICE	EXTENDED PRICE
A123		250	1,250.00	$312,687.50
A124		150	2,050.00	$307,500.00

TOTAL **$620,187.50**

continued

Exercise 1.2A *Continued*

2. Use DFU to enter the records shown in Table 1.2.

Table 1.2
Records to Create Table of Items Ordered

OLNUM	OLSEQ	OLPN	OLPRC	OLOQN	OLEDT	OLADT	OLAQN
000015	001	A123	1250.75	250	19980921	19980922	251
000015	002	A124	2050.00	150	19981030	19980922	150
000016	001	A123	1150.75	125	19981030	0	0
000017	001	A320	205.15	50	19981010	0	0
000017	002	A320	200.00	50	19981015	0	0
000017	003	A319	95.21	10	19981015	0	0
000018	001	A214	190.00	5	19980929	19980923	5
000018	002	A216	315.15	250	19981021	0	0
000018	003	A213	415.16	10	19981015	0	0

3. Create display file ORDD011C with the three records DSP01, DSP02, and FOOTER1. The subfile should display the fields OLNUM, OLSEQ, OLPN, OLPRC, OLOQN, and OLEDT in date format as well as a computed column, Extended Price (Extended Price = Price × Quantity) as shown in Figure 1.7. The subfile should be coded to display six records per page and have a maximum of six records in the subfile. The first record of the subfile should be displayed on line 7.

Figure 1.8 shows the screen design.

```
 USERID                 COMPUTERS ARE US PURCHASING              12/18/98
                           WORK WITH ORDER LINES

 ORDER  SEQ   PART          PRICE    QUANTITY      EXTENDED   EXPECTED
 NUMBER NUM   NUMBER                                  PRICE       DATE
 ============================================================================
 000015 001   A123         1,250.75       250     312,687.50   09/22/98
 000015 002   A124         2,050.00       150     307,500.00   10/30/98
 000016 001   A123         1,150.75       125     143,843.80   10/30/98
 000017 001   A320           205.15        50      10,257.50   10/10/98
 000017 002   A320           200.00        50      10,000.00   10/15/98
 000017 003   A319            95.21        10         952.10   10/15/98


 ============================================================================
 F3=Exit Subsystem
```

Figure 1.8
Computers Are US Purchase Order Line Data

4. View and enhance the layout using SDA.

Using a Subfile in RPG/400

Now that we have a well-designed display file — INVD011C — we are ready to develop the RPG program (INV011B) to load and display the subfile. The pseudocode for our design is provided in Figure 1.9.

Figure 1.9

Pseudocode for RPG
Program INV011B

Start
    Execute Load Subfile (LOAD) subroutine
    Do while user has not pressed the F3 key
                    Note: This loop is entered the first time
                    before the display has been sent to the
                    screen because the indicator associated
                    with the function key F3 (*IN03) is initially
                    off and cannot be pressed until the screen
                    is displayed and read.
        Display and read the subfile and the subfile control
    End do
    Close files
End

LOAD subroutine
    Clear subfile
    Load the subfile
        Read a record from INVPF
        Do while not EOF(INVPF) and fewer than eight records have been written
        to the subfile
            Populate the fields of the subfile record
        Add 1 to the subfile Relative Record Number (RRN)
        Write a record to the subfile
        End do
    Write footer
End subroutine

The value of the variable RRN is most critical to the performance of this or any subfile. This variable positions the "pointer" for the subfile to the correct subfile record to be used. In the pseudocode shown in Figure 1.9, 1 is added to the Subfile RRN just before a record is written to the subfile. If the value of this variable were zero, the number of an existing record, or greater than the subfile size when the WRITE (Write a Record to a File) operation was attempted, an error would occur.

Figure 1.10 contains the RPG code for program INV011B, with extensive internal comments. Read the code over carefully. Consider how it resembles the pseudocode in Figure 1.9.

```
*...1....+....2....+....3....+....4....+....5....+....6
**********************************************************************
*     Jefferson College     Professor Levinson 11/15/98
*     APPLICATION NAME          - Inventory System
*     PROGRAM NAME              - INV011B
*
*  DESCRIPTION  - 1. Clears Subfile   2. Loads Subfile  3. Displays Footer
*                 4. Exercises the Screen Display with the Subfile
*********************************************************************
*  L O G   O F   M O D I F I C A T I O N S
*
*  DATE        PGMR       DESCRIPTION
*  -------------------------------------------------------------------
*  /  /
**********************************************************************
*  F U N C T I O N   O F   I N D I C A T O R S
*  IND            FUNCTION
*  -------------------------------------------------------------------
*  03             USED TO EXIT DISPLAY
*  50             USED TO DISPLAY/CLEAR SUBFILE
*  90             EOF FLAG FOR INVPF
*  LR             LAST RECORD
**********************************************************************
*  S U B R O U T I N E   I N D E X
**********************************************************************
*  LOAD       - CLEAR AND ACTIVIATE SUBFILE DSP01
*  DISP       - DISPLAY SUBFILE
**********************************************************************
*  F I L E S
**********************************************************************
*                                    INVENTORY MASTER
FINVPF   IF E        K       DISK
*                                    DISPLAY FILE WITH SUBFILES
FINVD011CCF E                WORKSTN
F                            RRN   KSFILE DSP01
*
* note: The special continuation line - the variable RRN (9 0) - will
*       always contain the number of records in the subfile (SFILE) DSP01.
*       To enter this K (continuation) line, use the FK prompt format.
**********************************************************************
*    MAINLINE                 M A I N L I N E
**********************************************************************
*
C              EXSR LOAD                    LOAD INVENTORY SUBFILE
*
C       *IN03  DOWEQ*OFF                    Loop until F3 is pressed
*
C              EXFMTDSP02                    DISPLAY the SUBFILE
*                                            EXFMT the CONTROL Rec
C              ENDDO
*  END PROCESSING
C              MOVE *ON      *INLR
C              RETRN
*
**********************************************************************
*  LOAD - LOADS THE INVENTORY SUBFILE FROM THE DATAFILE INVPF
**********************************************************************
```

Figure 1.10
RPG Program INV011B

continued

Figure 1.10
Continued

```
*...1....+....2....+....3....+....4....+....5....+....6
C           LOAD      BEGSR
*
C                     MOVE *OFF      *IN50
C                     WRITEDSP02
*
*       We start by clearing the subfile -- even though it must be clear
*       at the moment because the program has just begun. However, clearing the
*       subfile whenever you are about to start loading records will avert
*       runtime errors and will be important as our code becomes more complex.
*
*       To clear the subfile, we write to the control record format DSP02 while
*       the conditioning indicator (50) is off. This does not display anything
*       on the workstation because the SFLDSP and SFLDSPCTL keywords are only
*       active when indicator 50 is on. It causes the SFLCLR keyword to be
*       exercised because that had a N50 conditioning indicator and that
*       causes the subfile to be cleared of all existing records.
*
C                     Z-ADD*ZERO     RRN       90
*
*       RRN is the variable name that I used above in the FK spec to
*       indicate the number of records in the subfile (currently zero).
*       the field size of RRN must be (9 0) as the "Key" into the subfile
*
*
C                     MOVE *ON        *IN50
*
*       Later, when we write the control record (EXFMT DSP02) with indicator
*       50 on, SFLDSP and SFLDSPCTL are enabled and both the subfile and the
*       display headings will appear on the workstation.
*
* Finally we start loading
C                     READ INVPF                     90
*
C           *IN90     DOWEQ*OFF                          Load until EOF INVPF
C           RRN       ANDLT8                             or the Subfile is full
C                     MOVE INPN      D1PN               -|
C                     MOVE INDESC    D1DESC              |Populate
C                     MOVE INQOH     D1QOH               |Subfile
C                     MOVE INUCST    D1UCST              |Fields
C           D1QOH     MULT D1UCST    D1LTOT             -|
C                     ADD  1         RRN                File position
C                     WRITEDSP01                        Write Rec to the SUBFILE
C                     READ INVPF               90 Read the next Inv Record
C                     ENDDO
* WRITE FOOTER RECORD
C                     WRITEFOOTER1                      Write Footer to display
C                     ENDSR
**********************************************************************************
```

Go back and read the RPG program code again. It seems rather long, but most of it is comments. When you write your programs, you should always include enough comments to make the logic and the details of the program clear to any programmer.

Figure 1.11 presents exactly the same code as Figure 1.10 but without comments. With the comments, the program seems long, but without comments the code comprises just 28 lines. The code without comments is harder to understand than the code with comments. Good comments are valuable. In fact, you will find that a large part of a programming job involves making changes to existing code — and it's much easier if the code includes good comments.

```
*...1....+....2....+....3....+....4....+....5....+....6
FINVPF    IF E           K           DISK
FINVD011CCF E                        WORKSTN
F                                            RRN   KSFILE DSP01
C                        EXSR LOAD
C            *IN03       DOWEQ*OFF
C                        EXFMTDSP02
C                        ENDDO
C                        MOVE *ON         *INLR
C                        RETRN
C            LOAD        BEGSR
C                        MOVE *OFF        *IN50
C                        WRITEDSP02
C                        Z-ADD*ZERO       RRN       90
C                        MOVE *ON         *IN50
C                        READ INVPF                    90
C            *IN90       DOWEQ*OFF
C            RRN         ANDLT8
C                        MOVE INPN        D1PN
C                        MOVE INDESC      D1DESC
C                        MOVE INQOH       D1QOH
C                        MOVE INUCST      D1UCST
C            D1QOH       MULT D1UCST      D1LTOT
C                        ADD  1           RRN
C                        WRITEDSP01
C                        READ INVPF                    90
C                        ENDDO
C                        WRITEFOOTER1
C                        ENDSR
```

Figure 1.11
RPG Program INV011B
Without Comments

Exercise 1.1B Computers Are US Inventory Project

Purpose

To learn to enter, debug, and test RPG code that loads and displays a subfile.

General Program Specifications

In step 5, you develop the RPG program INV011B to load and display the inventory display. In step 6, you test this program under severe conditions.

5. Enter, compile, and test the RPG program INV011B as shown in Figure 1.10. To test your program call INV011B.

> **Note:** If you have a problem compiling the program, remember that the library your *FILE objects are in must be included in your library list. You can use the DSPLIBL command to check your library list and the EDTLIBL command to add libraries to your library list. If you have further problems, remember that the compiler report in the spool file indicates the problems. You can view this when you edit in SEU by using F15 (Shift-F3) and then option 2.

continued

6. In this step, we will test the code to determine what happens if there are no records in the physical file. Testing is an important part of programming. It is the programmer's responsibility to develop virtually "bullet-proof" code.
    - Copy the file to INVPF2 (to save the records for later use) with the following command:

      ```
      CPYF YOURLIB/INVPF YOURLIB/INVPF2 CRTFILE(*YES)
      ```

    - Remove all records from the file: CLRPFM YOURLIB/INVPF.
    - Run the program. A runtime error occurs and the system displays an error screen — but don't despair. Solving this runtime error is the topic of the next section.

The No-Records Case

Our code works, but it won't pass quality control because it contains a ticking bomb: it will cause a runtime error under some special circumstances. If the inventory file is empty — which seems rather incredible for this particular file but is certainly possible in other subfile load situations — a runtime error occurs when the program attempts to display the subfile via the command EXFMT DSP02.

This error occurs when the subfile contains no record, and the system won't let you display a zero-record subfile.

The code shown in Figure 1.12 ensures that the subfile has at least one record, even if that record only displays the value NO RCDS. The code does so by testing the variable RRN, which is incremented every time a record is added. If the program flow reaches this code and RRN is zero, then this code writes the NO RCDS record to the subfile.

Figure 1.12
Code to Avoid the
No-Records Error

```
*...1....+....2....+....3....+....4....+....5....+....6
C                        ENDDO
 * NO RECORDS CODE
C          RRN           IFEQ *ZERO                        -- New Code
C                        MOVEL'NO RCDS' D1DESC      P         |
C                        MOVE *BLANKS   D1PN                  |
C                        Z-ADD*ZERO     D1QOH                 |
C                        Z-ADD*ZERO     D1UCST                |
C                        Z-ADD*ZERO     D1LTOT                |
C                        ADD  1         RRN                   |
C                        WRITEDSP01                           |
C                        ENDIF                             -- New Code
 * WRITE FOOTER RECORD
C                        WRITEFOOTER1
C                        ENDSR
 *
```

Exercise 1.1C Computers Are US Inventory Project

Purpose

To correct your code to remove a known error.

General Program Specifications

Finding and correcting errors is an important part of the programming process. Correct the inventory display program so that it does not fail when it encounters the no-records case.

7. Because you proved in step 6 that your code had a potential bug when it encountered the no-records case, you should correct it by adding the code presented in Figure 1.12.

   * Name your new program INV011C.
   * Test it with the empty file and print the screen.
   * Copy the data from INVPF2.
   * Once you've proven that your modified code works with no records, you must demonstrate that it still works with records. To do this, use the copy file command to copy your file with data back into your file:

   ```
   CPYF YOURLIB/INVPF2 YOURLIB/INVPF MBROPT(*REPLACE)
   ```

   * Test your program again to prove that it still works and print the screen.

Exercise 1.2B Purchase Order Line Project

Purpose

To reinforce your knowledge of the RPG needed to load and display subfiles and to get experience in restricting record selection when loading the subfile.

General Program Specifications

In steps 5 through 8 of the Purchase Order Project, you develop the code to display the purchase order line data. You use the physical file and display file that you created in Exercise 1.2, steps 1 through 4. Your code should include provisions for the no-records case. In steps 7 and 8, you create the code to restrict the selection of records further.

5. Write the RPG program to load the order-line data into subfile DSP01 and display it until F3 is pressed. Name the program ORDL21B. The expected date should be displayed in MM/DD/YY format. Print the compiler listing.
6. Call the program and print the screen.

continued

Exercise 1.2B *Continued*

7. For many of the uses that Computers Are US has for this data, the company is interested only in the PO lines that show orders that have not been delivered. As soon as the POs are marked as delivered, they are added to the inventory and show up on the inventory screens. If delivered lines continued to appear on the PO line screen, it might seem to indicate that more of these items still should be delivered.

   In this step, you will create a second program to display only those lines for orders that have not yet been delivered. Although the Order Line Data file (ORDLNP) does not contain a field that specifically indicates the line status, it does have a field that contains the actual delivery date. When the actual delivery date is zero, the order for that line has not been delivered.

   Copy program ORDL21B to ORDL21C. Modify ORDL21C so that it displays only records with OLADT = zero.

8. Call the program and print the screen.

Review

1. What is a subfile?
2. What is the role of the subfile record format?
3. How is the subfile record format specified?
4. What is the role of the subfile control record?
5. How is the subfile control record described?
6. Could you include the screen header and footer on the same format?
7. Define the following terms and their functions:

   • SFLDSP
   • SFLDSPCTL
   • SFLCLR
   • SFLSIZ
   • SFLPAG

8. Could the SFLSIZ be smaller than the SFLPAG? Larger?
9. What is different about the RPG F-spec for a subfile record?
10. Before loading the subfile, we turned off indicator 50 and wrote the control record. Why?
11. RRN is a variable that we assigned to indicate the relative record number of the subfile record. If we wanted to call it RRN01, indicate the lines that would be changed.
12. Why did we move NO RECRD to D1DESC instead of to another field?

Chapter 2

The Option Column, Windows, and File Maintenance

Chapter Overview

Chapter 2 helps you understand and demonstrate how to use

✓ the READC (Read the Next Changed Record) operation

✓ pop-up windows

✓ display-file code and RPG code for interactive file maintenance

✓ Add, Delete, and Change options

Subfiles: User Interaction

Your first experiments in creating subfiles displayed the subfile but did not allow user interaction. In this chapter, you add another column to the subfile description, one that lets users make an entry beside any of the records displayed.

Your program then responds to the users' selection of codes for add, delete, change, or display, by locating the corresponding record and displaying a pop-up window. After users make the appropriate entries or changes in the window, the program updates both the physical file and the display.

Updating files interactively is referred to as interactive file maintenance. Interactive file maintenance is not the only process that uses subfiles, but it is frequently encountered in interactive systems. In this chapter, you learn more about subfiles as you develop a simple file-maintenance system.

The chapter steps you through the process of developing an interactive file-maintenance system in the following sequence. You learn to

1. Describe and demonstrate the changes to the subfile description that are required to provide a user-input-capable column.
2. Describe and demonstrate the development of window formats in the display file.
3. Develop the display file for the inventory maintenance system for Computers Are US.
4. Develop the display file for the purchase order line maintenance system for Computers Are US.
5. Describe and demonstrate the RPG code to detect and process a change request.
6. Develop the RPG code for the inventory maintenance system for Computers Are US to display the screen, support user selection, detect an entry, and process change requests.

7. Add the add, delete, and display capabilities to the inventory maintenance system for Computers Are US.
8. Develop the RPG code for the Computers Are US purchase order line maintenance system to display the screen; allow user selection; detect an entry; and process add, delete, change, and display requests.

Adding an Option Column

Figure 2.1 presents the inventory maintenance screen for Computers Are US.

Figure 2.1
Computers Are
US Inventory
Maintenance Display

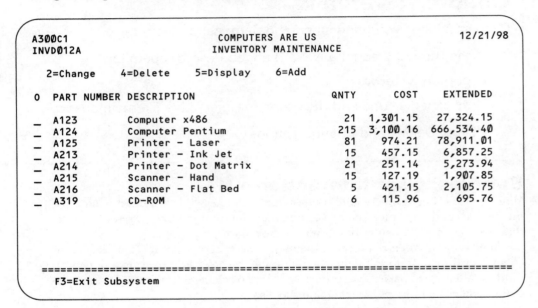

```
A300C1                      COMPUTERS ARE US                          12/21/98
INVD012A                  INVENTORY MAINTENANCE

  2=Change     4=Delete     5=Display      6=Add

O  PART NUMBER DESCRIPTION                      QNTY      COST      EXTENDED

_  A123        Computer x486                      21   1,301.15    27,324.15
_  A124        Computer Pentium                  215   3,100.16   666,534.40
_  A125        Printer - Laser                    81     974.21    78,911.01
_  A213        Printer - Ink Jet                  15     457.15     6,857.25
_  A214        Printer - Dot Matrix               21     251.14     5,273.94
_  A215        Scanner - Hand                     15     127.19     1,907.85
_  A216        Scanner - Flat Bed                  5     421.15     2,105.75
_  A319        CD-ROM                              6     115.96       695.76




==============================================================================
  F3=Exit Subsystem
```

This screen shown in Figure 2.1 is similar to the screen shown in Figure 1.2 (Chapter 1) except for the following:

- The display-file name (INVD012A) has been added on row 2. (Having an identification field on every screen is helpful both for user support in general and for tracking users' problems in particular.)
- The screen name on row 2 has been changed to Inventory Maintenance.
- A line has been added to the heading indicating how to select the Add, Change, and Delete options.
  - An option column has been added on the far left side of the subfile record. (This column is input capable.)
  - The column headings now have an O over the option column.
  - The column headings and subfile columns have been moved a few characters to the right to accommodate the new column.

The modified subfile code is shown in Figure 2.2. Only one line has been added — to accommodate the new field, D1PICK. Notice that D1PICK is input capable and that the other fields have been shifted to the right to accommodate it.

You also need to make cosmetic changes to the heading area of the control record. These changes include the column headings in the control record DSP02.

I've used an O as the heading for the option column because it fits easily above the column. I've also added a line to the heading that presents the definitions of the available options, option 2=change, etc.

```
*...1....+....2....+....3....+....4....+....5....+....6
A* Subfile example DDS  - INVD012A
A* by Phil Levinson
A*******************************************
A                                    PRINT
A                                    CF03(03)
A*******************************************
A
A          R DSP01                   SFL
A            D1PICK      1A  I  8  2
A            D1PN       11A  O  8  4
A            D1DESC     30A  O  8 16
A            D1QOH       5Y 0O  8 47EDTCDE(1)
A            D1UCST      6Y 20  8 55EDTCDE(1)
A            D1LTOT      8Y 20  8 65EDTCDE(1)
A*******************************************
```

Figure 2.2

Subfile Definition Including the Input-Capable Option Field D1PICK

Adding Windows

Your file-maintenance screen responds to the selection of an option by displaying a pop-up window. The window appears over part of the earlier display, and when an action is completed, disappears, revealing the entire earlier display. Figure 2.3 (page 26) presents a sample display with the change window "open."

A window is defined as a separate record format within the same display file as the screen. Its definition is similar to the definition of a screen except that it begins with the WINDOW keyword. The parameters of this keyword define the location and size of the window.

A special keyword that can be used only with windows, WDWBORDER (Window Border), controls the color and appearance of the window's border.

The position of text and variables in the window is measured from the upper left-hand corner of the window, not the upper left-hand corner of the display.

For the inventory project, a single window could be used for all of the options, but it's a little simpler to design a separate window for each option. Table 2.1 contains a list of the formats needed in the INVD01xx display file. DSP02 must immediately follow DSP01, but the rest of the formats can be entered in any order.

Table 2.1
Window Names

Format Name	Format Function	Related to
DSP01	Subfile record	
DSP02	Subfile control record for DSP01	
FOOTER1	Displays the function key definitions	
WINDOW2	Change window	User option 2
WINDOW4	Delete window	User option 4
WINDOW5	Display window	User option 5
WINDOW6	Add window	User option 6

Figure 2.3

Work with
Inventory Lists
That Have Pop-Up
Change Windows

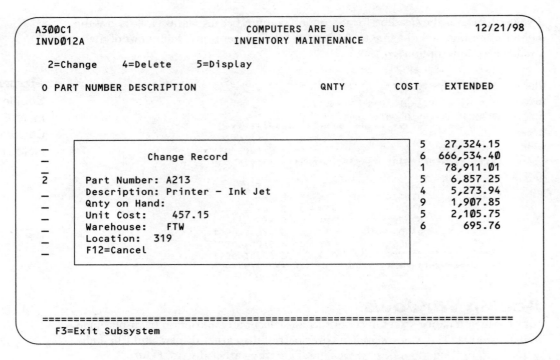

Figure 2.4 contains the window definition for the change window (WINDOW2). WINDOW2 contains a record-level keyword command function (CF) that enables function key F12 and turns on indicator 12 when that function key is pressed. As a record-level declaration, this function is only available in those records in which it is declared. The F12 key is used to exit the window and cancel the change.

Figure 2.4

Window2: The Change
Window

```
*...1....+....2....+....3....+....4....+....5....+....6

A*********************************************
A** Window2 - Change data *****************
A*********************************************
A           R WINDOW2
A                                 CF12(12 )
A                                 WINDOW(8 5 12 52)
A                                 WDWBORDER((*DSPATR HI RI) +
A                                 (*CHAR '        ') (*COLOR RED))
A                               1 13'Change Record'
A                               3  3'Part Number:'
A           W2PN      11A  B  3 17
A                               4  3'Description:'
A           W2DESC    30A  B  4 17
A                               5  3'Qnty on Hand:'
A           W2QOH      5Y 0B  5 17EDTCDE(1)
A                               6  3'Unit Cost:'
A           W2UCST     6Y 2B  6 17EDTCDE(1)
A                               7  3'Warehouse:'
A           W2WH       3A  B  7 17
A                               8  3'Location:'
A           W2WHL      5A  B  8 17
A                              10  3'F12=Cancel'
A                                 DSPATR(HI)
A*********************************************
```

The format for WINDOW2 — as shown in total in Figure 2.4 and in small segments in Figures 2.4A, 2.4B, and 2.4E — provides a good model for discussing the window keywords, including how to use them in designing windows.

The keyword WINDOW, shown in Figure 2.4A, is what declares to the system that this is a window (the record name WINDOW2 was fine, but had no special meaning to the system and gave the system no information). The complete command is WINDOW(*row column height width*). Thus, the window pops up with the upper left-hand corner at row 8 column 5; it will be 12 rows high and 52 columns wide. You must subtract three rows from the width and two columns from the height for the working width and height. The three "lost" rows are the top and bottom borders, as well as a line for error messages. The two "lost" columns are the right and left borders.

```
*...1....+....2....+....3....+....4....+....5....+....6

A*********************************************
A**  Window2 - Change data ******************
A*********************************************
A          R WINDOW2
A                                 CF12(12)
A                                 WINDOW(8 5 12 52)
```

Figure 2.4A
The Window Keyword
from WINDOW2

The inner, usable portion of our window comprises 9 rows (12 – 3) — with row 10 reserved for messages — and 50 columns (52 – 2). We position our text and fields in this area as if the window were a little display. The words Change Record appear in row 1 of the window (not row 1 of the physical display) and in column 13 of the window (not column 13 of the display).

The Window Border keyword, WDWBORDER (Figure 2.4B), lets you define the frame around the window.

```
*...1....+....2....+....3....+....4....+....5....+....6

A                                 WDWBORDER((*DSPATR HI RI) +
A                                 (*CHAR '         ')( *COLOR RED))
```

Figure 2.4B
The Window Border
Keyword from WINDOW2

The WDWBORDER keyword is not required (the default is shown in Figure 2.4C).

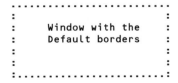

```
: ............................ :
:                              :
:      Window with the         :
:      Default borders         :
:                              :
:                              :
: ............................ :
```

Figure 2.4C
Window with the
Default Borders

Also, the optional *CHAR part of the WDWBORDER can be used to redefine the characters used for the corners, top, bottom, and sides. The sequence for defining the eight positions is shown in Table 2.2.

Table 2.2
Window Position Default Characters

Window Position	Default	Position in definition *CHAR('12345678')
Top left corner	.	1
Top border	.	2
Top right corner	.	3
Left border	:	4
Right border	:	5
Bottom left corner	:	6
Bottom border	.	7
Bottom right corner	:	8

The optional *CHAR part of the WDWBORDER keyword can be used, as shown in Figure 2.4D, to create another border pattern.

Figure 2.4D
Window with
*CHAR('/-\ | |\-/')

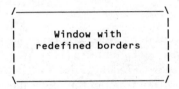

In the code for WINDOW2 (Figure 2.4) the *CHAR('   ') is filled with eight blanks, which means that there will be blank spaces around the border.

The color of the border can also be changed — with the optional *COLOR component of the WDWBORDER keyword. In Figure 2.4B, (*COLOR RED) makes the border red. The list of colors comprises BLU, GRN, WHT, RED, TRQ, YLW, and PNK. Actual colors vary based on the display unit.

The *DSPATR function of the WDWBORDER keyword offers three additional options for borders. These are high intensity (HI), reverse image (RI), and blinking (BL). Blinking makes the border characters blink and therefore has no effect if the border characters are blanks. Some displays may create different colors when HI is on. The latter function was shown in Figure 2.4B.

The rest of the code for WINDOW2 is shown in Figure 2.4E. This code is exactly the same as it would be if this were a simple screen instead of a window.

The row and column positions are all measured from the upper left corner of the window, not the screen, and all of the fields and text must fit within the border area of the window — or the compile of the display file will fail. Because this is the change window, the usage of all fields has been set to B, which allows both input and output.

When you use this window, the RPG program that is introduced in the next section of this chapter

- loads the selected record's data into the window field values
- issues the operation EXFMT WINDOW2 to display and read the window format
- transfers the values in the W2xxx fields to the file (unless F12 has been pressed)

```
*...1....+....2....+....3....+....4....+....5....+....6
A                                   1 13'Change Record'
A                                   3  3'Part Number:'
A           W2PN          11A  B    3 17
A                                   4  3'Description:'
A           W2DESC        30A  B    4 17
A                                   5  3'Qnty on Hand:'
A           W2QOH          5Y 0B    5 17EDTCDE(1)
A                                   6  3'Unit Cost:'
A           W2UCST         6Y 2B    6 17EDTCDE(1)
A                                   7  3'Warehouse:'
A           W2WH           3A  B    7 17
A                                   8  3'Location:'
A           W2WHL          5A  B    8 17
A                                   9  3'F12=Cancel'
A                                     DSPATR(HI)
A*******************************************
```

Figure 2.4E
WINDOW2
Remaining Code

Exercise 2.1A Computers Are US Inventory Project

Purpose
To create or modify an existing display file and test the modified display. The modifications add an option column in the subfile format and add windows for add, change, delete, and display of file data.

General Program Specifications
Create display file INVD012A for the Computers Are US inventory file-maintenance screen, as outlined in the steps that follow.

1. Copy member INVD011C to new member INVD012A, and make the changes to DSP01 and DPS02. Add the code for the WINDOW2 format. Compile the DDS.

   If you have problems, remember that the compiler makes a report. This spooled file will indicate the problems. You can view this report when you edit in SEU by using F15 (Shift-F3) and selecting option 2. Print the compiler listing.

2. Design and add the source code to define WINDOW4 (confirm delete); this should display the record to be deleted in output mode only. Also, add WINDOW5 (display record) at this point; both WINDOW4 and WINDOW5 are similar to WINDOW2, so some code can be copied and modified.

   Because WINDOW4 and WINDOW5 will be similar to WINDOW2, you can copy WINDOW2 code and modify it as needed. To copy multiple lines of code in SEU, mark the block by typing CC in the sequence number area of the first and the last lines to be copied. An A in the sequence number area of the destination indicates that you want the copy placed after that line; a B in place of the A indicates that you want the copy before that line.

   Compile and print the compiler listing.

3. Design and add the DDS definition for WINDOW6 (add record).

Exercise 2.2A Purchase Order Line Project

Purpose

To design screens and windows and create the code to support the designs. You will use the design functions to modify existing designs, adding an option column in the subfile format and adding windows for add, change, delete, and display of file data.

General Program Specifications

Create the display file ORDD022A for the Computers Are US Order Line File-Maintenance screen as outlined in the steps that follow.

1. Copy member ORDD021C to new member ORDD022A, make the following changes, and print:
   - Add a one-character input field to the left of other subfile fields.
   - Add appropriate heading information to define the options.
   - Print the compiler listing.
2. Modify the DDS for this project to add WINDOW2 (change), WINDOW4 (delete), WINDOW5 (display), and WINDOW6 (add) to ORDD022A. The change window should have all fields designated as Both except the order number and the sequence-of-line number. The order number and sequence-of-line number should be display only.

Copying WINDOW2 Code

As we mentioned earlier, WINDOW2 is similar to the windows in the previous project, and it might save time to copy WINDOW2 from INVD012A into the ORDD022A member. To do so, edit ORDD022A, press F15 (Shift F3), choose option 1, and change the browse/copy member name to INVD012A. Edit now displays the file you were editing in the edit window at the top of the screen and the browse/copy member in the browse window at the bottom of the screen. You can find the format that you want to copy in the Browse window by typing WINDOW2 on the SEU==> line of the browse member. Press F16 to search that member. Mark the code that you want to copy with CC in the sequence-number area on the first and last lines. Move your cursor to the Edit window and type either an A or B (for after or before) to specify where you want to locate the copied code. Press F12 to close the Browse window. Of course, the field names and text must be changed for this project.

3. Users are not allowed to delete records that are not closed. Therefore, add a window (WBADDEL) for this type of bad delete request. The window should display the highlighted record data as well as highlight the following message:

   The requested record cannot be deleted because it is not closed.

Interactive File Maintenance: RPG/400

In the previous section of the chapter, you developed the display file INVD012A, the Computers Are US inventory file-maintenance display. It contained an option column in the subfile and windows for the change, display, delete, and add options. Now we explore the RPG code needed to manage the expanded system. During the exploration, you will learn how to read from the subfile, load, and display windows, as well as how to code the change option. In subsequent exercises, you will design and develop the additional coding for the display, delete, and add options.

The pseudocode expanded design is provided in Figures 2.6A, 2.6B, and 2.6C. Only minor changes are required to the program design from Chapter 1; these changes are bolded in Figure 2.6A. Two new subroutines are added to the design. The Respond subroutine processes user responses to the initial display (Figure 2.6B) and calls the appropriate subroutine to service the request. The Change (CHG) subroutine (Figure 2.6C) processes change requests.

Start
    Execute LOAD subroutine
    Display and read the subfile and the subfile control
    Do while user has not pressed the F3 key
        Execute the Respond (RESPD) subroutine
        Display and read the subfile and the subfile control
    End do
    Close files
End

LOAD subroutine
    Clear subfile
    Position to the top of INVPF
    Load the subfile
        Read a record from INVPF, but do not lock the record
        Do while not EOF(INVPF) and fewer than eight records have been written to the subfile
            Populate the fields of the subfile record
            Add 1 to the subfile relative record number (RRN)
            Write a record to the subfile
        End do
    Write footer
End subroutine

Figure 2.6A
Pseudocode for RPG Program, Modified Code

Figure 2.6B

Pseudocode for the
RESPD Subroutine

RESPD subroutine
    Set the update flag to off (this flag will be set on if a change requires that the subfile be reloaded).
    Read the first changed record in the subfile (a changed record must have a new value in D1PICK field because that's the only field the user can change)
    Do while changed records exist
      Do selection
        Select when D1PICK is 2 (Change)
          Execute the Change (CHG) subroutine
      End selection
      Read the next changed record in the subfile
    End do
    If the update flag is on
        Execute the LOAD subroutine
    End if
End subroutine

Figure 2.6C

Pseudocode for the
CHG Subroutine

CHG subroutine
    Find and lock the correct record in the inventory physical file
    If inventory record found
      Move fields of the inventory record to the corresponding fields of WINDOW2
      Write and read the window (EXFMT WINDOW2)
      If neither F3 nor F12 was pressed
        Move the fields of WINDOW2 to the inventory physical file record fields
        Update the inventory physical file record
        Move the fields of WINDOW2 to the subfile record fields
        Update the subfile record
      Else
        Unlock the record
      End if
    End if
End subroutine

Now that you've looked over the changes to the pseudocode for the inventory-maintenance system, it's time to look at the actual RPG code. Throughout the next few pages, segments of the RPG code are presented, followed by discussion about each segment.

Figure 2.7A shows our first change — not surprisingly in the first active line of the program. To post changes to this file, we must open it in update mode. Later, when you add the add function, you will have to put an A code in the add-record column. However, because for the moment we are just tackling the change option, only the update status is necessary.

```
*******************************************************************
*    JEFFERSON COLLEGE  PROFESSOR LEVINSON 12/16/98
*    APPLICATION NAME - INVENTORY SYSTEM
*    PROGRAM NAME - INVØ12A
*
*    DESCRIPTION - 1. CLEARS SUBFILE 2. LOADS SUBFILE 3. DISPLAYS FOOTER
*         4. EXERCISES THE SCREEN DISPLAY WITH THE SUBFILE
*         5. RECEIVES USER RESPONSES
*         6. PROCESSES CHANGE REQUESTS
*         7. REPEATS THE DISPLAY
*****************************************************
*    FILES
*********************************************
**
FINVPF    UF  E          K         DISK
```

Figure 2.7A

Program Heading and
F-Spec for Physical
File Access

Notice that the display declaration (Figure 2.7B) is unchanged except for the use of the new display name. The display file used in Chapter 1 contains three record formats; this display contains seven. In your compiled listing, you will see information on all seven formats, including structural information on the fields in each. The listing of the display formats in the compiled listing can be a convenience. It lets programmers know what they have to work with in their program.

```
*...1....+....2....+....3....+....4....+....5....+....6

FINVDØ12ACF E                     WORKSTN
F                                          RRN   KSFILE DSPØ1
```

Figure 2.7B

F-Spec for Display Station

The changes to the mainline code are shown in Figure 2.7C. The sequence — in which an initial execution of the display is followed by a loop to process the user response and redisplay the main screen — makes the DOW statement do double duty. The first time it is encountered — just after the initial screen is displayed and the user releases the screen by pressing Enter or F3 — the DOW acts as an IF statement, preventing entry to the looped code if F3 has been pressed. Once the loop is entered, it acts as a DOW, testing the status of indicator 03 after each return from the display screen.

```
*...1....+....2....+....3....+....4....+....5....+....6

C                    EXSR LOAD
C                    EXFMTDSPØ2                initial display
C          *INØ3     DOWEQ*OFF
 *                                              process response
C                    EXSR RESPD
 *
C                    EXFMTDSPØ2                next display
C                    ENDDO
C                    MOVE *ON      *INLR
C                    RETRN
```

Figure 2.7C

Changes to the
Mainline Code

In the previous chapter, the LOAD subroutine left the record pointer in INVPF after the eighth record. Because we will now be reusing this subroutine to reload the subfile whenever we make an addition or deletion, we must reset this pointer. For now, we always want to load the subfile with the *first* eight records of INVPF.

Therefore, we reset the file pointer to the top of the file (TOF) using *LOVAL SETLL INVPF (Figure 2.7D) to position the INVPF file at the top every time the LOAD subroutine is called. Regardless of the key, or even without a key, you can position to the TOF with *LOVAL SETLL file name.

Figure 2.7D
Beginning of the
LOAD Subroutine

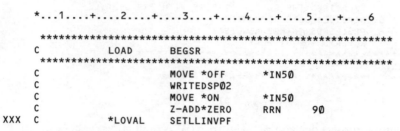

```
*...1....+....2....+....3....+....4....+....5....+....6

**************************************************************
C           LOAD        BEGSR
**************************************************************
C                       MOVE *OFF       *IN50
C                       WRITEDSP02
C                       MOVE *ON         *IN50
C                       Z-ADD*ZERO       RRN        90
XXX C           *LOVAL      SETLLINVPF
```

When option 2 is selected and records are changed, we do not need to rebuild the subfile because we can use the UPDATE operation to update both the subfile record and the physical file.

Mod-Marks

Notice the XXX that I put to the left of the specification type on one of the lines in Figure 2.7D. The compiler does not use positions 1 through 5 of every RPG and DDS specification, so those positions can be used to indicate which lines were changed as part of a specific modification. This tool can be valuable in maintenance programming; it is very helpful to know when and why specific lines of code were modified.

The standard for indicating modifications varies widely from one organization to the next, but a good standard includes the following elements:

1. The modification is described at the beginning of the program, along with the date, the programmer's name, and the reason for the change. These comments use the same Mod-Marks that are used in the subsequent code.

2. The Mod-Mark can be an IS work-request number. It should be some combination of letters and digits that differentiates this change from others in the program. In many standards, the length of the Mod-Mark is restricted to four characters or digits.

3. The Mod-Mark is preceded by a letter designating the action taken, such as A for add or D for delete.

Note: According to some shop standards, lines cannot be changed. This ensures that the original code and the nature of the changes are not hidden from future programmers. Changes are made by using the Delete Mod-Mark and an asterisk (*) in column 7 to declare the line a comment. A new line is then added with the corrected code. Using Delete Mod-Mark and retaining the old code as comments lets programmers see what changes occurred, but it can cause confusion if a programmer fails to realize that the line is no longer active.

The READ statement in Figure 2.7E includes a modifier to the READ operation that we haven't used often. The N in the H/P/N column indicates that this read does not lock the record. This feature is required because we now open the file in the F-spec for update, which causes READ statements to lock the record until the next READ, CHAIN, UPDAT, or DELET. At the moment, our only objective is to read the records and transfer the data to the subfile. We have no intention of updating or deleting this record immediately; therefore, we use the N in the H/P/N column.

```
*...1....+....2....+....3....+....4....+....5....+....6
C                    READ INVPF                N    90
```

Figure 2.7E
LOAD Subroutine: Read of
Physical File Without
Locking the Record

As Figure 2.7F shows, when we load the subfile, we clear the new field, D1PICK, by moving blanks to it.

```
*...1....+....2....+....3....+....4....+....5....+....6
C          *IN90     DOWEQ*OFF
C          RRN       ANDLT8
C                    MOVE *BLANKS   D1PICK
```

Figure 2.7F
LOAD Subroutine
(Continued)

The final section of the LOAD subroutine is shown in Figure 2.7G. This code requires only a single change from the code in Chapter 1. Like the initial or primary read shown in Figure 2.7E, the secondary read in Figure 2.7G must contain the N to unlock the record.

```
*...1....+....2....+....3....+....4....+....5....+....6
C                    MOVE INPN      D1PN
C                    MOVE INDESC    D1DESC
C                    MOVE INQOH     D1QOH
C                    MOVE INUCST    D1UCST
C          D1QOH     MULT D1UCST    D1LTOT
C                    ADD  1         RRN
C                    WRITEDSP01
C                    READ INVPF                N    90
C                    ENDDO
C          RRN       IFEQ *ZERO
C                    MOVE 'NO RECRD'D1DESC
C                    ADD  1         RRN
C                    WRITEDSP01
C                    ENDIF
C                    WRITEFOOTER1
C                    ENDSR
```

Figure 2.7G
LOAD Subroutine
(Continued)

The RESPD subroutine (Figure 2.7H) processes all user requests that were entered on the main screen when Enter was pressed. It initially sets the update flag (UPDFLG) off, then loops through all the requests. If the Add or the Delete subroutine turned the flag on, then at the end of the RESPD subroutine, the subfile is reloaded.

READC and CHAIN (Random Retrieval from a File, based on a record number) are the only input operations that let you access the subfile record. The READC operation in Figure 2.7H reads the first record that was changed and drops the flag for that record. The READC shown later in Figure 2.7J reads subsequent changed records.

Figure 2.7H
Beginning of
RESPD Subroutine

```
*...1....+....2....+....3....+....4....+....5....+....6

*************************************************************
* PROCESS RESPONSES TO SUBFILE
*************************************************************
C           RESPD       BEGSR
C                       MOVE *OFF       UPDFLG    1
C                       READCDSP01                        94
```

The indicator comes on at the EOF (when no more changed records exist). If the user changes any field in the record, the flag is set. In our case, only the D1PICK field can be changed, so we will check that field to see what option was requested.

A selection structure is used in the RESPD subroutine (Figure 2.7I-1) to branch to the various options selected by the user.

Figure 2.7I-1
RESPD Subroutine
(Continued)

```
*...1....+....2....+....3....+....4....+....5....+....6

C           *IN94       DOWEQ*OFF
C                       SELEC
C           D1PICK      WHEQ '2'
C                       EXSR CHG
C***
C                       ENDSL
```

If the changed record that was just acquired with the READC operation has a 2 in D1PICK, we run the CHG subroutine. You can imagine how to modify this code for options 4, 5, and 6, but remember that options 4 and 6 must turn on UPFLG if they actually write or delete a record.

Walk through the code and see whether you can determine how it will respond when someone types an option value of 6 or any other value that isn't coded.

Your users may prefer to use a C for change, but to be consistent with standard AS/400 screens, you also want to respond to a 2 for change. This can be easily accommodated in the selection structure in either of two ways, as shown in Figures 2.7I-2 and 2.7I-3. The code shown in Figure 2.7I-2 uses two When clauses, each calling the same subroutine. If either is true, the CHG subroutine is executed.

Figure 2.7I-2
Selection Structure with
Two Values Using Two
WHEN Clauses for
the CHG Subroutine

```
*...1....+....2....+....3....+....4....+....5....+....6

C           *IN94       DOWEQ*OFF
C                       SELEC
C           D1PICK      WHEQ '2'
C                       EXSR CHG
C           D1PICK      WHEQ 'C'
C                       EXSR CHG
C***
C                       ENDSL
```

The code in Figure 2.7I-3 uses a complex When/Or to accomplish the same task. A selection structure with complex When/And or When/Or clauses can create clear and simple code, which is especially useful when the alternative is nested Ifs or nested Selects.

```
*...1....+....2....+....3....+....4....+....5....+....6
C              *IN94     DOWEQ*OFF
C                        SELEC
C              D1PICK    WHEQ '2'
C              D1PICK    OREQ 'C'
C                        EXSR CHG
C***
C                        ENDSL
```

Figure 2.7I-3
Selection Structure
with Two Values Using
Complex WHEN Clause
for the CHG Subroutine

You will recall that the READC operation shown in Figure 2.7J reads subsequent changed records and sets the indicator on at the EOF (when no more changed records exist). If the user changes any field in the record, the update flag (UPFLG) is set on.

```
*...1....+....2....+....3....+....4....+....5....+....6
C                        READCDSP01                94
C                        ENDDO
C              UPDFLG    IFEQ *ON
C                        EXSR LOAD
C                        ENDIF
C                        ENDSR
```

Figure 2.7J
End of the RESPD
Subroutine

Because the code shown in Figures 2.7I through 2.7J loops until the READC finds no more changed records, the RESPD subroutine processes all requested changes before it reloads the subfile (if necessary) and returns to the mainline code. The mainline code then redisplays the main screen.

The CHG subroutine is shown in Figure 2.7K (page 38). This subroutine is called from the Respond subroutine when the user requests a change.

The READC operation in the RESPD subroutine locks the record, allowing an UPDAT of the record in the subfile. The value of D1PN, the part number of the record acquired by the READC operation, is used at the beginning of the CHG subroutine to CHAIN into the inventory file (which was conveniently keyed on — you guessed it — part number). This chain acquires the physical-file record and locks it for subsequent update.

The CHG subroutine loads the window's fields from the physical-file record and executes the window. When control returns to the program from the window and the user has not pressed F12 or F3, the design assumes that the values of one or more fields were changed. The code would be somewhat more efficient if the fields were compared and updates done only if a change actually occurred, but the performance improvement would be minor. If no changes were made, the code updates the file and subfile, and — if no damage has been done to the files since — the record looks exactly the same before and after the operation.

The processing continues by moving the returned window fields to the physical-file fields and updating the physical file. Then the returned window fields are moved to the subfile fields and that record is updated. Because the subfile is updated in this subroutine, the update flag that would update the subfile by reloading it is unnecessary. That flag, however, is necessary with adds or deletes.

If the user presses F12 or F3 to cancel or exit the process, the inventory physical-file record that was locked is unlocked.

Figure 2.7K
CHG Subroutine

```
*...1....+....2....+....3....+....4....+....5....+....6

***************************************************************
* PROCESS CHG REQUEST
***************************************************************
C           CHG         BEGSR
 *
C           D1PN        CHAININVPF                      93
C           *IN93       IFEQ *OFF
 *  COPY RECORD TO BE CHANGED TO WINDOW2 FIELDS
C                       MOVE INPN       W2PN
C                       MOVE INDESC     W2DESC
C                       Z-ADDINQOH      W2QOH
C                       Z-ADDINUCST     W2UCST
C                       MOVE INWH       W2WH
C                       MOVE INWHL      W2WHL
 *  DISPLAY CHANGE WINDOW
C                       EXFMTWINDOW2
 *  UNLESS EXIT OR CANCEL MOVE WINDOW VALUES TO BUFFER AND UPDATE RECORDS
C           *IN12       IFEQ *OFF
C           *IN03       ANDEQ*OFF
 *  prepare the physical file record data for update
C                       MOVE W2PN       INPN
C                       MOVE W2DESC     INDESC
C                       Z-ADDW2QOH      INQOH
C                       Z-ADDW2UCST     INUCST
C                       MOVE W2WH       INWH
C                       MOVE W2WHL      INWHL
 *  and update the record in the physical file
C                       UPDATINVPFR
 *  prepare the subfile record data for update
C                       MOVE W2PN       D1PN
C                       MOVE W2DESC     D1DESC
C                       Z-ADDW2QOH      D1QOH
C                       Z-ADDW2UCST     D1UCST
C           D1QOH       MULT D1UCST     D1LTOT
 *  and update the subfile record
C                       UPDATDSP01
C                       ELSE
 *  if cancel or exit unlock record
C                       UNLCKINVPF
C                       ENDIF
C                       ENDIF                           *IN93
C                       ENDSR
***************************************************************
```

Exercise 2.1B Computers Are US Inventory Project

Purpose

To create or modify and test RPG program code that

- loads and displays a subfile
- receives user input from the subfile
- branches to the appropriate subroutine based on the value of the user selection
- performs changes to the data
- performs display, delete, and add functions on the data

General Program Specifications

Create the maintenance program INV012A, which provides interactive file maintenance on the Computers Are US inventory file. The program uses the screen INVD012A. The steps of the process follow.

4. Copy source member INV011C to new member INV012A and make the changes as outlined in Figures 2.7A through 2.7K.

   - Test and debug.
   - Print the compiler listing.
   - Print the screens as well as a "before" and an "after" example of a change.

5. Design and develop the display components of the RPG code.

   - Test and debug.
   - Print the compiler listing.
   - Print the display screen.

6. Design and develop the delete components of the RPG code.

   - Test and debug.
   - Print the compiler listing.
   - Print the screens and a "before" and "after" example of a change.

7. Design and develop the add components of the RPG code.

   - Test and debug.
   - Print the compiler listing.
   - Print the screens and a "before" and "after" example of a change.

Exercise 2.2B Purchase Order Line Project

Purpose
To design and code an interactive file-maintenance system with subfiles, basing it upon a similar solution.

General Program Specifications
Create RPG program ORDL22A, which displays *all* purchase order lines. It lets the user
- select records to add, delete, change, or display
- change all of the fields except the order number and line sequence
- delete records that have been delivered with OLADT not equal to zero
- if the user requests a delete of a record with OLADT equal to zero, display a window that presents the record and informs the user that the line cannot be deleted because the record is not closed

4. Copy source member ORDL21C to new member ORDL22A. Make the modifications equivalent to the modifications in Figures 2.7A through 2.7K. The CHG subroutine should not change the values of the order number or sequence number fields, but they should be displayed on the change window.
   - Test and debug.
   - Print the compiler listing.
   - Print the screens and a "before" and "after" example of a change.

5. Add the display capability to the program.
   - Test and debug.
   - Print the compiler listing.
   - Print the screen.

6. Add the delete capability to the program.
   - Only delete records with a OLADT not equal to zero.
   - If OLADT is equal to zero load and display the Bad Delete Window.
   - Test and debug.
   - Print the compiler listing.
   - Print demonstrations of a good delete and a bad delete.

7. Add the add capability to the program.
   - Test and debug.
   - Print the compiler listing.
   - Print demonstrations of an add.

Review

1. What does the READC do? What does it mean when the READC indicator is on?
2. Write the code change necessary to allow entry of 2 *or* C, 4 *or* D, and 5 *or* A.
3. Write the DDS code for the following window:

```
                         DELETE ORDER REQUESTED

         OK to Delete ORDER NO:_____

         and all ORDER LINES?

         Enter=Accept    F12=Cancel
```

4. F3 was opened as a file-level function key: CF03. What would happen if F3 were pressed on the Delete window?

   a. How would you code the Delete subroutine so that this key cancels the request but does not exit the program?

   b. How would you code the Delete subroutine so that the application ends if F3 is pressed on the delete Window?

5. F12 was used to cancel an option; however, if pressed, F12 remains on.

   a. What happens to subsequent options?

   b. How can that be avoided?

6. You should be familiar with the option column.

   a. What happens when someone puts a 7 in the option column?

   b. Write the window definition and the changes to the RPG code to send the following message: You have chosen an invalid code _____! (The window should display the actual code that the user typed.)

7. Step by step, identify what the program does if no options are selected and the Enter key is pressed.
8. Describe why the Change option doesn't require that the subfile be rewritten.
9. If the N were left off the READ statement in the LOAD subroutine, what would happen if a second user attempted to load the same screen from the same physical file?
10. Why must you reload the subfile after an add or delete?

Chapter 3

Managing Multipage Subfiles

Chapter Overview

Chapter 3 helps you understand the implications of the following three subfile load options and be able to demonstrate their use:

✓ Subfile load option 1 — for loading all records

✓ Subfile load option 2 — for a growing subfile

✓ Subfile load option 3 — for a single-page subfile

When you complete the chapter, you will also be able to demonstrate how to use the following keywords

✓ SFLEND (Subfile End)

✓ ROLLUP (Roll Up) and ROLLDOWN (Roll Down)

✓ SFLRCDNBR (Subfile Record Number)

Managing Multipage Subfiles

As you studied the first two chapters, you also created some useful code. Your programs load and display subfiles and provide fully operational file-maintenance systems with pop-up windows for the options. The code you have developed has, however, one serious limitation: it displays and processes only the number of records that fit on a single screen. In this chapter, you learn how to develop code that manages a multipage subfile and lets the user move through the file.

We explore the following three options for managing a multipage subfile. Table 3.1 (page 44) presents code-related and user-related issues for all options.

- Subfile load option 1, which loads the entire file into a large subfile before displaying the first screen.
- Subfile load option 2, which loads the records to fill a single page and displays the subfile. It adds a page of records to the subfile when the last page of loaded records is displayed and the user requests more data by pressing the Page down key.
- Subfile load option 3, which loads a single page of records and displays the subfile. It replaces the current page with the next page whenever the user presses the Page down key and replaces the current page with the previous page whenever the user presses the Page up key.

Table 3.1
Subfile Load Options

Subfile Load Option	Code Issues	User Issues
1. Load entire file.	Simplest code. Limit of 9999 records.	• User has to wait until entire file is loaded. • Data is only updated when a user makes a change that requires reloading the subfile. • Changes made to the data by other users or other programs after the subfile is loaded will not be apparent.
2. Add a page at a time.	Code is more complex. Limit of 9999 records.	• Brief delay whenever a page is loaded. • Pages added when the Page down key is pressed are updated at the time they are added to the subfile. However, subsequent changes to the data made by other users or programs are not displayed until a user makes a change that requires reloading the subfile.
3. Replace the page with the next or previous page of data.	Most complicated code. Uses least memory. No size limit.	• Brief delay whenever the Page up key or the Page down key is pressed. • Data is always updated at the time of processing a Page up/Page down request.

Subfile Size and Subfile Page

Before we examine the details of the three load options, we will explore how each subfile load option controls the subfile's size. You recall that in Chapters 1 and 2, we worked with a single page only and declared the subfile size and the subfile page size as equal (Figure 3.1A). Subfile load option 3, covered later in the chapter, also works with single pages, and, as in the previous chapters, it, too, uses the same value for subfile size and subfile page.

Figure 3.1A
Subfile Size=Subfile Page

```
*...1....+....2....+....3....+....4....+....5....+....6
A                                       SFLSIZ(08)
A                                       SFLPAG(08)
```

Subfile load options 1 and 2 require a subfile that is larger than a single page. The subfile page value remains the number of records that are to be displayed on a single page, but the subfile size has a larger value than the page size.

A fixed-size subfile can be declared by putting the maximum size of the subfile in the subfile size field. Figure 3.1B shows this declaration with a maximum subfile size of 250 records. When the file is opened, a block of memory large enough to accommodate 250 records is claimed. This method of defining a subfile size works well when the maximum number of records is known and does not change.

```
*...1....+....2....+....3....+....4....+....5....+....6
A                                   SFLSIZ(250)
A                                   SFLPAG(08)
```

Figure 3.1B
Subfile Size=Maximum
Number of Records
in Subfile

A growing subfile is declared by setting the subfile size as one greater than the subfile page value (Figure 3.1C). A growing subfile can increase up to 9999 records.

```
*...1....+....2....+....3....+....4....+....5....+....6
A                                   SFLSIZ(09)
A                                   SFLPAG(08)
```

Figure 3.1C
Subfile Size Is One
Greater Than Subfile Page

As the subfile grows, the system gives the program new blocks of memory. This method of defining subfile size works well whenever you code load options 1 or 2.

More Than 9999 Records

Only subfile load option 3 accommodates more than 9999 records. The code that we introduce for subfile load option 1 loads the entire file if it is fewer than 9999 records or the first 9999 records of the file. Subfile load option 2 loads a page each time the user request a new page until either the entire file is loaded or 9999 records are loaded.

If the program displays eight records (like our sample program), then the user would have to press the Page down key 1,250 times to run into the limitation of options 1 and 2. And that number brings up another point. Obviously, when users work with large files, they need a quick way to move to a specific area of the file. Chapter 5 introduces a way to design the capability to quickly locate a record, and using it makes either load option 1 or load option 2 an effective solution for virtually all subfiles.

I recommend using subfile load option 1 for any file smaller than a few hundred records and subfile load option 2 for any larger files. If possible, avoid subfile load option 3, with its complex code. However, because you must be ready to do maintenance on existing code and to develop new code to the specifications of your organization, we will explore all three options.

Subfile Load Option 1: Loading All the Records (Up to 9999) at One Time

The coding of subfile load option 1 requires only minor changes to the code developed in the previous chapters. You change the SFLSIZ value to one more than the subfile page value. Because the SFLSIZ value is greater than the SFLPAG value, the system adds a page of records whenever needed — up to 9999 records. In the Load subroutine, you change the RPG loop control code to limit the value of RRN LT 9999, which keeps the program from attempting to load more than 9999 records. The loop control also ends at the end of file (EOF) of the physical file.

Exercise 3.1A Computers Are US Inventory Project

Purpose
To modify existing code to develop and test a simple multiple-page subfile display.

General Program Specifications
Create maintenance program INV013A and display file INVD013A. The program loads all of the records in the inventory file INVPF into the subfile (up to 9999 records) using subfile load option 1.

1. Copy display file INVD012A into the new member INVD013A and increase the subfile size by one.
2. Copy program INV012A into the new member INV013A and change the limit in the Load subroutine from 8 records to 9999 records.
3. Add the 10 records shown in Table 3.2 to the file, using either the Add option that you created in the last chapter or Display File Utility (DFU).

Table 3.2
Ten Records to Be Added to the File

A325	14" MULTI-SYNC MONITOR	00025	021500	STL	SL1
A326	15" MULTI-SYNC MONITOR	00006	027500	STL	SL2
A327	17" MULTI-SYNC MONITOR	00005	037500	FTW	F21
D2115	3½" DISK DRIVE	00127	002141	STL	S27
D2116	DISK DRIVE - 5¼ "	00007	002141	STL	211
CP07	CABLE PRINTER 7'	00015	000575	STL	S1L
CP10	CABLE PRINTER 10'	00019	000325	STL	S42
CS10MM	CABLE SERIAL 10' MALE–MALE	00015	000412	DAL	D21
D511	511 MBYTE HARD DISK	00023	015715	STL	S15
D1022	1.022 GIG-BYTE HARD DISK	00047	025319	DAL	D25

Compile and test. Note that you must compile the DSPF first and get a "clean" compile before you compile the RPG.

Test the effects of the Page up and Page down keys.

Using + or MORE...

The program that you just created works, but users might find it hard to know when they can press the Page down key. Therefore, as long as pressing the Page down key will show more records, the standard display on the AS/400 displays the term More... in the lower right-hand corner of the display. When the display shows the last available records, it says Bottom.

The subfile end keyword (SFLEND) can be added to the control record in the display file as in Figures 3.2A and 3.2B. The SFLEND keyword — when entered without the *MORE parameter (Figure 3.2A) — displays a plus sign (+) in the rightmost column of the subfile display whenever there are more records.

```
*...1....+....2....+....3....+....4....+....5....+....6

A  90                              SFLEND
```

Figure 3.2A
Subfile End Keyword
with No Parameter

When the *MORE parameter is added to the SFLEND keyword (Figure 3.2B), the keyword displays the term More... on the rightmost end of the line immediately below the end of the subfile display. When no more records are available for display, either the + is removed or More... becomes Bottom.

```
*...1....+....2....+....3....+....4....+....5....+....6

A  90                              SFLEND(*MORE)
```

Figure 3.2B
Subfile End Keyword
with *MORE

The display file determines whether there are more records based on two rules.

1. If the conditioning indicator (in this example, the conditioning indicator is 90) is off, there are more records — because more records can be loaded from the source file. This indicator is usually the same indicator used to sense the end of the physical or logical file that is the source of records to be loaded into the subfile. In our inventory example, that file is INVPF and the indicator used in the READ statements is 90.

2. If the conditioning indicator is on, the display shows + or More... when the subfile is positioned above the last page of records.

Exercise 3.1B Computers Are US Inventory Project

Purpose

To modify existing code to add the subfile end keyword to a simple multiple-page subfile display.

General Program Specifications

Create maintenance program INV013A and display file INVD013A. The program loads all of the records in the inventory file INVPF into the subfile (up to 9999 records) using subfile load option 1. The program indicates to users whether more records are available to view.

4. Modify INVD013A. Add the subfile end keyword without parameters to the control record. Compile the display and the RPG program and test. Print out the display with the + and without it.

5. Modify INVD013A. Add the subfile end keyword with the *MORE parameters to the control record. Compile the display and the RPG program and test. Print out the display with More... and with Bottom. Using the MORE* parameter will be our standard throughout the remainder of this text.

Exercise 3.2A Purchase Order Line Project

Purpose

To design and code a subfile that loads using subfile load option 1.

General Program Specifications

Create the RPG program ORDL23A, which displays all purchase order lines. It lets the user press the Page down key to perform maintenance on the data and loads and displays the word More... when there are more records to be displayed.

1. Copy the display file source member ORDD022A to a new member, ORDD023A. Make the necessary modifications to prepare this display file for subfile load option 1. Your modification should include More.../Bottom on the subfile display. Compile and test the display.

2. Copy the source member ORDL22A to new member ORDL23A. Make the necessary modifications to load all of the records in the file using subfile load option 1.

   - Test and debug.
   - Print the compiler listing.
   - Print the screens and a "before" and "after" example of a change.

3. Add the records shown in Table 3.3 to the order line file.

continued

Exercise 3.2A *Continued*

Table 3.3
Order Line File

OLNUM	OLSEQ	OLPN	OLPRC	OLOQN	OLEDT	OLADT	OLAQN
000019	001	A123	1175.00	50	19981114		0
000019	002	A124	2000.00	50	19981114		0
000020	001	A320	150.00	75	19981115	0	0
000021	001	A124	1900.10	50	19981201	0	0
000021	002	A320	200.00	50	19981201	0	0
000021	003	A319	95.21	10	19981201	0	0
000022	001	A214	200.00	15	19981229	19980923	5
000022	002	A216	305.15	200	19981229	19980923	200
000022	003	A213	415.16	10	19981229	0	0
000023	001	A214	200.00	25	19981222	0	0
000023	002	A216	305.15	150	19981222	0	0
000023	003	A213	415.16	12	19981222	0	0
000023	004	A319	100.00	14	19981222	0	0
000023	005	A320	150.15	225	19981222	0	0
000023	006	A321	400.16	1	19981222	0	0

Subfile Load Option 2: Adding a Page at a Time

Although subfile load option 1 is accomplished with the simplest code, the option could cause a significant waste of processing time in loading records beyond those needed. It could also mean that users would have to wait an unacceptably long time for the display to appear on their screen.

Subfile load option 2 minimizes the wait for the first screen because only the first page of records is loaded. However, there is a slight wait for each new page to be added to the subfile. (This wait is not repeated when the user is paging through any data already loaded.)

Only two changes to the display file are required. Both changes require that new keywords be added to the control record DSP02. The first keyword activates the Page down key and turns on an indicator when the key is pressed.

The keyword ROLLUP, shown in Figure 3.3A, is equivalent to the keyword PAGEDOWN. (IBM display terminals use the term roll up to mean the same thing that page down means on PCs; either keyword can be used with either type of display.) When the last page of the subfile has been displayed and either the Rollup or Page down key has been pressed, the display-file code will turn on the indicator enclosed in parentheses (in Figure 3.3A, indicator 25) and return control to the RPG program.

We will not want this keyword active once all the records in the physical file have been loaded into the subfile. The PAGEDOWN and ROLLUP keywords can be controlled by a conditioning indicator that the RPG program can set to a false condition when the physical file has been completely loaded. In Figure 3.3A, this control value is N90. When indicator 90 is off, the keyword is active, and when indicator 90 is on, the keyword is inactive. When the subfile is loaded from physical file INVPF, the RPG program uses indicator 90 as the EOF. As long as the RPG program has not encountered the end of the physical file, indicator 90 is off and the keyword is active (when the program comes to the end of physical file INVPF, indicator 90 is turned on and the keyword is inactive).

Figure 3.3A
Rollup Keyword Returns
Indicator 25 On When
Indicator 90 Is Off

```
*...1....+....2....+....3....+....4....+....5....+....6

A N90                                  ROLLUP(25)
```

The second keyword that must be added to the control record is used to control which page of the subfile is displayed and which record the cursor is located on when the subfile is displayed. The SFLRCDNBR keyword receives a value from the program through a variable defined on the same line with the keyword. This variable, which in the example shown in Figure 3.3B is named SFLRCD, must be signed (4 0), and its usage must be (H) hidden.

Figure 3.3B
Subfile Record Number
Locates the Cursor

```
*...1....+....2....+....3....+....4....+....5....+....6

A           SFLRCD      4S 0H       SFLRCDNBR(CURSOR)
```

A hidden variable is one whose value is available to the display file and the RPG program, but it is not displayed on the screen. The RPG program must include code that determines which record should be displayed at the top of the screen whenever a new page is added. The RPG program loads this value into the variable associated with the SFLRCDNBR keyword before it displays the subfile. That value is the relative record number (RRN) of the first record of the page displayed. Keywords with variables must appear after the general subfile keywords, as shown in Figure 3.3C.

Figure 3.3C
Subfile Control Record
for Subfile Load
Option 2

```
*...1....+....2....+....3....+....4....+....5....+....6

A****************************************************************
A           R DSP02                   SFLCTL(DSP01)
A 90                                   SFLEND(*MORE)
A                                      SFLSIZ(0009)
A                                      SFLPAG(0008)
** The rollup function will turn on the desired indicator when the
** rollup (Display station words for PageDown) key is pressed
** IN25 is turned when PgDn is pressed..but this command is only
** in effect until indicator 90 is on.
```

continued

```
*...1....+....2....+....3....+....4....+....5....+....6
** If IN90 is off and PgDn is pressed, the screen returns IN25 on.
** If 90 is on, the PgDn key will be processed by the screen code,
** either displaying the next page or a message warning about bottom
** of data.  We will use IN25 to detect when another page should be
** loaded.
*
A N90                              ROLLUP(25 'ROLLUP OR PGDN')
A                                  OVERLAY
A  50                              SFLDSP
A  50                              SFLDSPCTL
A N50                              SFLCLR
**
** We've taken more control of the system and must now take control of
** the cursor. Otherwise, the PgDn key will load another page but we
** will still display the first page. As we load the subfile, the RPG
** code will compute new values for the CURSOR location. The value
** will be loaded into the variable SFLRCD as a hidden value. The
** compiler gets "upset" if it encounters the SFLRCDNBR keyword
** before the SFLDSP and SFLCLR keywords.
*
A            SFLRCD        4S 0H     SFLRCDNBR(CURSOR)
A                                  1 31'COMPUTERS ARE US'
A                                  2 31'WORK WITH INVENTORY LISTS'
A                                  1  2USER
A                                  1 71DATE
A                                     EDTCDE(Y)
A                                  6  4'PART NUMBER'
A                                  6 16'DESCRIPTION'
A                                  6 47'QNTY'
A                                  6 55'COST'
A                                  6 65'EXTENDED'
A                                  6  2'0'
A                                  4  3'2=Change'
A                                  4 15'4=Delete'
A                                  4 27'5=Display'
```

Figure 3.3C
Continued

The pseudocode for the RPG program for subfile load option 2 is shown in Figures 3.4A through 3.4C. The Respond (RESPD) subroutine (Figure 3.4A) has been modified to call the subroutine to locate the position of the physical file just beyond the last record previously loaded, read the next record from the physical file, and load a page whenever indicator 25 is on. If indicator 25 is off, the subroutine works just as it did in Chapter 2.

Figure 3.4A

Pseudocode for the
Respond (RESPD)
Subroutine with
the Subfile Load
Option Added

RESPD subroutine

> If indicator 25 is on (the Page down key was pressed at the current bottom of the subfile)
>
> > Position in the physical file immediately after the last record loaded
> >
> > Read the record
> >
> > Execute the Load Page (LOADPG) subroutine
>
> ELSE
>
> > Set the update flag to off (this flag will be set on if a change requires that the subfile be reloaded)
> >
> > Read the first changed record in the subfile (a changed record must have a new value in D1PICK field because that's the only field the user can change)
> >
> > Do while changed records exist
> >
> > > Do selection
> > >
> > > > Select when D1PICK is 2 (Change)
> > > >
> > > > > Execute the Change (CHG) subroutine
> > >
> > > End selection
> > >
> > > Read the next changed record in the subfile
> >
> > End do
> >
> > If the update flag is on
> >
> > > Compute the number of pages up to the last changed record
> > >
> > > Execute the Clear Subfile (CLRSF) subroutine
> > >
> > > Repeat for the number of pages up to the last changed record
> > >
> > > > Execute the LOADPG subroutine
> > >
> > > If SFL>RRN then SFLRCD=RRN (occurs only if the last records were deleted)
> >
> > End if
>
> End if

End subroutine

Figure 3.4B shows the pseudocode for the LOADPG subroutine, which includes most of the LOAD subroutine from the previous examples. The code to clear the subfile is moved to another subroutine, CLRSF, because that code will only be used when you initially create or rebuild the subfile.

The LOAD subroutine needs a few additional variables: (load count) is used to count the number of records loaded during this execution of the subroutine. RRNHLD contains the number of records in the subfile. This value, obtained from the value of RRN at the end of each execution of the LOADPG subroutine, lets RRN be set to the number of records that are in the subfile prior to adding the next page. RRN must point at the EOF of the subfile whenever records are added. Between executions of this subroutine, the value of RRNs will change to point at the record accessed with a READC (Read Next Changed Record) operation in the Respond subroutine. RRN must be reset every time this subroutine runs to make certain that it is pointing to the EOF; this is accomplished at the beginning of the routine by moving the value of RRNHLD to RRN.

LOADPG subroutine
    Initialize load count to zero
    Move the value of the relative record number hold area (RRNHLD) to the relative record number (RRN)
    Set subfile record to one greater than the previous RRN
    Do while not EOF and load count < 8 and RRN < 9999
        Load source file fields into SFL record fields
        Add 1 to load count
        Add 1 to RRN
        Write subfile record
        Save the value of the last part number loaded
        Read the next record from the source file
    End do
    IF RRN = 0
        Create a 'no records' record
        Add 1 to RRN
        Write subfile record
    End if
    Set RRNHLD = RRN
End subroutine

Figure 3.4B
Pseudocode for the LOADPG Subroutine

The value of the key (part number) of the last record loaded into the subfile is stored in the variable LASTPN. This variable is used when the Page down key is pressed to position the physical file to the first record for the next page.

The LOAD subroutine also sets the value into SFLRCD, the variable used in the display file by the SFLRCDNBR keyword. Loading the RRN of the first record of the new screen into SFLRCD causes the display file to position the cursor on the first record of the new screen.

Figure 3.4C shows the pseudocode for the CLRSF subroutine. It contains the code to clear the subfile, reset the value of RRN, and position and read the first record from the physical file.

CLRSF subroutine
    Turn indicator 50 *off
    Write to Dsp02 (clear the subfile)
    Turn indicator 50 *on
    Set RRN and RRNHLD to zero
    Position INVPF at the top of file (TOF)
    Read the first record from INVPF
End subroutine

Figure 3.4C
Pseudocode for the CLRSF Subroutine

Because the LOAD subroutine has been replaced with the LOADPG and CLRSF subroutines, the mainline of our code is changed to call both subroutines, as shown in Figure 3.5A.

Figure 3.5A
Mainline Code for
Subfile Load
Option 2

```
*...1....+....2....+....3....+....4....+....5....+....6

****************************************************************
*    MAINLINE                 M A I N L I N E
****************************************************************
*
A3B  C                        EXSR CLRSF
A3B  C                        EXSR LOADPG
     C                        EXFMTDSP02
     *
     C            *IN03       DOWEQ*OFF
     *
     C                        EXSR RESPD
     *
     C                        EXFMTDSP02
     C                        ENDDO
     * END PROCESSING
     C                        MOVE *ON     *INLR
     C                        RETRN
```

Figure 3.5B contains the code for the RESPD subroutine for subfile load option 2. When the update flag has been set by the Delete or Add subroutines, the subfile will be reloaded from record 1 to the page containing the last change. To do that, the number of pages (LOOPC) is computed by dividing the RRN (which contains the location of the last READC performed by the RESPD subroutine) by the number of lines per page. The result is the number of complete pages. If the division has a remainder, one additional page must be loaded.

Figure 3.5B
Code for RESPD
Subroutine for Subfile
Load Option 2

```
*...1....+....2....+....3....+....4....+....5....+....6

****************************************************************
*    PROCESS RESPONSES TO SUBFILE
****************************************************************
*
     C            RESPD       BEGSR
     *
A3B  C            *IN25       IFEQ *ON
A3B  * position after last record previously loaded and read first rec
A3B  C            LASTPN      SETGTINVPF
A3B  C                        READ INVPF              N   90
A3B  C                        EXSR LOADPG
A3B  C                        ELSE
     C                        MOVE *OFF    UPDFLG  1
     C                        READCDSP01                    94
     C            *IN94       DOWEQ*OFF
     C                        Z-ADDRRN     SFLRCD
     C                        SELEC
     *
     C            D1PICK      WHEQ '2'
     C            D1PICK      OREQ 'C'
     C                        EXSR CHG
     * -- other options would follow
     *
```

continued

Figure 3.5B
Continued

```
*...1....+....2....+....3....+....4....+....5....+....6
       C                      ENDSL
       C                      READCDSP01                          94
       C                      ENDDO
        *
       C          UPDFLG      IFEQ *ON
A3B     * Compute the number of pages to load
A3B    C          RRN         DIV  8          LOOPC   40
A3B    C                      MVR             LOOPM   10
A3B    C          LOOPM       IFGT 0
A3B    C                      ADD  1          LOOPC
A3B    C                      ENDIF
A3B    C                      EXSR CLRSF
A3B    C                      DO   LOOPC
A3B    C                      EXSR LOADPG
A3B    C                      ENDDO
A3B    C          SFLRCD      IFGT RRN
A3B    C                      Z-ADDRRN        SFLRCD
       C                      ENDIF
       C                      ENDIF
A3B    C                      ENDIF
       C                      ENDSR
```

Figure 3.5C contains the CLRSF subroutine, which resembles the first portion of the LOAD subroutine used in previous programs.

Figure 3.5C
The CLRSF Subroutine
for Subfile Load
Option 2

```
*...1....+....2....+....3....+....4....+....5....+....6
A3B    *****************************************************************
A3B    *    CLRSF- CLEARS THE SUBFILE
A3B    *****************************************************************
A3B    C          CLRSF       BEGSR
        *
       C                      MOVE *OFF        *IN50
       C                      WRITEDSP02
       C                      MOVE *ON         *IN50
       C                      Z-ADD*ZERO       RRN    40
A3B    C                      Z-ADD*ZERO       RRNHLD 40
       C          *LOVAL      SETLLINVPF
       C                      READ INVPF              N   90 NOT LOCKED
        * write footer record
       C                      WRITEFOOTER1               Write footer
        *
A3B    C                      ENDSR
```

Figure 3.5D contains the LOADPG subroutine. It varies from the LOAD subroutine used before in two ways. First, clearing the file and reading the first record has been moved to the CLRSF subroutine. Second, the loop used to load records now tests three conditions:

- The end of the source file (indicator 90)
- The count of records added to this page (LOADCT)
- The maximum size of the subfile (9999)

Figure 3.5D
The LOADPG
Subroutine for
Subfile Load
Option 2

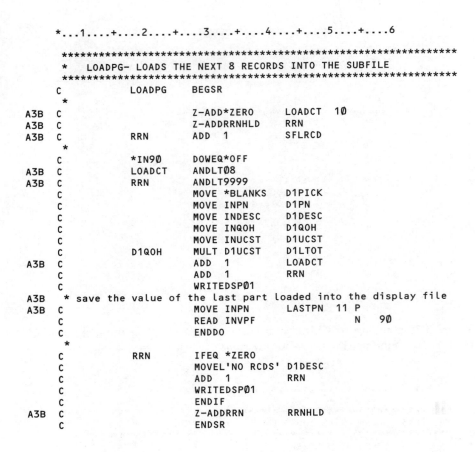

```
*...1....+....2....+....3....+....4....+....5....+....6

**********************************************************************
*   LOADPG- LOADS THE NEXT 8 RECORDS INTO THE SUBFILE
**********************************************************************
       C           LOADPG      BEGSR
       *
A3B    C                       Z-ADD*ZERO      LOADCT  10
A3B    C                       Z-ADDRRNHLD     RRN
A3B    C           RRN         ADD  1          SFLRCD
       *
       C                       *IN90    DOWEQ*OFF
A3B    C           LOADCT      ANDLT08
A3B    C           RRN         ANDLT9999
       C                       MOVE *BLANKS    D1PICK
       C                       MOVE INPN       D1PN
       C                       MOVE INDESC     D1DESC
       C                       MOVE INQOH      D1QOH
       C                       MOVE INUCST     D1UCST
       C           D1QOH       MULT D1UCST     D1LTOT
A3B    C                       ADD  1          LOADCT
       C                       ADD  1          RRN
       C                       WRITEDSP01
A3B    * save the value of the last part loaded into the display file
A3B    C                       MOVE INPN       LASTPN  11 P
       C                       READ INVPF                    N   90
       C                       ENDDO
       *
       C           RRN         IFEQ *ZERO
       C                       MOVEL'NO RCDS'  D1DESC
       C                       ADD  1          RRN
       C                       WRITEDSP01
       C                       ENDIF
A3B    C                       Z-ADDRRN        RRNHLD
       C                       ENDSR
```

Exercise 3.1C Computers Are US Inventory Project

Purpose
To modify existing code to add the subfile end keyword to a growing multiple-page subfile display.

General Program Specifications
Create maintenance program INV013B and display file INVD013B. The program loads one page at a time into the Subfile DSP01 using subfile load option 2. The program lets users know whether there are more records available to view.

6. Copy display file INVD013A to new member INVD013B and modify it. Add the subfile keywords ROLLUP and SFLRCDNBR. Compile the display and test it.

7. Copy program INV013A to new member INV013B, modify the mainline code and the RESPD subroutine, and replace the LOAD subroutine with the CLRSF and LOADPG subroutines shown in Figures 3.5A through D. Compile the RPG program and test it.

Exercise 3.2B Purchase Order Line Project

Purpose
To design and code a subfile using subfile load option 2.

General Program Specifications
Create the RPG program ORDL23B, which displays all purchase order lines. It lets users press the Page down key to perform maintenance on the data, and it displays the word More... when there are more records available to be displayed.

4. Copy the display file source member ORDD023A to a new member ORDD023B. Make the necessary modifications to prepare this display file for Subfile Load Option 2. Compile and test the display.

5. Copy the source member ORDL23A to a new member, ORDL23B. Make the necessary modifications to load all of the records in the file using subfile load option 2.

   • Test and debug.
   • Print the compiler listing.

Except for the changes to the LOAD subroutine — which was replaced by the CLRSF and LOADPG subroutines, as well as the RESPD subroutine and mainline — the other subroutines developed in Chapters 1 and 2 need not be altered to work with subfile load option 2.

Subfile Load Option 3: Loading a Single Page

In subfile load option 3, the subfile is never more than a single page long. Whenever the user presses the Page up or the Page down key, the program clears the subfile and loads the next or previous page.

With this option, we programmatically manage the file as blocks of eight records (remember that eight was an arbitrary number based on how many records would look good on the screen layout). When the user presses the Page down key, the program clears the subfile and loads the next page. When the user presses the Page up key, the program clears the subfile and repositions a sufficient number of records above the current page in the physical file to cause the previous page to be loaded. This load option allows fast access to each page of data but requires a good deal of coding to determine and locate the records to load when a Page up or Page down key is pressed.

This option is preferred for working with dynamic data. All the subfile load options show the data as it existed at the time that the page displayed was actually loaded, regardless of the subsequent changes made by other users or other programs. Because every PageUp/PageDown request causes this option to reload that page from the physical data, the display always shows data that was up-to-date the last time that the Page up or Page down keys were pressed. To make certain that a page loaded by this option is up-to-date, a user could simply press the Page down key and then press the Page up key.

The description and code samples for subfile load option 3 specify only differences from subfile load option 2.

In addition to the ROLLUP keyword used in the display file in option 2, a ROLLDOWN keyword is used to activate the Page up key. This keyword is conditioned by an indicator that indicates when the top of the file has been reached (Figure 3.6).

Figure 3.6
Page Up and
Page Down Keys

```
*...1....+....2....+....3....+....4....+....5....+....6
A N90                                ROLLUP(25 'ROLLUP OR PGDN')
A N91                                ROLLDOWN(26 'ROLLDN OR PGUP')
```

In subfile load option 3, the subfile is never longer than one page. Therefore, the subfile page size and subfile file size both equal the number of records displayed on a single screen. Finally, the SFLRCDNBR keyword is unnecessary. (This keyword was used in subfile load option 2 to control which page is displayed.) It is unnecessary because only a single page of subfile records exists in subfile load option 3.

The pseudocode for subfile load option 3 is shown in Figures 3.7A through 3.7C. The LOAD subroutine resembles the LOAD subroutine from Chapters 1 and 2 in that it clears the subfile and loads a single page. The LOAD subroutine stores the part numbers of the first and last records in the current page of the subfile. This makes it easy to locate the physical file properly when the next page is loaded or the current page updated.

To load the previous page, the program selects a point before the first record of the current page, reads back the number of records in a screen plus one additional record, and then reads that record. (Initially, the first record will be read in the mainline code, which you will see in Figure 3.8A, page 61.)

The RESPD subroutine has been modified as shown in Figure 3.7A. When the BACKUP subroutine is called, it reads backwards in the physical file until it reaches the point where the previous screen begins.

If the Page down key is pressed, *IN91 is turned off. Indicator 91 is used to signal the TOF, and if we've gone down one or more pages, we are no longer at the top of the physical file. Also, the physical file is positioned after the last record in the current subfile page and that record is read.

Both Page up and Page down cause the LOAD subroutine to be called, which loads the next page from the current record in the physical file.

Near the end of the RESPD subroutine, the update flag is tested to determine whether the subfile page has changed and needs to be reloaded. To reload the current page, the physical file is positioned just above the first record of the current page and that record is read and the LOAD subroutine is called.

Figure 3.7B shows the pseudocode for the LOAD subroutine. This subroutine includes most of the LOAD subroutine that appears in Chapters 1 and 2, including the code to clear the subfile.

RESPD subroutine
    If either indicator 25 or 26 is on (page down or page up)
        If indicator 26 is on (page up)
            Execute the BACKUP subroutine
        Else (page down)
            Move *off to indicator 91 (top-of-file (TOF) indicator)
            Position the physical file just beyond the last record loaded into the subfile page
            Read the next record from the physical file
        End if
            Execute the LOAD subroutine

    Else
        Set the update flag to off (this flag is on if a change requires that the subfile be reloaded)
        Read the first changed record in the subfile (a changed record must have a new value in D1PICK field because that's the only field the user can change)
        Do while changed records exist
            Do selection
                Select when D1PICK is 2 (Change)
                    Execute the CHG subroutine
            End selection
            Read the next changed record in the subfile
        End do
        If the update flag is on
            Position the physical file just above the first record loaded into the subfile page
            Read the next record from the physical file
            Execute the LOAD subroutine
        End if
    End if
End subroutine

Figure 3.7A

Pseudocode for the RESPD Subroutine with Subfile Load Option 3 Added

Figure 3.7B

Pseudocode for the
LOAD Subroutine

LOAD subroutine
    Clear the subfile
    Set RRN, relative record number hold area (RRNHLD), and load count to zero
    Write the footer
    Do while not EOF and load count <8
        Load source file fields into subfile record fields
        Add 1 to load count
        Add 1 to RRN
        Write subfile record
    End if
    Set RRNHLD = RRN
End subroutine

The LOAD subroutine uses the same variables as in subfile load option 2. Load Count (LOADCT) is used to count the number of records loaded during this execution of the subroutine.

The RRNHLD value contains the number of records in the subfile, which is obtained from the value of RRN at the end of the previous execution of the LOAD subroutine. Because this could be a partial page from the end of the data file, this value will be used to process the page-up requests. FRSTPN is the part number of the first record loaded into the current page. LASTPN is the part number of the last record loaded into the current page.

Figure 3.7C shows the pseudocode for the BACKUP subroutine. It uses the READP operation code to read backwards through the file until either the TOF is reached or the file has been positioned at the correct location. It then does the initial read from the data file preparing the data for the LOAD subroutine.

Figure 3.7C

Pseudocode for the
BACKUP Subroutine

BACKUP subroutine
        Position physical file above first record loaded into the current subfile
        page
        Set indicator 90 off
    Do while indicator 91 is off (TOF) and the count is less than the page size+1
        Read the previous record from the data file
        Add 1 to count
    End do
    If indicator 91 is on (TOF)
        Position at TOF
    End if
    Read from the data file
End subroutine

If either the top of the data file (during backup) or the bottom of the data file (during load) is encountered, the record pointer must be repositioned to the TOF or EOF for subsequent read or read previous operations to be successful. These tests and the SETLL (Set Lower Limit) or SETGT (Set Greater Than) operations are also included in the BACKUP subroutine.

The RPG code for the mainline code, and the RESPD, LOAD, and BACKUP subroutines are shown in Figures 3.8A through 3.8D.

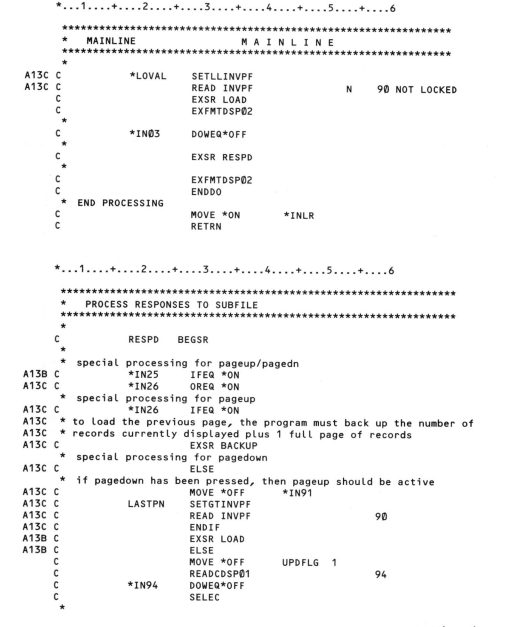

```
      *...1....+....2....+....3....+....4....+....5....+....6
      *****************************************************************
      *    MAINLINE                      M A I N L I N E
      *****************************************************************
      *
A13C  C           *LOVAL     SETLLINVPF
A13C  C                      READ INVPF                     N    90 NOT LOCKED
      C                      EXSR LOAD
      C                      EXFMTDSP02
      *
      C           *IN03      DOWEQ*OFF
      *
      C                      EXSR RESPD
      *
      C                      EXFMTDSP02
      C                      ENDDO
      *  END PROCESSING
      C                      MOVE *ON        *INLR
      C                      RETRN
```

Figure 3.8A
Mainline Code for Subfile Load Option 3

```
      *...1....+....2....+....3....+....4....+....5....+....6
      *****************************************************************
      *    PROCESS RESPONSES TO SUBFILE
      *****************************************************************
      *
      C           RESPD      BEGSR
      *
      *  special processing for pageup/pagedn
A13B  C           *IN25      IFEQ *ON
A13C  C           *IN26      OREQ *ON
      *  special processing for pageup
A13C  C           *IN26      IFEQ *ON
A13C  * to load the previous page, the program must back up the number of
A13C  * records currently displayed plus 1 full page of records
A13C  C                      EXSR BACKUP
      *  special processing for pagedown
A13C  C                      ELSE
      * if pagedown has been pressed, then pageup should be active
A13C  C                      MOVE *OFF        *IN91
A13C  C           LASTPN     SETGTINVPF
A13C  C                      READ INVPF                          90
A13C  C                      ENDIF
A13B  C                      EXSR LOAD
A13B  C                      ELSE
      C                      MOVE *OFF        UPDFLG  1
      C                      READCDSP01                          94
      C           *IN94      DOWEQ*OFF
      C                      SELEC
      *
```

Figure 3.8B
RESPD Subroutine Code for Subfile Load Option 3

continued

Figure 3.8B
Continued

```
*...1....+....2....+....3....+....4....+....5....+....6
       C           D1PICK      WHEQ '2'
       C           D1PICK      OREQ 'C'
       C                       EXSR CHG
        *  other options would follow
        *
       C                       ENDSL
       C                       READCDSP01                        94
       C                       ENDDO
        *
       C           UPDFLG      IFEQ *ON
        * position the physical file to the top of the page
A13C   C           FRSTPN      SETLLINVPF
A13C   C                       READ INVPF                        90
       C                       EXSR LOAD
       C                       ENDIF
       C                       ENDIF
       C                       ENDSR
       ****************************************************************
```

Figure 3.8C
LOAD Subroutine
Code for Subfile
Load Option 3

```
*...1....+....2....+....3....+....4....+....5....+....6

       ****************************************************************
       C           LOAD        BEGSR
        * clear the subfile
       C                       MOVE *OFF    *IN50
       C                       WRITEDSP02
       C                       MOVE *ON     *IN50
       C                       Z-ADD*ZERO   RRN      40
       C                       Z-ADD*ZERO   RRNHLD   40
       C                       Z-ADD*ZERO   LOADCT   30
A13    C                       MOVE INPN    FRSTPN 11 P
        * write footer record
       C                       WRITEFOOTER1                       Write footer
        *
       C           *IN90       DOWEQ*OFF
       C           LOADCT      ANDLT08
       C                       MOVE *BLANKS D1PICK
       C                       MOVE INPN    D1PN
       C                       MOVE INDESC  D1DESC
       C                       MOVE INQOH   D1QOH
       C                       MOVE INUCST  D1UCST
       C           D1QOH       MULT D1UCST  D1LTOT
       C                       ADD  1       LOADCT
       C                       ADD  1       RRN
       C                       WRITEDSP01
        * capture the value of the last part number loaded to page
A13    C                       MOVE INPN    LASTPN 11 P
       C                       READ INVPF               N       90
       C                       ENDDO
        *
       C           RRN         IFEQ *ZERO
       C                       MOVE 'NO RCDS' D1DESC
       C                       ADD  1       RRN
       C                       WRITEDSP01
       C                       ENDIF
       C                       Z-ADDRRN     RRNHLD
       C                       ENDSR
```

```
*...1....+....2....+....3....+....4....+....5....+....6

*********************************************************************
*    BACKUP - ROLL BACK THE NUMBER OF RECORDS DISPLAYED
*             PLUS THE NUMBER OF COMPLETE PAGES IN BACKPG (0 OR 1)
*********************************************************************
C           BACKUP    BEGSR
* position the physical file to the top of the current page
C           FRSTPN    SETLLINVPF
C                     MOVE *OFF    *IN90
C                     Z-ADD*ZERO   LOADCT
* read back through the file to the top of the previous page
C           *IN91     DOWEQ*OFF
C           LOADCT    ANDLT9
C                     READPINVPF             N   91
C                     ADD  1       LOADCT
C                     ENDDO
* if top of file has been reached the file must be repositioned
* with setll and the indicator turned off
C           *IN91     IFEQ *ON
C           *LOVAL    SETLLINVPF
C                     ENDIF
* perform initial read
C                     READ INVPF             N   90
*
C                     ENDSR
```

Figure 3.8D
BACKUP Subroutine Code
for Subfile Load Option 3

Exercise 3.1D Computers Are US Inventory Project

Purpose
To modify existing code to add the subfile end keyword to a growing multiple-page subfile display.

General Program Specifications
Create the maintenance program INV013C and the display file INVD013C. The program loads one page at a time into the subfile DSP01, using subfile load option 3. The program indicates to users whether there are more records to be displayed.

8. Copy display file INVD013A to new member INVD013C and modify it. Add the subfile keywords ROLLUP and ROLLDOWN. Compile and test the display.

9. Copy program INV013A to new member INV013C. Modify the mainline code as well as the RESPD and LOAD subroutines and add the BACKUP subroutine shown in Figures 3.8A through 3.8D. Compile and test the RPG program.

Exercise 3.2C Purchase Order Line Project

Purpose
To design and code a subfile that loads using subfile load option 3.

General Program Specifications
Create RPG program ORDL23C, which displays all purchase order lines. It lets the user press the Page down key to perform maintenance on the data and displays the word More... when there are more records to be displayed.

6. Copy the display-file source member ORDD023A to a new member, ORDD023C. Make the necessary modifications to prepare this display file for subfile load option 3. Compile and test the display.

7. Copy the source member ORDL23A to a new member ORDL23C. Make the necessary modifications to load all of the records in the file using subfile load option 3.

   - Test and debug.
   - Print the compiler listing.

Review

1. For each of the subfile load options, state what is displayed if — after the initial load and while a user is viewing the first screen — another program deleted all of the records. What would happen with each load option if the Page down key were pressed? What would happen if the Page up key were pressed?

2. If we have a small number of records to display, which option would be most appropriate? Why?

3. Explain how the BACKUP subroutine works. Why is it necessary to use a SETLL on the physical file if the TOF is encountered during backup?

4. The bottom of the physical file is displayed and the Page up key is pressed. What happens in the RPG code for each of the following load options?

   a. Option 1
   b. Option 2
   c. Option 3

5. The first page is displayed, there are more physical records available to load, and the Page down key is pressed. What happens in the RPG code for each of the following load options?

   a. Option 1
   b. Option 2
   c. Option 3

6. The first page is displayed, the user has already pressed the Page down key once followed by the Page up key, there are more physical records available to load, and the Page down key is pressed. What happens in the RPG code for each of the following load options?

   a. Option 1
   b. Option 2
   c. Option 3

Chapter 4

Adding Drop and Fold Capabilities and Using the Header and Footer

Chapter Overview

When you finish Chapter 4, you will be able to describe and use

✓ the SFLDROP (Subfile Drop) and SFLFOLD (Subfile Fold) keywords

✓ the SFLPAG (Subfile Page) keyword with the SFLDROP and SFLFOLD keywords

✓ the SFLCSRRRN (Subfile Cursor Relative Record Number) keyword

✓ the layout of the SFL record to accommodate drop and fold

✓ the layout of the SFL record to place a blank row between records

✓ the Input, Output, or Both fields on the header record

✓ the Output fields on the footer record

Introduction to Drop and Fold

The data to be displayed on a screen frequently exceeds the space available to display it. This is especially true when you design displays with subfiles that are usually limited to a single row of 80 characters. The first part of the chapter introduces a new display-file keyword that lets the user press a function key and expand the display of each record from a single-row layout to a multiple-row layout. Adding this feature to a subfile display lets the screen designer lay out the first row with the frequently viewed data and subsequent rows with data that users would view less often.

Figure 4.1 (page 66) shows the inventory file maintenance screen. The display is well laid out, easy to read, and presents the most frequently needed data. However, the inventory file (INVPF) contains fields for warehouse and warehouse location that are not shown. Although these fields are included in the display window (option 5), this isn't convenient for users who need to scan the data for items in a particular warehouse or location.

Figure 4.2 (page 66) shows the display after the user presses F6 to display the additional fields. F6 works like a toggle for the user; pressing it again switches the display shown in Figure 4.2 back to the display shown in Figure 4.1.

Figure 4.1
Initial Display with
SFLDRP Keyword

```
A300C1                          COMPUTERS ARE US                    12/21/98
INVD012A                     INVENTORY MAINTENANCE

   2=Change      4=Delete     5=Display      6=Add

O   PART NUMBER      DESCRIPTION            QNTY          COST      EXTENDED

_   A123            Computer x486            21       1,301.15    27,324.15
_   A124            Computer Pentium        215       3,100.16   666,534.40
_   A125            Printer - Laser          81         974.21    78,911.01
_   A213            Printer - Ink Jet        15         457.15     6,857.25
_   A214            Printer - Dot Matrix     21         251.14     5,273.94
_   A215            Scanner - Hand           15         127.19     1,907.85
_   A216            Scanner - Flat Bed        5         421.15     2,105.75
_   A319            CD-ROM                    6         115.96       695.76
                                                                  More ...

===============================================================================
   F3=Exit Subsystem         F6=Display Details
```

Figure 4.2
Display After
F6 Is Pressed

```
A300C1                          COMPUTERS ARE US                    12/21/98
INVD012A                     INVENTORY MAINTENANCE

   2=Change      4=Delete     5=Display      6=Add

O   PART NUMBER      DESCRIPTION                 QNTY        COST    EXTENDED

_   A123            Computer x486                 21     1,301.15   27,324.15
                      WAREHOUSE: DLS   LOCATION: 15A
_   A124            Computer Pentium             215     3,100.16  666,534.40
                      WAREHOUSE: FTW   LOCATION: 21901
_   A125            Printer - Laser               81       974.21   78,911.01
                      WAREHOUSE: DLS   LOCATION: X19
_   A213            Printer - Ink Jet             15       457.15    6,857.25
                      WAREHOUSE: FTW   LOCATION: 319
                                                                    More ...

===============================================================================
   F3=Exit Subsystem         F6=Display Details
```

The subfile keyword that initially displays only the first line of the subfile records (as in Figure 4.1) and reacts to a function key by switching into a multiline format (as in Figure 4.2) is **SFLDROP**. Conversely, the keyword **SFLFOLD** initially displays the subfile in a multiline format (as in Figure 4.2) and reacts to a function key by switching to a single-line format (as in Figure 4.1). These keywords are mutually exclusive; only one of them should be used in a subfile control record.

Creating the Subfile Record
for Subfile Drop and Fold

To add drop and fold, the additional fields are added to the subfile record as shown in Figure 4.3. Fields to be displayed on the first line are entered with the first line number of the subfile (8 in this example). Fields to be displayed on the second line are coded with the next line number (9). If a third or fourth line were needed, the line numbers would be 10 and 11. If you look back at Figure 4.2, you can see that

'WAREHOUSE:' and 'LOCATION:' precede the fields on the second line of each record. The coding for these constants is shown shaded in Figure 4.3. Because these constants are to be displayed on the second line of each subfile record, they are entered with the line position of the second line of the first record (9).

```
*...1....+....2....+....3....+....4....+....5....+....6

A* Subfile example DDS  - INVD014A
A* by Phil Levinson
A*******************************************
A                                  PRINT
A                                  CF03(03)
A*******************************************
A
A           R DSP01                    SFL
A             D1PICK       1A  I  8  2
A             D1PN        11A  O  8  4
A             D1DESC      30A  O  8 16
A             D1QOH        5Y 00  8 47EDTCDE(1)
A             D1UCST       6Y 20  8 55EDTCDE(1)
A             D1LTOT       8Y 20  8 65EDTCDE(1)
A                                 9 18'WAREHOUSE:'
A             D1WH         3A  O  9 29
A                                 9 34'LOCATION:'
A             D1WHL        5A  O  9 44
A*******************************************
```

Figure 4.3
Subfile Record Definition
Including Drop/Fold Fields

Creating the Subfile Control Record for Subfile Drop and Fold

A sample subfile control record is shown in Figure 4.4 (page 68). Although this is the control record for subfile load option 2, the same two changes would be required in any subfile control record. The SFLDROP keyword has been added, followed by CF06. CF06 is the function key that causes the display file to switch from the drop (single-line format) to the fold (multiline format).

The subfile page size (SFLPAG) has been changed to the number of folded records that can be displayed. The value of SFLPAG has been changed to 4 (four two-line records occupy eight lines). In drop mode, eight records are displayed per page; in folded mode, only four records are displayed per page.

Figure 4.4
Subfile Control Record for
Subfile Load Option 2
with Subfile Drop

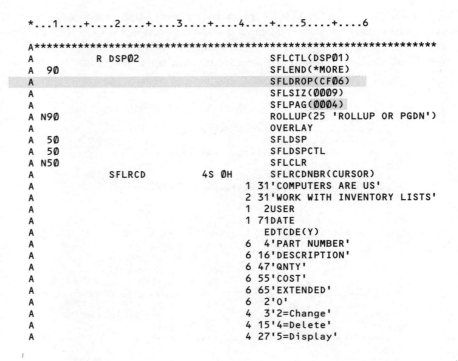

```
*...1....+....2....+....3....+....4....+....5....+....6

A****************************************************************
A           R DSP02                    SFLCTL(DSP01)
A    90                                 SFLEND(*MORE)
A                                       SFLDROP(CF06)
A                                       SFLSIZ(0009)
A                                       SFLPAG(0004)
A    N90                                ROLLUP(25 'ROLLUP OR PGDN')
A                                       OVERLAY
A    50                                 SFLDSP
A    50                                 SFLDSPCTL
A    N50                                SFLCLR
A           SFLRCD         4S 0H        SFLRCDNBR(CURSOR)
A                                     1 31'COMPUTERS ARE US'
A                                     2 31'WORK WITH INVENTORY LISTS'
A                                     1  2USER
A                                     1 71DATE
A                                       EDTCDE(Y)
A                                     6  4'PART NUMBER'
A                                     6 16'DESCRIPTION'
A                                     6 47'QNTY'
A                                     6 55'COST'
A                                     6 65'EXTENDED'
A                                     6  2'0'
A                                     4  3'2=Change'
A                                     4 15'4=Delete'
A                                     4 27'5=Display'
```

Modifying the Footer Record for Drop and Fold

The footer record is used to display function key definitions to the user. Because the drop or fold is going to be activated by pressing F6, the footer record should inform the user about that.

Modifying the RPG Program for Drop and Fold

Because the display file manages the fold-and-drop process without returning to the RPG program, the only modifications to the RPG program are in the subroutines that write or update the subfile records. The subfile records contain some new fields (D1WH and D1WHL). Therefore, the subroutines that write or update the subfile records must be modified to move the appropriate data into these fields along with the rest of the subfile fields prior to the write or update process.

Adding a Blank Line Between Records

The folded screen can sometimes be difficult to read. A blank line between folded records makes the screen easier to read, as is apparent in Figure 4.5.

Creating the folded record layout with a blank line between the records (Figure 4.5) requires two changes to the display file. The first change is to the subfile record. One additional field is added, as shown in shaded type in Figure 4.6.

The other change that might be required is in the definition of page size in the subfile control record. Because the folded record now takes more rows, you may have to reduce the page size. The display shown in Figure 4.5 was created with a subfile page size of 3. If, however, your program uses subfile load options 2 or 3 and loads

```
A300C1                     COMPUTERS ARE US                    12/21/98
INVD012A                 INVENTORY MAINTENANCE

   2=Change       4=Delete      5=Display      6=Add

O  PART NUMBER   DESCRIPTION                 QNTY     COST      EXTENDED

_  A123          Computer x486                 21  1,301.15    27,324.15
                    WAREHOUSE: DLS  LOCATION: 15A

_  A124          Computer PentIUM             215  3,100.16   666,534.40
                    WAREHOUSE: FTW  LOCATION: 219

_  A125          Printer - Laser               81   974.21     78,911.01
                    WAREHOUSE: DLS  LOCATION: X19

                                                            More ...
======================================================================
   F3=Exit Subsystem        F6=Display
```

Figure 4.5
Folded Display with a Blank Line Between Records

Figure 4.6
Subfile Record Definition Including Drop and Fold Fields

```
*...1....+....2....+....3....+....4....+....5....+....6

A* Subfile example DDS  - INVD014A
A* by Phil Levinson
A**********************************************
A                                    PRINT
A                                    CF03(03)
A**********************************************
A
A       R DSP01                      SFL
A         D1PICK        1A  I  8  2
A         D1PN         11A  0  8  4
A         D1DESC       30A  0  8 16
A         D1QOH         5Y 00  8 47EDTCDE(1)
A         D1UCST        6Y 20  8 55EDTCDE(1)
A         D1LTOT        8Y 20  8 65EDTCDE(1)
A                              9 18'WAREHOUSE:'
A         DIWH          3A  0  9 29
A                              9 34'LOCATION:'
A         D1WHL         5A  0  9 44
A                             10  1' '
A**********************************************
```

eight records at a time, then in folded mode, you will see two pages of three followed by one page of two. This accounts for the eight records loaded into the subfile.

The next use of the Page down key causes the program to load eight more records — and, in folded mode, you will again see two pages of three records each followed by one page of two records. The pattern of 3-3-2-3-3-2 is not a technical problem, but users might find it distracting. If we modify the LOAD subroutine to load nine records at a time instead of eight, then the display will show nine dropped records or three pages of three folded records.

Exercise 4.1A Computers Are US Inventory Project

Purpose

To modify existing code to develop and test a subfile with subfile fold capability.

General Program Specifications

Create the maintenance program INV014A and the display file INVD014A. The program and display are modified to display the folded record when the user presses F6.

1. Copy display file INVD013B into the new member INVD014A. Modify INVD014B by adding the additional fields from the inventory file to a second line of the subfile record. Add SFLDROP(CF06) to the control record and modify the footer record to indicate that Function key 6 will display details. Modify the SFLPAG value to 4.
2. Copy program source member INV013B into new member INV014B. Modify your program to load additional fields into the subfile in the LOAD subroutine.
3. Compile and test your program. Select folded mode (multiline record). Select option 5 to display a record. Did the screen remain folded after you exited the display window?
4. Modify your code to provide a blank line between records, as shown in Figure 4.5.

Exercise 4.2A Purchase Order Line Project

Purpose

To demonstrate that you can add drop and fold capabilities to subfiles.

General Program Specifications

Create the RPG program ORDL24A, which will display all purchase order lines. This file will have drop and fold capabilities.

1. Copy the display file source member ORDD023B to new member ORDD024A. Add the fields in the file ORDLPF that were not previously included in the subfile display. Make the necessary modifications to prepare this display file for subfile display fold. Include a blank line between records when they are folded.
2. Copy the source member ORDL23B to a new member ORDL24A. Make the necessary modifications to load the additional fields.

Review

1. Describe two differences between SFLDROP and SFLFOLD.
2. Describe how to compute the SFLPAG value when you use drop or fold.
3. What is the impact of leaving out the SFLDROP and the SFLFOLD keywords with a multiline subfile?

Maintaining the Subfile Mode

With drop and fold, you've added a nice feature to your code. However, you may have noticed in testing it that every time the program loops and executes the format DSP02, the drop and fold reverts to its default setting. For some applications, that might be fine, but it is possible to keep the drop and fold mode the way that the user sets it. This requires a few changes and one new keyword.

Changes to the Subfile Control Record to Maintain the Subfile Mode

To take control of the subfile drop and fold, the RPG program needs to know what mode the display was in when it turned over control to the program. The keyword that passes the drop and fold mode to the program is SFLMODE (Subfile Mode). This keyword, shown in Figure 4.7, is followed by an ampersand (&) and the name of a one-character hidden variable: SFLMODE(&SFLMD). When you code display-file keywords, the name of a field that transfers data from the display file to the program is preceded by an &. The field SFLMD is defined on the next specification after the SFLMODE keyword. This variable must be one character long and hidden.

Table 4.1 shows the meaning of the values of the variable associated with SFLMODE.

Table 4.1
SLFMODE Values

Value	Subfile mode
'0' or *OFF	Folded (multiline)
'1' or *ON	Dropped (single line)

The subfile control record also contains both the SFLDROP and SFLFOLD keywords. They are conditioned by opposite modes of the same indicator. In Figure 4.7, this indicator is 55. If indicator 55 is on, the screen appears in drop (single-line) format because the SFLDROP keyword is conditioned with 55. If indicator 55 is off, the screen appears in fold (multiline) format because the SFLFOLD keyword is conditioned with N55.

Figure 4.7
Subfile Control Record
with Subfile Drop
Default and
SLFMODE Keyword

```
*...1....+....2....+....3....+....4....+....5....+....6

A***************************************************************
A          R DSP02                       SFLCTL(DSP01)
A   90                                    SFLEND(*MORE)
A   55                                    SFLDROP(CF06)
A  N55                                    SFLFOLD(CF06)
A                                         SFLSIZ(0009)
A                                         SFLPAG(0003)
A  N90                                    ROLLUP(25 'ROLLUP OR PGDN')
A                                         OVERLAY
A   50                                    SFLDSP
A   50                                    SFLDSPCTL
A  N50                                    SFLCLR
A                                         SFLMODE(&SFLMD)
A            SFLMD         1A  H
A            SFLRCD        4S 0H          SFLRCDNBR(CURSOR)
A                                    1 31'COMPUTERS ARE US'
A                                    2 31'WORK WITH INVENTORY LISTS'
A                                    1  2USER
A                                    1 71DATE
A                                         EDTCDE(Y)
A                                    6  4'PART NUMBER'
A                                    6 16'DESCRIPTION'
A                                    6 47'QNTY'
A                                    6 55'COST'
A                                    6 65'EXTENDED'
A                                    6  2'0'
A                                    4  3'2=Change'
A                                    4 15'4=Delete'
A                                    4 27'5=Display'
```

Changes to the RPG Program to Maintain the Subfile Mode

Figure 4.8 shows the mainline code for subfile load option 2. Before the initial display of the screen, indicator 55 should be set on if the screen should be shown initially in SFLDROP mode. Later in the same subroutine, the mode value returned at the completion of the previous execution of the display is used to set the value of indicator 55 appropriately, so the display will be activated in the same mode in which it ended.

Figure 4.8
Mainline Code for Subfile
Load Option 2 with
Subfile Mode Control

```
*...1....+....2....+....3....+....4....+....5....+....6

    *****************************************************************
    *    MAINLINE                    M A I N L I N E
    *****************************************************************
    *
    C                          EXSR CLRSF
    C                          EXSR LOADPG
    * set indicator 55 to initially display the file in SFLDROP mode
A14 C                          MOVE *ON       *IN55
    C                          EXFMTDSP02
    *
    C          *IN03           DOWEQ*OFF
    *
    C                          EXSR RESPD
    *
    * set indicator 55 to initially display the file in SFLDROP mode
A14 C                          MOVE SFLMD     *IN55
    C                          EXFMTDSP02
    C                          ENDDO
    * END PROCESSING
    C                          MOVE *ON       *INLR
    C                          RETRN
```

Exercise 4.1B Computers Are US Inventory Project

Purpose
To modify existing code to develop and test a subfile that maintains the subfile display mode.

General Program Specifications
Create the maintenance program INV014B and the display file INVD014B. The program and display will be modified to display the folded record when the user presses F6 and to maintain the latest selection of mode.

5. Copy display file INVD014A into new member INVD014B. Modify INVD014B by adding the SFLMODE keyword and its variable. Also include both SFLDROP and SFLFOLD conditioned with the opposite values of the same indicator.

6. Copy RPG source member INV014A into new member INV014B. Modify your program to bring the subfile up initially in SFLDROP mode and to maintain the user's preferred mode.

7. Test your program carefully. Switch into folded mode and press the Enter key. While still in folded mode, press the Page down key to move to the next set of records. Press the Enter key. What records are displayed each time you press the Enter key?

Exercise 4.2B Purchase Order Line Project

Purpose

To demonstrate that you can add drop and fold capabilities to subfiles and maintain the user-selected subfile display mode.

General Program Specifications

Create the RPG program ORDL24B, which will display all purchase order lines. This file will have drop and fold capabilities. Initial display mode should be folded.

3. Copy the display file source member ORDD024A to the new member ORDD024B. Make the necessary modifications to prepare this display file for subfile display fold. Include a blank line between records when they are folded.

4. Copy the source member ORDL24A into new member ORDL24B. Make the necessary modifications to initially show the display file in fold mode and then maintain the user's selected mode.

Review

4. Describe the use of SFLMODE, as well as the use of conditioning indicators on SFLDROP and SFLFOLD.

5. What modifications are required in the RPG program to control the subfile mode?

Using the Subfile Cursor Keyword to Improve Screen Control

In Exercise 4.1, step 7, you saw that pressing the Enter key

- returned the cursor to the top of a page
- caused a different page to be displayed occasionally

In subfile load option 2, the RPG program controls the cursor position by setting the value of the variable associated with the SFLRCDNBR (Subfile Record Number) keyword in the subfile control record. The current page can be kept on the display and the cursor can be returned to its correct location. To do so, set the value of this variable to the record number of the record the cursor was pointing to when a user action caused the screen to turn over control to the RPG program.

The subfile control keyword SFLCSRRRN returns to the RPG program the number of the subfile record that the cursor is pointing to when control returns to the program. If the cursor is not pointing to a subfile record, then SFLCSRRRN returns a zero. This keyword identifies a field that transfers data to the program. In Figure 4.9, the field to transfer the subfile record cursor location is CSRLOC, and the variable name is preceded with an ampersand (&) in the keyword to indicate that it transfers data to the program. As shown in Figure 4.9, this variable must be defined in the display file (as 5 0 signed and hidden).

```
*...1....+....2....+....3....+....4....+....5....+....6
A****************************************************************
A          R DSP02                  SFLCTL(DSP01)
A 90                                 SFLEND(*MORE)
A 55                                 SFLDROP(CF06)
A N55                                SFLFOLD(CF06)
A                                    SFLSIZ(0009)
A                                    SFLPAG(0003)
A N90                                ROLLUP(25 'ROLLUP OR PGDN')
A                                    OVERLAY
A 50                                 SFLDSP
A 50                                 SFLDSPCTL
A N50                                SFLCLR
A                                    SFLMODE(&SFLMD)
A                                    SFLCSRRRN(&CSRLOC)
A          SFLMD        1A  H
A          CSRLOC       5S  0H
A          SFLRCD       4S  0H        SFLRCDNBR(CURSOR)
A                                    1 31'COMPUTERS ARE US'
  * code continues as in previous examples
```

Figure 4.9
Subfile Control
Record with
Subfile Cursor
Relative Record
Number Keyword

The RPG program (shown in Figure 4.10) uses the value the SFLCSRRRN keyword creates (if it is not zero) to set the subfile record variable. The subfile record variable is used by the SFLRCDNBR keyword to locate the cursor on the subsequent EXFMT (Execute Format) operation. If this is done immediately after the execution of the display, as shown in Figure 4.10, no other changes to the RPG program are needed.

```
*...1....+....2....+....3....+....4....+....5....+....6

****************************************************************
 *   MAINLINE                M A I N L I N E
****************************************************************
 *
C                     EXSR CLRSF
C                     EXSR LOADPG
 * set indicator 55 to initially display the file in SFLDROP mode
A14 C                 MOVE *ON        *IN55
C                     EXFMTDSP02
 *
C          *IN03      DOWEQ*OFF
 *
 *   Set the value of the subfile record number to the current sfl pos
C          CSRLOC     IFNE *ZERO
C                     Z-ADDCSRLOC     SFLRCD
C                     ENDIF
 *
C                     EXSR RESPD
 *
 * set indicator 55 to initially display the file in SFLDROP mode
A14 C                 MOVE SFLMD      *IN55
C                     EXFMTDSP02
C                     ENDDO
 * END PROCESSING
C                     MOVE *ON        *INLR
C                     RETRN
```

Figure 4.10
Mainline Code for
Subfile Load Option 2
Loading Current Subfile
Position into SFLRCD

After the subfile record number is set, the remainder of the processing cycle takes place. Based on the subsequent processing, a better location might be computed for the cursor (i.e., when a new page is added to the subfile). The last value of the variable SFLRCD when the subfile is displayed again will control the position of the cursor. Therefore, setting the value at this point ensures that a good value will be in the SFLRCD variable, but it will leave the opportunity for it to be changed by later processing.

Exercise 4.1C Computers Are US Inventory Project

Purpose
To modify existing code to develop and test a subfile that maintains the cursor position.

General Program Specifications
Modify the inventory maintenance program INV014B and the display file INVD014B. The program and display are modified to maintain the correct records on the display and keep the cursor in the correct position.

8. Modify display file INVD014B to return the subfile cursor position as shown in Figure 4.9.

9. Modify the program INV014B to return the cursor to the correct position when redisplaying the screen. Refer to the code sample in Figure 4.10.

10. Test your program carefully. Switch into folded mode and press the Enter key. While still in folded mode, press the Page down key to move to the next set of records. Press the Enter key. Move the cursor to the top of the page and press Enter.

Exercise 4.2C Purchase Order Line Project

Purpose
To demonstrate that you can apply the SFLCSRRRN keyword to control the cursor location.

General Program Specifications
Modify the RPG program ORDL24B, which will display all purchase order lines. Add the SFLCSRRRN keyword and the necessary program modifications to control the cursor location.

5. Make the necessary modifications to display file ORDD024B to include the SFLCSRRRN keyword.

6. Make the necessary modifications to ORDL24B to control the cursor location.

Review

6. Describe the SFLCSRRRN keyword and its use in subfile processing.

The Screen Header

In the past few chapters, we've concentrated on the subfile. However, the screen also has a header area, which we've defined in the subfile control record, and a footer area defined in the footer record. These screen areas can play a role in communicating a more complete set of information to users or in making the programs easier to use.

Frequently, an input field is added to the header that lets users indicate a value to which they want to position the subfile. I will explore this tool in Chapter 5.

Output fields can also be added to the header area of the display to provide information that applies to the whole set of records displayed. The example in Figure 4.11 displays the general information about an order in the header, and the subfile contains the "lines" of the order.

```
A300C1                    Jefferson College                    10/24/98
                          Bookstore Order

ORDER NUMBER:  2113               Order Status: 0
TO:       DUKE PRESS                          SHIP TO:  BOOKSTORE
          221 E. 29TH STREET                            JEFFERSON COLLEGE
          LOVELAND, CO 80538                            1000 VIKING ROAD
                                                        HILLSBORO, MO 63050
SHIPPING INSTRUCTIONS: FASTEST WAY        ORDER DATE:   10/25/98

1=Add 2=Change 4=Delete 5=Display
                                                                    *
O    PART#        Description        Quantity    Cost    Extended

_    ISBN1245A    RPG/400 by Judy Yaeger     30   60.00    1,800.00
_    ISBN2144B    Advanced RPG by P.Levinson 20   45.00      900.00
_
_
_

                               Total               2,700.00
   --------------------------------------------------------------
F3= Exit       F6=Display Detail     F12= Cancel
```

Figure 4.11
Display File with Subfile, Data Fields in the Header Area, and a Grand Total in the Footer Area

If the header is included in the subfile control record, then the fields in the header can be output capable, input capable, or both. When the RPG program issues an EXFMT (Execute Format) operation on the control record, all input and both fields in the header are returned — along with values for which we have already coded. This provides the user with a large number of options and the programmer with more processing options to accommodate in the code.

The user can

- change any input-capable field on the header
- select options by entering values into the options field
- press the Page up or Page down keys
- press any activated function key

The Footer

The footer can contain output fields, such as the Total field in Figure 4.11. This value was accumulated as the subfile was loaded. For the total to be correct, the entire subfile must be loaded (load option 1).

To keep the total up-to-date when changes, deletes, or adds occur, its value must be recomputed or corrected. The simplest way to do this is to reload the subfile whenever any type of change occurs. The subfile routine would begin by setting the value of the Total field to zero and subsequently add the extended price of each line as it is computed to the total.

Whenever the Total field is recomputed, the footer record must be rewritten to the screen, or it continues to show the old value. We do this by including the WRITE FOOTER statement at the end of the Load Subfile (LOAD) subroutine. We've been including this write in the LOAD subroutine from the beginning, but now you know why.

The header can have input or both fields included in the control record. The fields work because we do an EXFMT operation on the control record. EXFMT causes the control record to return its input and both fields, function keys, and subfile changes.

You cannot use input or both fields in the footer record because it will be written to but never read from (with a READ or an EXFMT operation).

Exercise 4.1D Computers Are US Inventory Project

Create INV014C and INVD014C, which will be similar to INV013A.

1. Load entire subfile (load option 1).
2. Display the extended total in the footer properly labeled and formatted and in reverse image and color.
3. Total should be updated whenever changes, deletes, or adds occur.

Purpose

To modify existing code to develop and test a program that loads and displays all records in a subfile and that displays a grand total field in the footer.

General Program Specifications

Create maintenance program INV014C and display file INVD014C. These programs should function like INV013A, but they display the extended price total in the footer. The total should be updated when records are added, deleted, or changed.

11. Copy display file INVD013A to member INVD014C and add the Grand Total field to the footer record.

12. Copy RPG source member INV013A to new member INV014C. Modify the code to compute and display the total. Test the program to make certain that the total is correct when records are added, deleted, and changed.

Review

7. Consider the program developed in Exercise 4.1D, steps 11 and 12. It displays a grand total on the footer record. If the user changes a record, it is possible to execute that change without reloading the subfile. Use a flowchart or pseudocode of the Change (CHG) subroutine to demonstrate how that subroutine can keep the total up-to-date without reloading the subfile.

Chapter 5

Positioning the Subfile and Selecting Records

Chapter Overview

Chapter 5 teaches you the programming techniques you need to load records from the correct position in a physical file by

✓ using a selection screen

✓ using a selection field in the header record

You will also learn techniques for

✓ locating records based on various fields and loading the subfile from different logical files

✓ creating a display file and writing a program with more than one subfile

Loading Records from the Physical File

Although you have learned a lot about programming subfiles in the first four chapters, there are many additional techniques to learn. In this chapter, we explore various ways of determining which records in the physical file are to be loaded and displayed.

In the real world, physical files contain thousands — sometimes millions — of records. With large files, your users' Page down keys could wear out long before they reach the records they need. Clearly, there has to be a better way.

Instead of displaying the first page of records to the user, the program begins by displaying a selection screen (Figure 5.1, page 82). Once the user enters a part number, the RPG program will position the file to that part. The program will then load the subfile from that position in the file and display the first page. For example, if the user typed the part number A214 on the selection screen, the RPG program would locate the file at A214, and the first record loaded and displayed would be A214. If the user types the partial value A3, the first record that would be loaded and displayed would be the first record with a part number equal to or greater than A3.

The file will be positioned using the SETLL (Set Lower Limits) operation. This operation positions the file at the record that is equal to or greater than the specified value. If the user leaves the selection field blank, then the SETLL operation positions the file at the first part number.

Once the file is positioned, we can use any of the load options. Remember, however, that load option 1 shouldn't be used for large loads and a subfile cannot contain more than 9999 records.

By pressing F12, the user can exit the subfile display screen and return to the selection screen. F3 exits the program from either screen.

Figure 5.1
Selection Screen

```
 A300C1                      COMPUTERS ARE US                    09/21/98
                    INVENTORY PART NUMBER SELECTION SCREEN



       Locate Part Number:_____




    =======================================================================
    * F3=Exit Subsystem
```

Using the Selection Screen

Selection screens are used frequently because they are both easy to program and simple to use. Users can enter the first part of or the entire entry of interest, and the subfile is loaded and displayed beginning at that value.

The screen definition is a simple record with one field designated as both (input and output), which will be in the same display file as the subfile record, the subfile control record, and the footer record. The field should be the same size and type as the key to the physical file. The subfile control record must be changed to activate function key F12.

The RPG program must be altered to

- display the selection screen
- use the value from the input screen instead of *LOVAL to position the physical file before reading records and loading the subfile
- if F12 is pressed, display the selection screen
- if F3 is pressed, exit the program

All of the changes to the RPG program will be located in the mainline code. These changes appear in boldface in the pseudocode shown in Figure 5.2.

Mainline

    Execute the select screen format

    Do while indicator 03 is off

        Position the file with the setll operation using the value from the select screen

        Read the first record

        Execute the Load (LOAD) subroutine

        Use the EXFMT (Execute Format) operation to display the control record and the subfile (DSP02)

            Do while indicators 03 and 12 are off

                Execute the Respond (RESPD) subroutine

                Execute the format display screen and subfile (DSP02)

            End do

        If indicator 03 is off

            Execute the select screen format

        End if

    End do

End program

Figure 5.2

Mainline Pseudocode for Subfile Load Option 3 with Selection Screen

---

Exercise 5.1A Computers Are US Inventory Project

Purpose
To modify existing code to add a selection screen.

General Program Specifications
Create maintenance program INV015A and display file INVD015A. The program will display a selection screen (Figure 5.1) and use subfile load option 3.

1. Copy display file INVD013C into new member INVD015A. Modify INVD015A by
   - adding a new record for the selection screen
   - adding CA12(12) to the subfile control record so function key F12 can be used

2. Copy program source INV013C into new member INV015A. Modify your program's mainline code as shown in the pseudocode in Figure 5.2. Compile and test your program.

Exercise 5.2A Purchase Order Line Project

Purpose
To design and add a selection screen to a subfile program.

General Program Specifications
Create RPG program ORDL25A, which displays all purchase order lines. This program uses a selection screen to locate the correct records to load and display. Records are loaded using subfile load option 2.

1. Copy the display file source member ORDD024B to new member ORDD025A. Design and add a record for the selection screen (Figure 5.3).

Figure 5.3
Selection
Screen

```
USERID                      COMPUTERS ARE US PURCHASING              09/21/98
                                Order Lines Selection


                  Locate Order Number:  _____


     ==========================================================================
        F3=Exit Subsystem
```

2. Write the pseudocode for the necessary changes to incorporate the selection screen into the RPG program ORDL25A (from ORDL24B).
3. Copy the source member ORDL24B to new member ORDL25A. Modify ORDL25A to provide the selection-screen capabilities.

Review

1. How would you design the selection screen to for the following file keyed on CSTZIP, CSTLN, and CSTFN?

Customer File

Field	Size	Description
CSTZIP	10A	CUSTOMER'S ZIP CODE
CSTLN	25A	CUSTOMER'S LAST NAME
CSTFN	25A	CUSTOMER'S FIRST NAME
CSTA1	25A	CUSTOMER'S ADDRESS LINE 1
CSTA2	25A	CUSTOMER'S ADDRESS LINE 2
CSTCT	10A	CUSTOMER'S CITY
CSTST	2A	CUSTOMER'S STATE

Keyed on: CSTZIP, CSTLN, CSTFN

Adding a Selection Field to the Screen Header

With the selection screen, we've provided a quick way for users to locate the first record that they need. However, whenever users need to move to another location in this file, our current design requires that they press F12, then key the new value on the selection screen. We can provide users with a simpler way to locate records by adding a selection field to the header section of the display (Figure 5.4).

```
     USERID                  COMPUTERS ARE US                   09/21/98
                          WORK WITH INVENTORY LISTS

        2=Change      4=Delete      5=Display       6=Add

        Locate Part Number: A
    O   PART NUMBER DESCRIPTION          QNTY        COST      EXTENDED

        _  A123        Computer x486        21     1,301.15    27,324.15
        _  A124        Computer PentIUM    215     3,100.16   666,534.40
        _  A125        Printer - Laser      81       974.21    78,911.01
        _  A213        Printer - Ink Jet    15       457.15     6,857.25
        _  A214        Printer - Dot Matrix 21       251.14     5,273.94
        _  A215        Scanner - Hand       15       127.19     1,907.85
        _  A216        Scanner - Flat Bed    5       421.15     2,105.75
        _  A319        CD-ROM                6       115.96       695.76



    ===================================================================
        F3=Exit Subsystem
```

Figure 5.4
Inventory List with Selection Field

The selection field that is added to the header record in Figure 5.4 is the same type and size as the key field of the physical file. This field is coded as both input and output capable.

The code in the RPG program must be able to determine whether the user has changed the value in the selection field. One way to determine whether the value has been changed is to maintain a selection hold field. In the Respond (RESPD) subroutine, the current value of the selection field and the hold field are compared. If the values are different, the program will

- reposition the file to the new location and read the first record
- load a page
- update the hold value with the new value

These steps can be included in the RESPD subroutine. The pseudocode for this subroutine using subfile load option 3 is shown in Figure 5.5. Because there are now three positioning options (Page up, Page down, and Locate), the new pseudocode uses a select structure rather than the if-then-else structure the previous code used.

Figure 5.5

Pseudocode for the
RESPD Subroutine
with Subfile Load
Option 3 and a
Select Value Field

RESPD Subroutine

If indicator 25 or 26 is on (page down or page up) **or SELPN is not equal to SELPNH**

Do selection

Select when indicator 26 is on (page up)   Note: if/then/else structure replaced with selection structure

Execute the Backup (BACKUP) subroutine

Execute the LOAD subroutine

Select when indicator 25 is on (page down)

Move *off to indicator 91 (top of file indicator)

Position the physical file just beyond the last record loaded into the subfile page

Read the next record from the physical file

Execute the LOAD subroutine

Select when SELPN is not equal to SELPNH

Position the physical file just before SELPN

Read the next record from the physical file

Execute the LOAD subroutine

Update SELPNH to value of SELPN

End select

Else

Set the update flag to off

Read the first changed record in the subfile

Do while changed records exist

Do selection

Select when D1PICK is 2 (change)

Execute the Change (CHG) subroutine

Logic continues with other options

End selection

Read the next changed record in the subfile

End do

If the update flag is on

Position the physical file just above the first record loaded into the subfile page

Read the next record from the physical file

Execute the LOAD subroutine

End if

End if

End subroutine

Exercise 5.1B Computers Are US Inventory Project

Purpose
To modify existing code to add a selection field.

General Program Specifications
Create maintenance program INV015B and display file INVD015B. The program will display a selection screen (Figure 5.1) and use subfile load option 3. It will also have a selection field (Figure 5.4).

3. Copy display file INVD015A into new member INVD015B. Modify INVD015B by adding text and the selection field to the subfile control record (Figure 5.4).

4. Copy program source INV015A into new member INV015B. Modify your program by adding the RESPD subroutine as shown in the pseudocode shown in Figure 5.5. Compile and test your program.

Exercise 5.2B Purchase Order Line Project

Purpose
To design and add a selection field to a subfile program (the program will not have a selection screen).

General Program Specifications
Create RPG program ORDL25B, which will display all purchase order lines. This program will use a selection field to locate the correct records to load and display. Records will be loaded using subfile load option 2.

4. Copy the display-file source member ORDD024B to new member ORDD025B. Design and add the text and selection field.

5. Write the pseudocode for the necessary changes to incorporate the selection field into the RPG program ORDL25B (from ORDL24B).

6. Copy source member ORDL24B to new member ORDL25B. Modify ORDL25B to provide the selection field capabilities.

Review

2. What differences are there in handling the user input from a selection screen and a selection field?

Locating Data on Other Fields

In the Computers Are US example, we've provided a quick way to locate a record if the user knows the part number. However, users find the program hard to use when they don't know the part number. To make this program more useful, users have requested that it be able to locate and load records based on either the part number or the part description.

Users often need more than one way to access records. In an employee file, Human Resources users might need access by social security number or name, and in a customer file, users might need access by customer number or customer name.

In the Computers Are US example, the RPG program could search the physical file INVPF and load only those records that matched the desired description into the subfile. However, if the file is large, this could take quite awhile. Online programs must be quick and easy to use. To get good performance, we need a logical file that provides an alternative sequence keyed on the other field or fields.

About Logical Files

Logical files are real winners from the perspective of online performance, but they have their own performance costs. Whenever a physical file record is updated, added, or deleted, the logical files over that physical file must also be posted. (The only exception to this rule is logical files with maintenance values of REBUILD or DELAY.) However, to meet our quick response needs, our logical files must have a maintenance value of IMMEDIATE, which means that they are kept up-to-date at all times.

In the real world, we don't create a logical file until we check to see whether one that can serve our needs might already exist. You can check on existing logical files with the CL command DSPDBR (Display Database Relations), which lists logical files for the physical file with which you are working. The DSPDBR command (Figure 5.6) can be run from any command line.

Figure 5.6
CL Command Display
Database Relations

```
Parameters or command
===> DSPDBR FILE(INVPF)
```

The results of the DSPDBR command are shown in Figure 5.7. This report shows that the file INVPF has a dependent file INVLF1.

Figure 5.7
List of Dependent (Logical)
Files Created with the
DSPDBR Command

```
Number of dependent files . . . . . . . . :          1
   Files Dependent On Specified File

   Dependent File      Library                        Dependency   JREF
Constraint
      INVLF1           A300C1_BOK         Data
```

The next step is to check each logical file to determine whether any will meet our basic needs. If the source code for the logical files is available, it can be used, but the data we need on each logical file exists as a component of that file. The CL command DSPFD (Display File Description), shown in Figure 5.8, provides the information that we need to determine whether the logical file will meet our needs.

```
Parameters or command
===> DSPFD INVLF1
```

Figure 5.8
CL Command DSPFD
(Display File Description)

A lot of information is available from via the DSPFD command. Figure 5.9 shows data extracted from the display file description command for the file INVLF1. Each of the pieces of information about INVLF1 will be useful in determining whether this file suits our needs.

```
Access path maintenance . . . . . . . . . . : MAINT      *IMMED
    Record format . . . . . . . . . . . . . .:            INVPFR
        Key field . . . . . . . . . . . . . .:            INDESC
            Sequence . . . . . . . . . . . . :            Ascending
        Key field . . . . . . . . . . . . . .:            INPN
            Sequence . . . . . . . . . . . . :            Ascending
    Select/omit specified . . . . . . . . . .:            No


                          Record    Format Level
        Format    Fields  Length    Identifier
        INVPFR       6        60     2A224C68C1F19
```

Figure 5.9
Partial Listing of Output of DSPFD (Display File Description) for a Logical File

The logical file record format should have the same name, length, and format-level identifier as the record format in the physical file. If any of these things is different, the logical file may not access all of the fields of the physical file. This would limit our ability to use this logical file.

As shown in Figure 5.9, the logical file INVLF1 uses a composite key of the fields INDESC INPN. This composite key lets us find items by description, and items with the same description will be ordered by part number.

Finally, check the select/omit specifications, which indicate what rules are used to include or exclude records from the logical file. Excluded or omitted records that exist in the physical file are not available through the logical file. If there is a selection rule, only those records selected are available through the logical file. If these rules exclude some of the records that your application will need, then the logical file will not be useful in solving your problem.

If no logical file that meets the key and selection requirements exists, then one must be created. In the inventory project, we know that there are no logical files over the physical file INVPF. To provide quick access based on the description field, a new logical file must be created.

Exercise 5.1C Computers Are US Inventory Project

Purpose
To create a logical file that provides an alternate key to a physical file.

General Program Specifications
Users have requested that the inventory program locate records by descriptions as well as part number. Create logical file INVLF1, which provides an alternate key structure to the physical file INVPF. INVLF1 will be keyed on the description and the part number.

5. Enter the member INVLF1 logical file using the specifications shown in Figure 5.10. Compile the member.

Figure 5.10
Specifications
for INVLF1

```
*...1....+....2....+....3....+....4....+....5....+....6

*************** Beginning of data **************************************
0001.00     *  JEFFERSON COLLEGE    10/19/98   PHIL LEVINSON    INVLF1
0002.00     *  LOGICAL FILE INVLF1 OVER INVPF ON DESCRIPTION FIELD AND PART N
0003.00     A        R INVPFR                      PFILE(INVPF)
0004.00     A        K INDESC
0005.00     A        K INPN
***************** End of data ****************************************
```

6. Test how the logical file delivers records to our application by using DFU to view the data. A quick way to do this is with the UPDDTA command. Once the key fields are displayed on DFU, press the Page down (Roll up) keys on your keyboard to step through the file. This is the sequence in which these records will be presented to programs using read statements. You can also do the equivalent of a CHAIN by pressing F12 — so that just the fields for the key are shown — and typing in a value.

7. Enter the CL command DSPDBR and press F4 to prompt the command entry. Enter the file name INVPF and change the output to *Print. *Print directs the command to spool the DSPDBR report. Issue the command and print out the spool file with the DSPDBR report.

8. Enter the CL command DSPFD and press F4 to prompt the command entry. Enter the file name INVPF and change the output to *PRINT. *PRINT directs the command to spool the DSPFD report. Issue the command and print out the spool file with the DSPFD report.

Exercise 5.2C Purchase Order Line Project

Purpose
To design and create a logical file that provides an alternate key structure to a physical file.

General Program Specifications
Modify the purchase order line display program to locate and display records based on order number or part number. When you use part number to locate and display records, display only the records of orders that have not been received.

Create logical file ORDLNLF1. This file should provide an alternate key structure to the physical file ORDLNP. The key should be based on part number, order number, and sequence. It should include only records of items that haven't yet been delivered (i.e., the actual delivery date equals zero).

7. Enter member ORDLNLF1 as a logical file over physical file ORDLNP. This logical file should use the same record name and structure as the physical file. It should be keyed on the part number, order number, and sequence number fields. The logical file definition should contain a selection rule to limit the available records to those records for which the received date is equal to zero, as shown in Figure 5.11. Compile the member.

```
*...1....+....2....+....3....+....4....+....5....+....6
A           S OLADT                  COMP(EQ 0)
```

Figure 5.11
Specifications to Select Records with OLADT Equal to Zero

Review

3. Why are logical files used in conjunction with online processing?
4. What are the "costs" of logical files?

Loading the Subfile from One of Two Sources
In the inventory project, you've created a logical file because users needed to be able to find parts in the inventory by the description. Now that we have the logical file with the required keys, we need to modify the program INV015B to provide the necessary access. An easy way to do this would be to clone the program. The clone could be modified by substituting the logical file for the physical file and making a few other minor changes. That would be simple and effective, but there would be little learning involved.

Instead, we will modify our program to load the subfile from either the keyed physical file or a logical file based on the field on the selection screen (Figure 5.12) into which users enter data. Later, users can request repositioning of the subfile by entering the request in one of the two selection fields in the header (Figure 5.13). Each time that our program returns from the screen, we will check the fields. If either field has been changed, then our program will reload the subfile from the physical or logical file, depending on which field the user updated.

We need to modify our display program to provide the selection screen shown in Figure 5.12.

Figure 5.12
Selection Screen with Alternate Selection Fields

```
 A300C1                COMPUTERS ARE US                11/02/98
                  INVENTORY LIST SELECTION SCREEN




          Locate Part Number: _____

          or

          Locate Part Description: _____



     =================================================================
      F3=Exit Subsystem
```

The subfile control record must also be changed to allow entry into a selection field by either a part number or a part description (Figure 5.13). On both the selection screen and the control record, these fields are SELPN and SELDES.

Figure 5.13
Work with Inventory Lists with Selection Fields on Both Part Number and Part Description

```
 A300C1                 JEFFERSON COLLEGE                 11/02/98
                     Work with Inventory Lists

     1=Add      2=Change     4=Delete      5=Display

     Locate Part Number: B_____ or Part Descp: _____
 O PART NUMBER DESCRIPTION              QNTY     COST     EXTENDED

 _  CP07        CABLE PRINTER 7'          15      5.75        86.25
 _  CP10        CABLE PRINT 10'           19      3.25        61.75
 _  CS10MM      CABLE SERIAL 10' MALE-MALE 15     4.12        61.80
 _  D2115       3 1/2" DISK DRIVE        127  2,141.00    271,907.00
 _  D2116       DISK DRIVE - 5 1/4         7     21.41       149.87
 _  D511        512 MBYTE HARD DISK       23    157.15      3,614.45

                                                             Bottom


     ---------------------------------------------------------------
      F3=Exit Subsystem       F6=Display Details
```

The RPG program positions and reads from INVPF unless the user has changed the value in the Locate by Description field (SELDES). When the user changes the SELDES value, the display in part number order flag (DPNFLG) is turned off, and both positioning and reading are done from the logical file INVLF1. To control the source of data, the RPG code needs the following changes:

- Add an F-spec for the logical file INVLF1 (Figure 5.14).
- Add a call to a subroutine to position the file in the mainline code (Figure 5.15, page 94).
- Add a subroutine to position the file based on the value in either the selection part number or the selection description and set the flag DPNFLG on if part number is used (Figure 5.16, page 94).
- Modify the RESPD subroutine (Figure 5.17, page 95).
- Test the Description field.
- If there is a change in the Part Number field or the Description field, call the subroutine to position the file.
- If the update flag is on, reposition and read from file INVPF or INVLF1 based on the value of DPNFLG.
- Modify the LOAD subroutine (Figure 5.18, page 96).
- Read from either INVPF or INVLF1 based on the value of DPNFLG.
- Modify the BACKUP subroutine (subfile load option 3) to perform both the READ and READP operations from file INVPF when DPNFLG is on and from file INVLF1 when DPNFLG is off.

```
*...1....+....2....+....3....+....4....+....5....+....6....+....7

      ****************************************************************
      *  F I L E S
      ****************************************************************
      *                                    INVENTORY MASTER
      FINVPF   UF  E        K        DISK                       A
      *                                    INVENTORY MASTER PM DESCRPT
      *
A5D   FINVLF1  IF  E        K        DISK
A5D   F             INVPFR                        KRENAMEINVLFR
A5D   * note: The special continuation line - RENAMING RECORD FORMAT
```

Figure 5.14
F-Specs for Program INV015C with Logical File INVLF1 Added

Figure 5.14 shows the first minor change required. Using the logical file INVLF1 requires an additional F-spec (shaded). This file can be input only. The Change, Delete, and Add subroutines can continue to locate and update records in the physical file.

The third line in the RPG program is new. It is a continuation line, which gives this file a different record name within the program. RPG demands unique record names because commands such as UPDAT or DELET require the record name and must designate a single target file.

The task of positioning the file after the selection screen has been removed from the mainline code, as the crossed-out lines in Figure 5.15 illustrate. This task will be placed in a new subroutine.

Figure 5.15

Mainline Pseudocode for
Subfile Load Option 3
and a Selection Screen
with Two Fields

Mainline
    Execute the select screen format
    Do while indicator 03 is off
    ~~Position the file with the SETLL operation using the value from the select~~
    ~~screen~~
    ~~Read first record~~
        Execute the subroutine to position the file
        Execute the LOAD subroutine to load a page into the subfile
        Execute the format for the display screen and subfile
        Do while indicators 03 and 12 are off
            Execute the RESPD subroutine
            Execute the format for the display screen and subfile
        End do
        If indicator 03 is off
            Execute the select screen format
        End if
    End do
End program

The new subroutine for positioning the file (Figure 5.16) is called by the main routine — as is the RESPD subroutine.

Figure 5.16

Pseudocode for the
Position the File (POSFIL)
Subroutine

POSFIL subroutine
    If the Description Selection field (SELDES) is not equal to the Description
    Selection Hold field (SELDEH)
        Turn off the display on part number flag (DPNFLG)
        Update SELDEH with SELDES
        Position file INVLF1 with the set lower limits operation using SELDES
        Read INVLF1
    Else
        Turn on the display on part number flag (DPNFLG)
        Update SELPNH with SELPN
        Position file INVPF with the SETLL operation using SELDES
        Read INVPF
    End if
End subroutine

If the user has changed the Locate by Description field on the selection screen or on the main screen, the POSFIL subroutine will detect it because the SELDES field will not equal the value of SELDEH. The subroutine then sets the display on part number flag (DPNFLG) off, updates the hold area SELDEH, positions the logical file on the entered value, and reads the next record from the logical file.

If the POSFIL is called but the description has not changed, then the SELPN field is used to locate the physical file INVPF and the first record is read. The flag DPNFLG is set on and the hold area SELPNH is updated.

The RESPD subroutine (Figure 5.17) is changed to call the File subroutine if either the Locate on Part Number (SELPN) or the Locate on Description (SELDES) field has been changed.

RESPD Subroutine
    IF indicator 25 or 26 is on (Page down or Page up) or SELPN is not equal to SELPNH or SELDES is not equal to SELDEH
        Do Selection
            Select when indicator 26 is on (Page up)   note: if/then/else structure
                Execute the BACKUP subroutine   replaced with Selection
                Execute the LOAD subroutine
            Select when indicator 25 is on (Page down)
                Move *off to Indicator 91 (Top of File (TOF) indicator)
                Position the physical file just beyond the last record loaded into the subfile page
                Read the next record from the physical file
                Execute the LOAD subroutine
            Select when SELPN is not equal to SELPNH **or SELDES is not equal to SELDEH**
                Execute the POSFIL subroutine
                ~~Position the physical file just before SELPN~~
                ~~Read the next record from the physical file~~
                Execute the LOAD subroutine
                ~~Update SELPNH to value of SELPN~~
        END Select
    ELSE
        Set the update flag to off
        Read the first changed record in the subfile
        Do while changed records exist
            Do selection
                Select when D1PICK is 2 (Change)
                    Execute the CHG subroutine
                Logic continues with other options
            End selection
            Read the next changed record in the subfile
        End do
        If the Update flag is on
            If DPNFLG is on

continued

Figure 5.17
Pseudocode for the Respond Subroutine (RESPD) with Subfile Load Option 3 and Two Selection Fields

Figure 5.17
Continued

Position the file INVPF just above the first record loaded into the subfile page
Read the next record from the file INVPF
Execute the LOAD subroutine
Else
Position the file INVLF1 just above the first record loaded into the subfile page
Read the next record from the file INVLF1
Execute the LOAD subroutine
End if
End if
END IF
End subroutine

The update task in the RESPD subroutine is changed to position and read from the file INVPF if the flag DPNFLG is on and from the file INVLF1 if the flag is off.

The LOAD subroutine must be changed to read from either INVPF or INVLF1 based on the value of the flag DPNFLG (Figure 5.18; note shaded lines). The READ from file INVPF must contain the N for not locked, but the READ from file INVLF1 does not require the N because, as an input-only file, the READ does not lock the record when accessing it. The value of the DPNFLG field should be used to determine whether the physical file INVPF or the logical file INVLF1 is used in READ, READP, and CHAIN operations whenever records are accessed.

Figure 5.18
The Part of the Load Subroutine that Uses the Value of DPNFLG to Determine Which File to Read

```
     *...1....+....2....+....3....+....4....+....5....+....6
       C                       WRITEDSP01
 15D   C          DPNFLG       IFEQ *ON
       C                       READ  INVPF              N    90
 15D   C                       ELSE
 15D   C                       READ  INVLF1                  90
 15D   C                       ENDIF
       C                       ENDDO
```

Exercise 5.1D Computers Are US Inventory Project

Purpose
To modify a subfile program to load data from either of two access paths.

General Program Specifications
Users have requested that the inventory program locate records by description as well as part number. Modify display file INVD015C and program INV015C to locate and access data from file INVPF or file INVLF1.

9. Copy member INVD015B to INVD015C. Modify the selection screen to appear with the fields SELPN and SELDES, as shown in Figure 5.12. Also, modify the subfile control record to provide both fields, as shown in Figure 5.13.

10. Copy program source member INV015B to INV015C and modify it per the code in Figures 5.14 and 5.18 and the pseudocode in Figures 5.15 through 5.17. Modify the BACKUP subroutine to locate the correct record — in the file INVPF if the flag DPNFLG is on and in the file INVLF1 if the flag DPNFLG is off.

Exercise 5.2D Purchase Order Line Project

Purpose
To design and modify a subfile program to provide records via two access paths to the file.

General Program Specifications
The purchasing department needs to be able to enter a part number and see the display of order lines in part-number order, starting with the part number entered. They are interested in viewing only those parts that have not been received (Received date=0). Modify the pseudocode and the program to load the records from ORDLNPF or ORDLNLF1 based on a user's most recent entry in the Locate field.

8. Copy display-file source member ORDD025B to new member ORDD025C. Modify the subfile control record to add the text and selection fields for locating records by order number or by part number.

9. Write the pseudocode for the necessary changes to incorporate the two selection fields into the RPG program ORDL25C (from ORDL25B). Data is to be loaded from ORDLNPF or ORDLNLF1 based on the user's most recent entry in the Locate fields.

10. Copy the source member ORDL25B to new member ORDL25C. Modify ORDL25C to provide the selection field capabilities.

Eliminating the Initial Selection Screen
We have duplicated the function of the initial selection screen with the selection fields on the subfile control screens. To support this redundancy, we have had to add some redundant RPG code. Both the initial selection screen and the redundant code can be eliminated, in which case you depend exclusively on the selection fields on the control record to determine what should be displayed. This change can be accomplished by either of two alternative methods.

You've actually coded one of these alternatives — in ORDL25B and ORDL25C. In this case, the program initially loads and displays the first page of the physical file or loads the entire file from record 1 depending on the design of the load process. The user can then use the header fields to relocate the file to the desired position.

Eliminating the Initial Selection Screen with Finesse

The only criticism of the simple solution just described is its inefficiency: it requires the program to load a page of the subfile that is not likely to be of interest. An alternative is to begin the process by displaying the subfile control record without the actual subfile. This lets the user make an entry in one of the select fields.

Separating the display of the header from the display of the subfile requires a change to the DDS and a couple of lines of code.

First, the SFLDSP keyword in the control record is changed to use an additional control indicator, indicator 52 (Figure 5.19; note shaded number).

Figure 5.19
Portion of Subfile Control Record with SFLDSP Controlled by Two Conditioning Indicators

```
*...1....+....2....+....3....+....4....+....5....+....6

     A                                          OVERLAY
15E  A   50 52                                  SFLDSP
     A   50                                      SFLDSPCTL
     A  N50                                      SFLCLR
     A   90                                      SFLEND(*MORE)
```

Here's how the additional control indicator — indicator 52 — works:

IN50	IN52	RESULT
*OFF	*ON	SFLCLR clears subfile
*OFF	*OFF	SFLCLR clears subfile
*ON	*OFF	Control record is displayed
*ON	*ON	Control record and subfile are displayed

The mainline pseudocode shown in Figure 5.20 would initially display the main screen without the subfile. It displays the footer and the header (IN50 on) but not the subfile (IN52 off). But after the initial screen, the subfile is displayed (IN52 on).

Figure 5.20
Mainline Pseudocode for Subfile Load Option 3 Displayed Initially Without the Subfile

Mainline
Turn off indicator 52 (deactivate SFLDSP)
Execute the format footer
Execute the format to display the screen **without** the subfile (DSP02)
Turn on indicator 52 (activate SFLDSP)
Do while indicator 03 is off
    Execute the RESPD subroutine
    Execute the format to display the screen and the subfile (DSP02)
End do
End program

Exercise 5.1E Computers Are US Inventory Project

Purpose
To modify a subfile program to initially display the control record without the subfile.

General Program Specifications
Modify display file INVD015D and program INV015D to initially display the main screen without the subfile.

11. Copy member INVD015C to INVD015D. Remove the record for the selection screen. Also, modify the subfile control record to provide two conditioning indicators for the SFLDSP field (Figure 5.19).

12. Copy program source member INV015C to INV015D and modify the mainline code per the pseudocode in Figure 5.20.

Multiple Subfiles
We know we've got a good basic program, but users still want more. When they select to position based upon a description value, the screen is confusing if that description value is not in the leftmost column. Figure 5.21 shows a screen sequenced by description but with description in the second column.

```
A300C1              COMPUTERS ARE US                11/02/98

    1=Add   2=Change   4=Delete   5=Display

   Locate Part Number: _____ or Part Des: C_____
 O Part Number Description                 Qnty       Cost      Extended

 _ A124        Computer PENTIUM             300    2,100.16    630,048.00
 _ A123        Computer X486                 22    1,301.15     28,625.30
 _ CP10        CABLE PRINT 10'               19        3.25         61.75
 _ CP07        CABLE PRINTER 7'              15        5.75         86.25
 _ CS10MM      CABLE SERIAL 10' MALE-MALE    15        4.12         61.80
 _ A319        CD-ROM                         7      115.96        811.72
 _ A155        COMPUTER STAND                 4       21.00         84.00
 _ D2116       DISK DRIVE - 51/4              7       21.41        149.87
                                                              More...


    F3=Exit Subsystem     F6=Display Details
```

Figure 5.21
Description Displayed in Sequence in the Second Column

The screen would be easier to understand if the leftmost column were the description column. When the data is displayed in description sequence, users like the clarity of having the description in the leftmost column, as shown in Figure 5.22.

Figure 5.22

Description
Displayed in
Sequence in the
First Column

```
A300C1                      COMPUTERS ARE US                    11/02/98
                          Work with Inventory Lists

    1=Add      2=Change     4=Delete      5=Display

    Locate Part Des: C_____ or Part Number: _____
  O Description                 Part Number  Qnty        Cost        Extended

  _ Computer PENTIUM            A124          300     2,100.16      630,048.00
  _ Computer X486               A123           22     1,301.15       28,625.30
  _ CABLE PRINT 10'             CP10           19         3.25           61.75
  _ CABLE PRINTER 7'            CP07           15         5.75           86.25
  _ CABLE SERIAL 10' MALE-MALE  CS10MM         15         4.12           61.80
  _ CD-ROM                      A319            7       115.96          811.72
  _ COMPUTER STAND              A155            4        21.00           84.00
  _ DISK DRIVE - 51/4           D2116           7        21.41          149.87
                                                                       More...

  ----------------------------------------------
    F3=Exit Subsystem       F6=Display Details
```

Only a few minor changes are necessary to meet the users' request. We create two new records in the display file. DSP03 is a subfile record with the description in the leftmost column, and DSP04 is the subfile control record for DSP03. The RPG program writes the subfile records either to DSP01 or DSP03 and executes the format of DSP02 or DSP04 when it clears or displays the subfile.

The following changes are required:

1. Edit the display file by making copies of the subfile record format DSP01 and subfile control record format DSP02. Name the new formats DSP03 and DSP04. Change the field locations in DSP03. Change the column headings in DSP04. Change the SFLCTL reference from DSP01 to DSP03 in record DSP04.

2. In the RPG code, add the F-spec to key for the subfile DSP03 (Figure 5.23; note shaded line). Each subfile in a display file requires a continuation specification that identifies the field that will be used as the RRN. In this case, the same field can be used for both subfiles because only one or the other will be loaded and displayed.

Figure 5.23

Adding the F-Spec to
Subfile DSP03

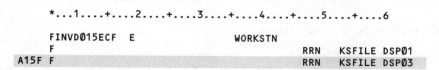

```
*...1....+....2....+....3....+....4....+....5....+....6

  FINVD015ECF  E                  WORKSTN
  F                                          RRN    KSFILE DSP01
A15F F                                       RRN    KSFILE DSP03
```

3. In the RPG code, make every reference to DSP01 conditional on the value of DPNFLG. When DPNFLG is on, use DSP01; when it is off, use DSP03.

4. In the RPG code, make every reference to DSP02 conditional on the value of DPNFLG. When DPNFLG is on, use DSP02; when it is off, use DSP04.

Exercise 5.1F Computers Are US Inventory Project

Purpose
To modify a subfile program to load and display one of two subfiles.

General Program Specifications
Modify display file INVD015E and program INV015E to display one of two subfiles.

13. Copy member INVD015D to INVD015E. Copy records DSP01 and DSP02 to DSP03 and DSP04. Modify records DSP03 and DSP04 to display the part-description column to the left of the part-number column, with the appropriate headings above the columns, as shown in Figure 5.22.
14. Copy program source member INV015D to INV015E and modify the program to use DSP01 and DSP02 when DPNFLG is on and DSP03 and DSP04 when DPNFLG is off.

Exercise 5.2E Purchase Order Line Project

Purpose
To design and modify a subfile program to load and display records in two different formats.

General Program Specifications
Users request that the order-line screen show the display with the column on which the data is sequenced to the left of all other data columns. For example, when an order number is entered, the order-number column should be shown to the left, and when a part number is entered, the part-number column should appear to the left. Modify ORDD025D and ORDL25D to add these screens.

11. Copy the display-file source member ORDD025C to new member ORDD025D. Add records DSP03 and DSP04 and modify these records to display the part number in the leftmost column.
12. Copy the source member ORDL25C to new member ORDL25D. Modify ORDL25D to use DSP01 and DSP02 when the user requests an order number and DSP03 and DSP04 when the user requests a part number.

Review

5. How can the headers and footers be displayed without the subfile? What would be the advantage of doing so?
6. What is the function of the RENAM FK-Specification?
7. Why is a logical file needed?
8. What are hidden fields used for?

Subfile Bookstore Order Project 1

Project Overview

To demonstrate that you can design, code, debug, and test a system with two
subfiles.

The Bookstore Order System

It's time for a new project that will serve as a good review. The bookstore system
will require a number of programs, but our task of the moment is a single program that creates the two displays shown in Figures SF1.1 and SF1.2.

When the system is started, SCREEN1 (Figure SF1.1) is displayed. This screen
lists and supports user interaction with bookstore orders.

```
A300C1                   Jefferson College                 10/24/98
SCREEN1                  Bookstore Orders


  1=Add 2=Change   5=Lines

O    ORDER STS  DATE      INSTR         TO

_    2112   O   11/23/98  UPS           BEST PUBLISHERS
_    2113   O   11/24/98  FASTEST WAY   DUKE PRESS
_    2114   C   11/25/98  FED X         BEST PUBLISHERS
_    2115   O   11/25/98  FED X         UNIVERSITY OF MISSOURI PRESS
_


  F3=Exit     F6=Display Details     F12=Cancel
```

Figure SF1.1
Subfile Project
Screen 1 —
List of Orders

When option 5 is selected on an order, the system loads and displays
SCREEN2 (Figure SF1.2).

```
A300C1                   Jefferson College                 10/24/98
                         Bookstore Order

ORDER NUMBER:  2113            ORDER STATUS: O
TO:       DUKE PRESS                    SHIP TO:   BOOKSTORE
          221 E. 29TH STREET                       JEFFERSON COLLEGE
          LOVELAND, CO 80538                       1000 VIKING ROAD
                                                   HILLSBORO, MO 63050
SHIPPING INSTRUCTIONS: FASTEST WAY       ORDER DATE:  10/25/98

1=Add 2=Change 4=Delete 5=Display
                                                        *
O   PART#      DESCRIPTION                     QUANTITY   COST   EXTENDED

_   ISBN1245A  RPG/400 by Judy Yaeger               30   60.00  1,800.00
_   ISBN2144B  Subfile Programming Essentials by P.Levinson  20   45.00    900.00
_
_
_
                                   Total              2,700.00
-----------------------------------------------------------------
F3= Exit      F6=Display Details     F12= Cancel
```

Figure SF1.2
Subfile Project
Screen 2 —
Order Details

continued

Subfile Project 1 *Continued*

SCREEN2 displays and lets users interact with and maintain the details of an order. The order selected on SCREEN1 is the one displayed on SCREEN2. The subfile on SCREEN2 is loaded with the lines of the order selected on SCREEN1.

Instructions

1. Create a file to hold the header information. This information occurs once per order whereas the line information is unique to each "line." Figure SF1.3 shows the header information for order 2113.

Figure SF1.3
Subfile Project —
Order Header

```
ORDER NUMBER: 2113              ORDER STATUS: O
TO:      DUKE PRESS            SHIP TO: BOOKSTORE
         221 E. 29TH STREET             JEFFERSON COLLEGE
         LOVELAND, CO 80538             1000 VIKING ROAD
                                        HILLSBORO, MO
63050
SHIPPING INSTRUCTIONS: FASTEST WAY    ORDER DATE: 10/25/98
```

This file, often referred to as the Order Header file, will be named **BSORH01** for Bookstore Order Header 01. It will be keyed on order number, which is unique.

Fields are

BSHON	4	A	TEXT('ORDER NUMBER')
BSHSTS	1	A	TEXT('STATUS O / C')
BSHODT	6	S 0	TEXT('ORDER DATE')
BSHSI	25	A	TEXT('SHIP INSTR')
BSHTO1	25	A	TEXT('TO: LINE #1')
BSHTO2	25	A	TEXT('TO: LINE #2')
BSHTO3	25	A	TEXT('TO: LINE #3')
BSHTO4	25	A	TEXT('TO: LINE #4')
BSHFM1	25	A	TEXT('FROM: LINE #1')
BSHFM2	25	A	TEXT('FROM: LINE #2')
BSHFM3	25	A	TEXT('FROM: LINE #3')
BSHFM4	25	A	TEXT('FROM: LINE #4')

2. Enter the following records into your file.

BSHON	2112	2113	2114	2115
BSHSTS	O	O	C	O
BSHODT	961123	961124	961125	961125
BSHSI	UPS	FASTEST WAY	FED X	FED X
BSHTO1	BEST PUBLISHERS	DUKE PRESS	BEST PUBLISHERS	UNIVERSITY OF MISSOURI PRESS
BSHTO2	21 BROADWAY	221 E. 29TH STREET	21 BROADWAY	PO BOX 1241
BSHTO3	NEW YORK, NY 29101	LOVELAND, CO 80538	NEW YORK, NY 29101	COLUMBIA, MO 63901
BSHTO4				

continued

Subfile Project 1 *Continued*

BSHFM1	BOOKSTORE	BOOKSTORE	BOOKSTORE	BOOKSTORE
BSHFM2	JEFFERSON COLLEGE	JEFFERSON COLLEGE	JEFFERSON COLLEGE	JEFFERSON COLLEGE
BSHFM3	1000 VIKING DRIVE	1000 VIKING DRIVE	1000 VIKING DRIVE	1000 VIKING DRIVE
BSHFM4	HILLSBORO, MO 63050	HILLSBORO, MO 63050	HILLSBORO, MO 63050	HILLSBORO, MO 63050

3. Create a file to hold the line information. This information occurs multiple times, once for each line of the order. Below is the type of information that it should hold.

ISBN1245A RPG/400 by Judy Yaeger	30	60.00
ISBN2144B Subfile Programming Essentials by Philip J. Levinson	20	45.00

The extended price is not included in the file because, as we know, it can be computed whenever needed.

The line file, which we'll name BSORL01, will contain the data on all orders. Therefore, it is necessary to include a way to tie the line to the parent order. We will accomplish this by including the order number in the line file. But F6=Display Details shows more about these lines, as you see below.

ISBN1245A RPG/400 by Judy Yaeger   30   60.00
LINE STATUS: O Date Received / / Actual
ISBN2144B Subfile Programming Essentials by Philip J. Levinson 20   45.00
LINE STATUS: C Date Received 11/15/98 Actual 19 44.50

The file **BSORL01** should be keyed on both the order number and the line number, and the key should be unique. The fields in this file are

BSLON	4	A		TEXT('ORDER NUMBER')
BSLLN	4	S	0	TEXT('LINE NUMBER')
BSLPN	12	A		TEXT('PART NUMBER')
BSLDS	30	A		TEXT('PART DESCRIPTION')
BSLQO	4	S	0	TEXT('QUANT ORDERED')
BSLOP	7	S	2	TEXT('ORDER PRICE')
BSLSTS	1	A		TEXT('LINE STATUS')
BSLRDT	6	S	2	TEXT('REC DATE')
BSLQA	4	S	0	TEXT('QUANT ACTUAL')
BSLAP	7	S	2	TEXT('ACTUAL PRICE')

continued

Subfile Project 1 *Continued*

4. Enter the data below into the file BSORL01.

BSLON	BSLLN	BSLPN	BSLDS	BSLQO	BSLOP	BSLSTS	BSLRDT	BSLQA	BSLAP
2112	1	ISBN414	ENGLISH I	250	4712	O			
2112	2	ISBN312	ENGLISH II	75	5300	O			
2113	1	ISBN1245A	RPG/400 by Judy Yaeger	30	6000	O	0	0	0
2113	2	ISBN2144B	SUBFILE PROGRAMMING ESSENTIALS by Philip J. Levinson	20	4500	C	961115	19	44.50
2114	1	ISBN912	HISTORY 1	300	6500	C	961201	300	65.00
2115	1	ISBN311	HISTORY 2	150	7200	O			

5. Create the display DDS for SCREEN1 with windows for Add Order, Delete Order, and Change Order. Make the SFL Size 1500. Name the DDS BSORDD01.

6. Develop the code to manage SCREEN1 using LOAD OPTION 1 (load all orders at one time). This code should provide all services to the header file (add, delete, and change). The only option that will not be activated is option 5 (detail), which will bring up SCREEN2 and will be coded as indicated in steps 7 and 8. The ADD option should assign the order number, which will be 1 higher than the highest order number previously assigned. The user will not be allowed to change the order number. Name this program BSORDR01.

7. Modify the DDS for BSORDD01, adding the displays for SCREEN2 with windows for Add Line, Delete Line, and Change Line. Make the SFL Size 500. Name the DDS as BSORDD01.

8. Modify the code BSORDR01 to service option 5 from SCREEN1. When it is selected, load the subfile for SCREEN2 with the lines for the selected order and provide code to handle the Add Line, Delete Line, and Change Line. When F12 is pressed on SCREEN2 the program should return to SCREEN1.

9. Add the field SELORD to SCREEN1 Header Control Record, as is shown in the screen at the top of page 107. If the user types in a new value to which the subfile is to be positioned, reload the subfile starting with that value. To test this function, add 15 or 20 header records to the file.

continued

Subfile Project 1 *Continued*

```
A300C1                    Jefferson College              10/24/98
SCREEN1                   Bookstore Orders
ORDER 2112
1=Add 2=Change   5=Lines
O   ORDER STS  DATE       INSTR        TO
_   2112   O   11/23/98   UPS          BEST PUBLISHERS
_   2113   O   11/24/98   FASTEST WAY  DUKE PRESS
_   2114   C   11/25/98   FED X        BEST PUBLISHERS
_   2115   O   11/25/98   FED X        UNIVERSITY OF MISSOURI PRESS
_


F3= Exit      F6=Display Details    F12= Cancel
```

10. Add the following three function keys to SCREEN1:

        F9 - Show All Orders
        F10 - Show Open Orders
        F11 - Show Closed Orders

    Only two of these definitions should be displayed at any time — the two that aren't currently used to select header records. When F10, F11, or F12 is selected, reload the header subfile with only the appropriate records from the header physical file.

11. Add a function key to SCREEN1 that works as a "switch" when the screen first appears:

        F7 - TO: Sequence

    The orders are now shown in sequence based on the values in the field BSHT01, which requires a logical file over the header file.

    Because record names must be unique within a program, if the logical file has the same record name as the physical file, you must use an FK format to rename the records for the logical file.

    When the data is redisplayed, the function key displays the message

        F7 - Order Num Sequence

    Selecting F7 again will bring the display back to the original status, order number sequence, and the footer message F7 - TO: Sequence.

Chapter 6

Developing User-Friendly Subfiles

Chapter Overview

Chapter 6 helps you understand and develop subfiles that let users change the data on the screen. When you complete the chapter, you will be able to

✓ understand and use hidden fields

✓ create prompts for fields

✓ add Help at field and screen levels

Updating Data Directly on the Screen

In the previous chapters, you've developed a fully functional system to support users who maintain data files. The system you've developed is typical of many in existence today. This chapter introduces some techniques that help you make the system more user friendly.

The subfiles that you have created have looked a lot like spreadsheets, but most users would find them harder to work with. End users experienced with spreadsheet software, such as Excel or Lotus 1-2-3, would complain that the subfile we've created makes it too difficult to make changes. Using our subfile, a user would have to move to the correct record, type a 2 for change, wait for the change screen, move to the field targeted for change, and finally make the change.

In the first part of this chapter, you will learn to modify your subfiles so they have much more of the look and feel of spreadsheets. This change lets users make changes directly on the subfile instead of on a change screen.

First, you will learn to modify the subfile record in the display file as follows:

1. Change all of the fields except the Key field from a designation of output to both. If you allow changes to the Key field, you won't be able to find the record in the physical file to update it!

2. The fields that are changed to Both should also have the CHANGE (Change) keyword added to them to determine whether a change has occurred. The CHANGE keyword is followed by an indicator number. This indicator is turned on when READC (Read the Next Changed Record) accesses a record that includes a field with the CHANGE keyword and that has, in fact, been changed. If we need to know *which* field has been changed, we can use a different indicator for each field.

Figure 6.1 shows the display file with the fields changed to use Both and the CHANGE keyword. Notice that to make the second line easier to read, the text 'WAREHOUSE' and 'LOCATION' is displayed.

```
*...1....+....2....+....3....+....4....+....5....+....6
A           R DSP01                     SFL
A             D1PICK       1A  I  8  2
A             D1PN        11A  O  8  4
A             D1DESC      30A  B  8 16
A                                       CHANGE(27)
A             D1QOH        5Y 0B  8 47EDTCDE(1)
A                                       CHANGE(27)
A             D1UCST       6Y 2B  8 55EDTCDE(1)
A                                       CHANGE(27)
A             D1LTOT       8Y 2B  8 65EDTCDE(1)
A                                       CHANGE(27)
A                                9 10'WAREHOUSE'
A             D1WH         3A  B  9 25
A                                       CHANGE(27)
A                                9 35'LOCATION'
A             D1WHL        5A  B  9 45
A                                       CHANGE(27)
```

Changes to the RPG program are primarily in the Respond (RESPD) subroutine and a new subroutine, the On-Screen Change (ONSCHG) subroutine. Indicator 27 will be the first test in the select structure (Figure 6.2); if indicator 27 is on, the ONSCHG subroutine (Figure 6.3) will be executed.

```
*...1....+....2....+....3....+....4....+....5....+....6
      C                   SELEC
A16   C           *IN27   WHEQ *ON                      ON-SCREEN
A16   C                   EXSR ONSCHG                   CHANGE
      *
      C           D1PICK  WHEQ '2'
      C           D1PICK  OREQ 'C'
      C                   EXSR CHG
      *--the other options have been omitted to save space
      *
      C                   ENDSL
```

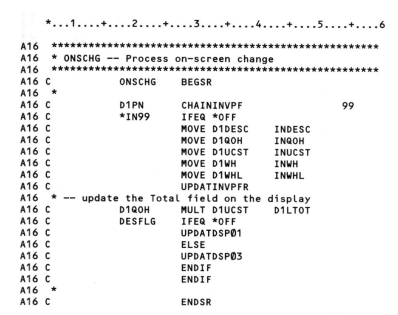

```
     *...1....+....2....+....3....+....4....+....5....+....6
A16  ******************************************************
A16  * ONSCHG -- Process on-screen change
A16  ******************************************************
A16 C          ONSCHG     BEGSR
A16  *
A16 C          D1PN       CHAININVPF                 99
A16 C          *IN99      IFEQ *OFF
A16 C                     MOVE D1DESC    INDESC
A16 C                     MOVE D1QOH     INQOH
A16 C                     MOVE D1UCST    INUCST
A16 C                     MOVE D1WH      INWH
A16 C                     MOVE D1WHL     INWHL
A16 C                     UPDATINVPFR
A16  * -- update the Total field on the display
A16 C          D1QOH      MULT D1UCST    D1LTOT
A16 C          DESFLG     IFEQ *OFF
A16 C                     UPDATDSP01
A16 C                     ELSE
A16 C                     UPDATDSP03
A16 C                     ENDIF
A16 C                     ENDIF
A16  *
A16 C                     ENDSR
```

Figure 6.3
On-Screen Change
(ONSCHG) Subroutine

The ONSCHG subroutine chains into the physical file on the part number and updates the fields in the physical file from the subfile update. Also, because the subfile contains a computed field, we need to recompute that field and update the subfile record to reflect changes in quantity or price.

On-Screen Changes: A Simpler Solution?

What might seem an even simpler solution to making on-screen changes involves the following elements:

1. Except for the key field, all of the fields in the subfile record DSP01 are defined with a usage of both.

2. The CHANGE keyword is not used.

3. Modify the RESPD subroutine by adding an OTHER clause at the end of the Selection structure. The OTHER clause, which is executed if none of the previously defined clauses are true statements, will be coded to call the ONSCHG subroutine shown in Figure 6.3.

There is, however, a potential problem with this solution: It gives preference to the value in D1PICK.

If any previous user interaction leaves a value in the field D1PICK (e.g., if a canceled delete leaves a 4 in D1PICK), and the user attempts to make an on-screen change to that record, the code would branch to the Delete subroutine instead of to the ONSCHG subroutine.

Because this is not a robust solution, I don't recommend it. It is included for your information.

Exercise 6.1A Computers Are US Inventory Project

Purpose

To modify existing code to provide on-screen edit capabilities.

General Program Specifications

Create the maintenance program INV016A and the display file INVD016A.

1. Copy display-file member INVD015E to new member INVD016A. Modify the code to designate the subfile fields (except for the Key field) as Both. Add the CHANGE keyword for these fields. Refer to Figure 6.1.

2. Copy RPG program source member INV015E to new member INV016A. Add the necessary code as shown in Figures 6.2 and 6.3.

Exercise 6.2A Purchase Order Line Project

Purpose
To design and code subfiles with on-screen change capability.

General Program Specifications
Create the RPG program ORDL26A, which lets users make on-screen changes.

1. Copy the display-file source member ORDD025D to new member ORDD026A. Make the necessary modifications to prepare this display for on-screen changes.

2. Copy the RPG source member ORDL25D to new member ORDL26A. Make the necessary modifications to add on-screen change capabilities to this program.

Use of Hidden Fields

With what you've done so far, life will be good for about 15 minutes — until users discover that they cannot modify the Key field (in our example, the part number field). We prevented a change to that field because it was the Key field to the physical file. We needed its value to chain into the physical file to find the record to update. If we let the user change the Key field, we would no longer be able to find the record.

In this section, we introduce a way to make even the Key field update capable. As you may suspect from the title of this section, that's where hidden fields come into play.

A hidden field is stored in the display file but not displayed to the user. Although hidden fields are not displayed on the screen, programs can treat them exactly the same way they treat fields designated as Both. Hidden fields are defined with a width, type, number of decimals, and a designation as hidden. On a hidden field, the Location Line and Position fields are left blank. If the field is defined in the subfile record, there will be one value of the hidden field for each subfile record.

To satisfy the users' additional need, we will have to change the field D1PN, designating it Both. We will also need a second copy of the original part number, which is used to chain into the physical file. Figure 6.4 shows the modified specifications for D1PN and D1PNH, the hidden copy of the part number in the subfile.

```
*...1....+....2....+....3....+....4....+....5....+....6
A           D1PN          11A  B  8  4
A                                        CHANGE(27)
A   88                                   DSPATR(RI)
A           D1PNH         11A  H
```

Figure 6.4

Adding the Hidden Field DIPNH to the Subfile Record

Two other changes are shown in Figure 6.4. First, the D1PN field has the field-level keyword CHANGE with the same indicator value as is used on the other fields defined in the subfile record. Second, indicator 88 causes the value in the Part Number field to be displayed in reverse video. The program turns this indicator on to warn users who attempt to change the part number listed in the Part Number field to a number that already exists. The file INVPF identifies a unique key of part number and will not allow an add or update operation that would create a second record with an existing part number. (Part number was established as a unique key because that fits the company's business rules.)

> **Note:** To establish what fields should be defined with unique keys, you must understand how the company operates. For example, when we establish that the key field INPN is unique in the file INVPF, we are interpreting a company business rule. The file INVPF defines the part, cost, quantity on hand, and warehouse location of stored parts. For this key field to work correctly, the business rule must be that any product (number) will be stored in only one of the organization's warehouses and in only one location within that warehouse.

Whenever our RPG program loads a value into D1PN, it loads the same value into the field D1PNH. Later, when the program reads changed records from the subfile, we can be certain that D1PNH will still contain the key value of the corresponding record in the physical file.

Keep in mind two additional issues:

1. Because INPN is a unique key, we must test the changed value against the file to prevent a change of the key value to that of an existing key.
2. If this field's value is used to relate this file to other files, you may want to prevent or at least test any change of the value to see that the necessary relationships are not destroyed. The code may need to change the value in both the current file and the related files. In the RPG code, as is shown in Figure 6.5, whenever the value of D1PN is updated, the value of the hidden field D1PNH is also updated.

Figure 6.5
Loading Fields
D1PN and D1PNH

```
*...1....+....2....+....3....+....4....+....5....+....6
        C                      MOVE INPN      D1PN
  16B   C                      MOVE INPN      D1PNH
```

The pseudocode for the ONSCHG subroutine shown in Figure 6.6 compares D1PN to D1PNH. If the values are different, the user has requested a change of the part number. The new part number is tested to determine whether it already exists in the file. (If the value already exists in the file, adding it would be an error.) The value of D1PN is reset to the original value, and the error indicator 88 is on. If the error indicator is off, the program chains into the physical file on the original value, which is stored in the hidden field.

The remainder of the ONSCHG subroutine is identical to the code in Figure 6.3 (page 111).

ONSCHG Subroutine

    Turn off the error on part number change (indicator 88)

    If the subfile part number is not equal to the subfile hidden part number (D1PN IFNE D1PNH)

        Test for the existence of a record in the physical file with the new part number (D1PN SETLLINVPF   39)

        If the new part number is equal to an existing part number (if the indicator in the Equals field of SETLL is on)

            Turn on the error on part number indicator (indicator 88)

            Move the old value back to the subfile (Move D1PNH to D1PN)

            Update the subfile

        End if

    End if

    If the indicator for an error on part number change (indicator 88) is off

        Chain into the physical file on the hidden field (D1PNH CHAININVPF)

        If the record is found

            Copy subfile fields to physical file fields (use D1PN, not D1PNH)

            Update physical file

        End if

        Compute the item total (quantity times cost)

        If the display in description order flag (DESFLG) is off

            Update subfile record DSP01

        Else

            Update subfile record DSP03

        End if

    End if

End subroutine

Figure 6.6

Pseudocode for ONSCHG Subroutine with Change of DIPN

Exercise 6.1B Computers Are US Inventory Project

Purpose

To modify existing code to provide on-screen edit capabilities for all fields (including the Key field).

General Program Specifications

Create the maintenance program INV016B and the display file INVD016B.

3. Copy display-file member INVD016A to new member INVD016B. Modify the code to designate the subfile fields (including the Key field) as both. Add the CHANGE keyword for these fields.

4. Copy RPG program source member INV016A to new member INV016B. Change the ONSCHG subroutine to allow changing the part number.

Exercise 6.2B Purchase Order Line Project

Purpose
To design and code subfiles with on-screen change capabilities.

General Program Specifications
Create RPG program ORDL26B, which will let users make on-screen changes, including changes to the Key field.
3. Copy display-file source member ORDD026A to new member ORDD026B. Make the necessary modifications to prepare this display for on-screen changes, including changes to the Key field.
4. Copy RPG source member ORDL26A to new member ORDL26B. Make the necessary modifications to add the on-screen change capabilities to this program.

Prompting on Non-Subfile Fields

You've already seen prompting used on various AS/400 screens. You point at an entry field and press F4, the Prompt function key, and a window or screen appears with options, further information, and an entry field. In theory, this is fairly easy to do.

For our first experiment, let's develop a prompt window for the header field Locate on Part Number (SELPN). When the user points to the Locate on Part Number field, we will display the window shown in Figure 6.7.

Figure 6.7
Prompt Window for
Locating on Part Number

```
          Locate Part Number
Type in the Part Number
or the first few digits of the Part Number:
_____
```

This prompting should happen only when users point the cursor to the field and press F4. To know that F4 has been pressed, we need to activate the key in the display-file description with the CF04(04 'F4=Prompt') keyword. If prompting is to be used on all records, the CF04 keyword should be placed at the file level (before the first record declaration). If prompting is to be used for specific screens, the CF04 keyword should be placed at the record level, after the record declaration of a record for which prompting will be provided. Because the command function keyword cannot be included in a subfile record, it is defined in the subfile control record to provide prompting for fields on the control record and the subfile record.

To provide the correct prompt, we need to know what field the cursor is pointing to when F4 is pressed. The field name is available through the display-file keyword RTNCSRLOC (Return Cursor Location). The keyword actually returns two values: the activated format and the activated field. As is shown in Figure 6.8, I named these fields CSRFMT and CSRFLD, and both must be 10 characters long. When the fields are used in the command itself, they are preceded by an ampersand (&). The RTNCSRLOC keyword should be added to every display-file record for which prompting is provided.

In the subfile control record that defines variables, display-file keywords must come after the general subfile control commands. Because the SFLRCDNBR (Subfile Record Number) keyword does both, it is the last subfile keyword. The RTNCSRLOC keyword must come after the general SFL commands but before SFLRCDNBR. Finally, the variable definitions must be added in the subfile control record variable definition area, which starts with the keyword SFLRCDNBR.

```
*...1....+....2....+....3....+....4....+....5....+....6
A                                       RTNCSRLOC(&CSRFMT &CSRFLD)
A          SFLRCD        4S ØH           SFLRCDNBR(CURSOR)
A          CSRFMT       1ØA  H
A          CSRFLD       1ØA  H
```

Figure 6.8

Part of the Subfile Control Record with the RTNCSRLOC (Return Cursor Location) Keyword and Its Related Field Definitions

In our experiments, we have two control records with different subfile column layouts. Because we want to provide the prompting on both screens, the CF04 and RTNCSRLOC keywords must be added to both subfile control records.

Finally, a window definition — as was shown in Figure 6.7 — must be added to the display file for the prompt window. The window can use the same field name as the control record field for Select Part Number (SELPN), and it should be designated Both.

The RPG program must be modified to execute the new prompt window when indicator 4 is on and the field name returned from the RTNCSRLOC keyword matches the name of the field on the control record (SELPN).

In the RESPD subroutine (Figure 6.9), we can check the status of IN04. If it is *ON and CSRFLD contains the value SELPN, we can execute a DDS record format named PMTPN window, which you will design. If the user changed the part number in the PMTPN window, then the code for Locate on Part Number (developed in a previous chapter) will find that the SELPN no longer matches the SELPNH field and will proceed to locate the correct position in the file and reload the subfile.

```
*...1....+....2....+....3....+....4....+....5....+....6
      *****************************************************************
      *    PROCESS RESPONSES TO SUBFILE
      *****************************************************************
      *
     C          RESPD       BEGSR
      *
A16C C          *INØ4       IFEQ *ON
A16C C                      MOVE *OFF      *INØ4
A16C C                      SELEC
A16C C          CSRFLD      WHEQ 'SELPN'              Window on
A16C C                      EXFMTPMTPN                Part Num
      * insert other prompt fields cases here
A16C C                      ENDSL
A16C C                      ENDIF                     *INØ4
      *
      *   The remainder of the subroutine as previously defined follows.
```

Figure 6.9

Part of the RESPD Subroutine with Prompt Cases

Exercise 6.1C Computers Are US Inventory Project

Purpose
To modify existing code to prompt for specific fields.

General Program Specifications
Create the maintenance program INV016C and the display file INVD016C to provide prompting on the Locate on Part Number and Locate on Description fields.

5. Copy display-file member INVD016B to new member INVD016C. Modify INVD016C to activate F4 for prompting. Add the RTNCSRLOC keyword to the control records. Add two new windows, one for prompting for part number and the other for prompting by description.

6. Copy RPG program source member INV016B to new member INV016C. Add the code to the RESPD subroutine shown in Figure 6.9.

Exercise 6.2C Purchase Order Line Project

Purpose
To design prompt screens.

General Program Specifications
Create RPG program ORDL26C, which provides prompting on the Locate on Order Number and Locate on Part Number fields.

5. Copy the display-file source member ORDD026B to a new member ORDD026C. Make the necessary modifications to prepare this display for prompting on Locate on Order Number as well as Locate on Part Number.

6. Copy the RPG source member ORDL26B to new member ORDL26C. Make the necessary modifications to add prompting on the two alternative selection fields.

F4=Prompt on Fields in the Subfile

Users might also need the prompt capability on fields in the subfile (as shown in Figure 6.10). As you will see in Chapter 7, prompts on these fields become more useful when the prompt window is changed to a list of values (a subfile in the window) that lets the user select the value instead of keying it.

Figure 6.10
Prompt for
Warehouse Field

```
Warehouse Code: STL    Enter Warehouse
                       Correct Values are:
                       STL, DLS, FTW
```

Just as in developing prompts for non-subfile fields, the RTNCSRLOC keyword returns the field that the cursor is on when the display file returns control to the program. However, when it works with the subfile, in addition to knowing which field is being prompted, the program must also know which subfile record is being prompted. The display-file keyword that identifies what subfile record the cursor is on — the SFLCSRRRN (Subfile Cursor Relative Record Number) keyword — was introduced in Chapter 4. SFLCSRRRN returns the number of the subfile record that the cursor is on, or a zero if the cursor is not pointing at a row of the subfile (Figure 6.11).

```
*...1....+....2....+....3....+....4....+....5....+....6
A                                    SFLCSRRRN(&CSRRRN)
A                                    RTNCSRLOC(&CSRFMT &CSRFLD)
A           SFLRCD        4S 0H      SFLRCDNBR(CURSOR)
A           CSRFMT       10A  H
A           CSRRRN        5S 0H
A           CSRFLD       10A  H
```

Figure 6.11
Extract from Subfile Control Record with the SFLCSRRRN Keyword

If indicator *IN04 is on and the value in CSRFLD is D1WH, we know that the cursor is pointing to the subfile record number stored in the variable CSRRRN and to the subfile field D1WH. Because we are likely to have a number of prompts to service, I have moved the prompt processing into a new subroutine, the Prompt (PROMPT) subroutine, shown in Figure 6.12. This subroutine is called from the RESPD subroutine whenever indicator 4 is on. Prompting of a subfile field requires chaining into the display file using the RRN returned by the SFLCSRRRN (Subfile Cursor Relative Record Number) keyword. Then the prompt window that uses the same field name as the field in the screen (i.e., D1WH) is executed. And unless the user presses F12 or F3, the value returned from the window is used to update the physical file and the display file.

Figure 6.12
PROMPT
Subroutine

```
*...1....+....2....+....3....+....4....+....5....+....6

**********************************************
*      Prompt Subroutine -- responds to prompt
**********************************************
C           PROMPT      BEGSR
C                       SELEC
 * -- prompt on warehouse code
C           CSRFLD      WHEQ 'D1WH'
 * -- position and read the subfile record where the user put the cursor
 * -- when the user pressed F4.
C           DESFLG      IFEQ *ON
C           CSRRRN      CHAINDSP01
C                       ELSE
C           CSRRRN      CHAINDSP03
C                       ENDIF
 * -- window WINWH uses the same field name D1WH
C                       EXFMTWINWH
C           *IN12       IFEQ *OFF
C           *IN03       ANDEQ*OFF
 * -- update the physical file
C           D1PNH       CHAININVPF                      92
C           *IN92       IFEQ *OFF
C                       MOVE D1WH       INWH
C                       UPDATINVPFR
C                       ENDIF
 * -- update the subfile record
C           DSPFLG      IFEQ *ON
C                       UPDATDSP01
C                       ELSE
C                       UPDATDSP03
C                       ENDIF
 ** prompt on other fields
C                       ENDSL
C                       ENDSR
```

Exercise 6.1D Computers Are US Inventory Project

Purpose
To modify existing code to prompt for subfile fields.

General Program Specifications
Create the maintenance program INV016D and the display file INVD016D to provide prompting on the Description, Quantity, and Cost fields in the subfile.

7. Copy display-file member INVD016C to new member INVD016D. Modify INVD016D to add the keyword SFLCSRRRN (Subfile Cursor Relative Record Number) to the control records. Add new windows to prompt for description, quantity, and cost.

8. Copy RPG program source member INV016C to new member INV016D. Modify the RESPD subroutine to call the PROMPT subroutine when F4 is pressed. Put all prompt servicing into the PROMPT subroutine.

Exercise 6.2D Purchase Order Line Project

Purpose
To design prompt screens.

General Program Specifications
Create the RPG program ORDL26D, which will provide prompting on all of the subfile fields.

7. Copy display-file source member ORDD026C to new member ORDD026D. Make the necessary modifications to prepare this display for prompting on Locate on all of the subfile fields

8. Copy RPG source member ORDL26C to new member ORDL26D. Make the necessary modifications to add prompting on all of the subfile fields.

Positioning the Cursor

In the previous two sections of this chapter, you developed prompt capabilities that let the user point to a position on the screen and press F4. A prompt window appeared and users entered the required data. The program then updated both the screen and the physical file when appropriate. Finally, the screen was redisplayed. However, users may notice that the cursor has wandered from where it was when they pressed F4. For example, users may have pressed F4 to prompt on the third field of the fourth record on the screen. They would expect the cursor to return to the point of origin or perhaps move to the next field or the next record. In this section, we explore how to return the cursor to the point at which it was when the prompt was requested.

We can find out the exact row and column of the cursor's location when F4 was pressed by making just a few changes to the RPG program. The cursor position is passed from the display file to the program in the file data structure. The file data structure contains a wealth of data about the display file and is updated and returned to the program whenever the display returns control to the program. To link the program with the file data buffer, you add another continuation specification to the F-spec for the display file, as shown in Figure 6.13.

```
*...1....+....2....+....3....+....4....+....5....+....6

FINVD16E CF   E                   WORKSTN
F                                      RRN   KSFILE DSP01
F                                      RRN   KSFILE DSP03
F                                            KINFDS FILDS
```

Figure 6.13
F-Spec with a Continuation Specification for the Data Structure

The continuation file data structure (INFDS) declares the name of a structure that will be defined in the I-specs. The structure defined in the specification in Figure 6.13 is FILDS. Figure 6.14 shows the I-specs that define this structure.

Figure 6.14
I-Spec for File Data
Structure (FILDS)

```
*...1....+....2....+....3....+....4....+....5....+....6

IFILDS         DS
I                                            B 370 3710CURPOS
```

The structure defined in Figure 6.14 extracts just 2 bytes of data from the large and complex structure that was passed from the display file to the program. These 2 bytes, representing a binary number, are in positions 370 and 371 of the structure. The binary number has zero decimal positions. In the example in Figure 6.14, the field mapped over these 2 bytes is named CURPOS. Whenever control is passed from the display file to the RPG program, the field CURPOS will contain a binary number that represents the cursor position and can be converted into the cursor row and column position.

A new subroutine will be added to the RPG program to compute the cursor location. The Locate Cursor (LOCCUR) subroutine, shown in Figure 6.15, extracts the row and column positions from the field that maps the display-file data structure, CURPOS.

Figure 6.15
The LOCCUR Subroutine
Computes the Row and
Column of the Cursor
from the Field CURPOS

```
*...1....+....2....+....3....+....4....+....5....+....6

*****************************************************************
* CURPOS Subroutine -- computes the row & column of the cursor
*                      from the field CURPOS, which is mapped over
*                      the file data structure of the display file
*****************************************************************
C           LOCCUR      BEGSR
C                       Z-ADDCURPOS    CURSA    50
C           CURSA       DIV  256       ROWPOS
C                       MVR            COLPOS
C                       MOVE *ON       *IN46
C                       ENDSR
```

The LOCCUR subroutine should be called at the beginning of the Prompt subroutine. (If it is called after a prompt window has been displayed, it computes the cursor position on the prompt window instead of on the original screen.)

Notice that the LOCCUR subroutine turns on indicator 46. Indicator 46 conditions a new display-file keyword, CSRLOC (Cursor Location), shown in Figure 6.16. CSRLOC receives two fields of data from the program. Because they have the same field names as the fields computed in the LOCCUR subroutine — ROWPOS and COLPOS — the CSRLOC keyword will locate the cursor at the current values of those fields. ROWPOS and COLPOS must be signed (3 0) and hidden (note shaded lines in Figure 6.16). The CSRLOC keyword will only have an effect on the cursor when the conditioning indicator 46 is on. When indicator 46 is off, the values of ROWPOS and COLPOS have no effect.

```
*...1....+....2....+....3....+....4....+....5....+....6
A                                   SFLCSRRRN(&CSRRRN)
A    46                             CSRLOC(ROWPOS COLPOS)
A                                   RTNCSRLOC(&CSRFMT &CSRFLD)
A          ROWPOS      3S  ØH
A          COLPOS      3S  ØH
A          CSRRRN      5S  ØH
A          CSRFMT     10A   H
A          CSRFLD     10A   H
```

Figure 6.16
CSRLOC Keyword Added
to Subfile Control Record

Indicator 46 should be turned off after the screen that is being controlled is displayed. If the subroutine to recompute the value is called again, it will be turned on for the next time that the display is executed. In our current design, indicator 46 can be turned off at the top of the RESPD subroutine.

Exercise 6.1E Computers Are US Inventory Project

Purpose
To modify existing code to return the cursor to its original location when the program returns to the main screen after a prompt window has been displayed.

General Program Specifications
Create maintenance program INV016E and display file INVD016E to return the cursor to its location at the time the user requested the prompt.

9. Copy display-file member INVD016D to new member INVD016E. Modify INVD016E to add the CSRLOC keyword.

10. Copy RPG program source member INV016D to new member INV016E. Add the continuation specification for INFDS and the data structure for CURPOS (Figures 6.13 and 6.14). Modify the RESPD subroutine to turn off indicator 46 at the beginning of the routine. Modify the PROMPT subroutine to call the new LOCCUR subroutine at the beginning of the PROMPT routine.

Exercise 6.2E Purchase Order Line Project

Purpose
To develop the code necessary to use CSRLOC to control cursor location.

General Program Specifications
Create the RPG program ORDL26E to to return the cursor to its position at the time the user selected a prompt.

9. Copy the display-file source member ORDD026D to a new member ORDD026E. Make the necessary modifications to add the CSRLOC keyword.

10. Copy the RPG source member ORDL26D to new member ORDL26E. Make the necessary modifications to control the cursor location.

F1=Help

A feature of most on-line systems on the AS/400 is an extensive Help service. Typically, a user can point to the top of any screen, press F1, and access general Help about the screen. The user can also point to any field, press F1, and see a Help screen for that field. Users who rarely use printed manuals often are willing to press the Help key if the Help system is consistently available and easy to use. The information on the Help screens needs to be clear. I will introduce three different methods for handling requests for Help, which I refer to as HELP1, HELP2, and HELP3.

The HELP1 method is functionally similar to the prompt system. You create Help records in the display file and use the command action keyword CA01(01'F1=Help') to activate a function key to be used to request Help (usually F1).

If the program returns 01 on, the CSRFLD field is checked and the correct Help record displayed. This is not a bad solution, especially because the code is basically the same as the code that you developed for prompting. Because this method is functionally identical to the prompt system discussed earlier in this chapter, I will not explore it in this section.

The HELP2 method, like HELP1, calls Help records that have been included in the display-file description. However, with HELP2, new display-file keywords program the display file to display the Help record. With this method, there are virtually no changes to the RPG code. I will explain the new display-file keywords that HELP2 uses in the next few pages.

The HELP3 method uses some of the same display-file keywords as HELP2 but requires a few new keywords. The Help screens are not included in the display file but coded in a new type of object, a panel-group object (PNLGRP). The resultant Help screens look and act exactly the same as others used throughout the operating system (Figure 6.17).

Figure 6.17
Example of
HELP3 Method

```
                           Print Key Output                          Page   1
         5763SS1 V3R2M0 960517              JEFFCIS1        08/03/98  11:36:07
         Display Device . . . . . :  TC10717S1
         User . . . . . . . . . . :  DEVELOPER
                              Work with Members Using PDM              JEFFCIS
         File . . . . . .  QDDSSRC
          Library . . . .  TEXTBOOK              Position to . . . . .
         Type options, press Enter.
          2=Edit        3=Copy  4=Delete 5=Display    6=Print    7=Rename
          8=Display description  9=Save 13=Change text 14=Compile 15=Create module..
         ....................................................................
         Opt :                        Options - Help                         :
             :                                                               :
             : Use this column to perform different operations on individual :
             : members. Type the option number next to a member and press Enter or :
             : F4=Prompt. You can type the same option next to more than one :
             : member at a time, and you can also type different options next to :
             : different members at the same time.                           :
             :                                                               :
             : Choose from the following:                                    :
             :                                                               :
         Par :                                                      More... :
         === : F2=Extended help    F10=Move to top   F11=Search Index  F12=Cancel :
         F3= : F13=Information Assistant   F20=Enlarge   F24=More keys   :
         F9= :                                                               :
             :...............................................................:
```

Changing Help text in panel groups is easy because it does not require changes to the program or the display file. The same panel group can contain Help panels for many programs and a Help panel can be used by many programs. All that is required to change Help text is to type the changes into the "text" PNLGRP member and recompile it.

HELP2: Using Help Records

Using Help records is an efficient and simple way to create Help screens. The changes required are entirely in the display file. The display file itself manages the Help. The RPG program will not need to be modified and will not know that the Help screen was displayed.

The four display-file keywords that we will explore are the following:

- HELP (Help) is a file-level keyword that activates the Help system.
- ALTHELP (Alternate Help) is a file-level keyword that redefines the Help key from the Scroll Lock to a function key (e.g., ALTHELP(CA01) and that defines Function key F1 as the Help key).
- HLPARA (Help Area) is a file and record-level keyword that defines the record, field, or area of the screen for which a Help definition will be created. Figure 6.18 shows samples of a Help area delared for 1) the area of the record footer, 2) the area of the field SELPN, and 3) the definition of a Help area of a rectangle. Remember that if the definition is at the record level, that definition exists only when that record is active.

HLPARA(*RCD FOOTER) — the area defined is the footer record

HLPARA(*FLD SELPN) — the area defined is the field SELPN

HLPARA(8 4 15 14) — the area defined is from row 8 column 4 to row 15 column 14

Figure 6.18
Three Examples
of HLPARA

- HLPRCD (Help Record) is a file and record-level keyword that identifies the record to display for a specific Help request (e.g., HLPRCD(SPNHLP) displays the display-file record format SPNHLP; you must create the record SPNHLP).

One new display-file tool needs to be introduced: the Help specification. An H in the type field identifies a record as beginning a Help definition. Typically, a Help definition occupies two lines. The first line has the H type and the HLPARA keyword, which defines what area of the screen is to be defined. The next line has a blank type and the HLPRCD definition. The pair of keywords identifies what record to display when the cursor is within the specified area and the Help key is pressed.

Help specifications cannot be included in subfile records though they can be included in every other type of record. To provide Help for subfile fields, put the Help specifications in the control record for the subfile. These specifications must identify the rectangle of each Help area (not the field names of subfile fields).

Figure 6.19 shows the use of the ALTHELP keyword and contains the default declaration of a Help record. The default record GENERAL is displayed whenever Help is requested (F1) unless another definition is in effect for the specific part of the screen that the cursor is pointing to at the time of the request. These are file-level declarations that must appear before the first record declaration.

Figure 6.19

Example of File-Level Declaration of Help Key and a Default Help Declaration That Will Display the Record GENERAL

```
*...1....+....2....+....3....+....4....+....5....+....6

*** added to File Level DDS
**-- makes F1 the Help key and HELP activates the help system
A                                    ALTHELP(CA01)
A                                    HELP
**-- at the file level, this will display the DDS record General
**-- whenever Help is called and no other further definition applies
A                                    HLPRCD(GENERAL)
```

Figure 6.20 demonstrates Help specifications. When the user points the cursor to the SELPN field and presses F1, the Help specification for the field SELPN displays the screen HLPSPN. If the cursor is located anywhere in the rectangle from row 8 column 4 to row 15 column 14 and F1 is pressed, the display record format HLPDPN is displayed.

Figure 6.20

Subfile Control Record Containing Help Specifications for the Field SELPN and the Area (8 4 15 14)

```
*...1....+....2....+....3....+....4....+....5....+....6

A         R DSP02                    SFLCTL(DSP01)
 *-- SFL keywords not shown
A                                    RTNCSRLOC(&CSRFMT &CSRFLD)
A                                    SFLCSRRRN(&CSRRRN)
A    46                              CSRLOC(ROWPOS COLPOS)

   *-- added to control record; must be after SFL keywords
   *-- and before variables are defined
   *-- if Help is requested while pointing at SELPN field then
   *--      The record named HLPSPN is displayed.
A         H                          HLPARA(*FLD SELPN)
A                                    HLPRCD(HLPSPN)

   *-- if Help is requested while pointing at rectangle row 8 col 4
   *--      to row 15 col 14. This is the area where the part number
   *--      is displayed. The record named HLPDPN is displayed.
A         H                          HLPARA(8 4 15 14 )
A                                    HLPRCD(HLPDPN)

A         SFLRCD        4S 0H        SFLRCDNBR(CURSOR)
A         ROWPOS        3S 0H
```

Exercise 6.1F Computers Are US Inventory Project

Purpose
To modify existing code to incorporate Help method HELP2.

General Program Specifications
Create maintenance program INV016F and display file INVD016F to provide general Help on the entire screen and specific Help on the fields SELPN and D1PN.

11. Copy display-file member INVD016E to new member INVD016F. Modify INVD016F to add the file-level and record-level Help keywords as shown in Figures 6.19 and 6.20. Create the display-file records GENERAL, HLPSPN, and HLPDPN, which give appropriate information about the purpose of the entire screen, the Locate on Part Number field, and the Part Number area of the subfile.

12. Copy RPG program source member INV016E to new member INV016F.

Exercise 6.2F Purchase Order Line Project

Purpose
To develop Help screens using the HELP2 method.

General Program Specifications
Create the RPG program ORDL26F. It should provide general Help on the entire screen, as well as specific Help on each field displayed and on the footer record.

11. Copy display-file source member ORDD026E to new member ORDD026F. Make the necessary modifications to add general Help on the entire screen, Help on each field, and Help on the footer record.

12. Copy RPG source member ORDL26E to new member ORDL26F.

HELP3: Using Help Panel Group

Only two new keywords beyond those used with the HELP2 are needed for the HELP3 method. The only change to the display-file description is replacing the HLPRCD with the HLPPNLGRP (Help Panel Group) keyword, as shown in Figure 6.21. The HLPPNLGRP keyword refers to records in the panel-group object not in the display file. Therefore, you can eliminate the Help records in the DDS.

Figure 6.21
Help Panel Group
Keyword and Help Panel
Group Title Replaces Help
Record Keyword

```
*...1....+....2....+....3....+....4....+....5....+....6
A                                          HLPRCD(GENERAL)
A                                          HLPPNLGRP(GENERAL INVP016G)
A                                          HLPTITLE('Inventory Help')
```

The HLPPNLGRP keyword identifies the record in the panel-group file and the name of the panel-group file. The HLPPNLGRP keyword identifies that the GENERAL record in the panel-group file INVP016G is to be called if Help is requested when no other Help applies.

The HLPTITLE (Help Panel Group Title) keyword provides a title to appear at the top of the Help screen. This will only be used if the panel definition has a blank panel title. The display-file description must contain at least one HLPTITLE keyword.

The Panel Group

You must create a new member of type PNLGRP, which will contain the Help text. You could create the source member in the file QDDSSRC or QUIMSRC. Members of type PNLGRP are text files with no prompting or syntax checking. Entries can be up to 80 characters long.

An example of a panel group is shown in Figure 6.22.

The panel-group definition begins with :PNLGRP. and ends with :EPNLGRP. The prefix E stands for End (e.g., End Panel Group, End Help).

The colons (:) and periods (.) are important. A colon (:) indicates a special panel-group command. A period (.) ends the command.

Each Help panel begins with the Help name, which is same as the name that was used in the HLPPNLGRP keyword in the display-file description:

```
:HELP NAME = D1PN.
```

Each panel ends with :EHELP.

The second line of each Help panel is the panel heading:

```
Part Number - Help Screen.
```

The third line of each Help panel is the highlighted topic name you'll find when you scan through expanded Help (F2) that identifies this as a topic heading:

```
:XH3.Part Number - Help
```

```
:PNLGRP.
:HELP NAME = GENERAL.

:P.
The Inventory Inquiry/Maintenance screen is designed to allow you to
view and update inventory amounts by location. You should be
careful not to change product numbers if orders exist for the
products.
:P.
This system has been developed by _____ for class _____.
:EHELP.
.****************************************************************
:HELP NAME = SELPN.
Select Part Number - Help Screen
:XH3.Select Part Number - Help
:P.
You can position the list to the part number that you need to view
by typing part of or the whole part number.
:EHELP.
.****************************************************************
:HELP NAME = D1PN.
Part Number - Help Screen
:XH3.Part Number - Help
:P.
You can change the part number in three ways.
:P.
 1. Move to the part number and type over it.
:P.
 2. Move to the part number and press F4 for prompting.
:P.
 3. Type a 2 in the option beside the record to be changed.
:P.
The number will not be changed if there is a current product with the
same number. You should not change the number if there are any
outstanding orders for the product.
:EHELP.
.****************************************************************
:EPNLGRP.
```

Figure 6.22
Panel Group INVP016G

The XH3 identifies the format that will be applied to the Part Number-Help.
The panel-group system provides fourteen different "formats," each of which will be
displayed differently. The formats are numbered XH1, XH2, and so forth, up
to XH14.

Each paragraph begins with :P.

It's that easy. The body of the Help text is typed in a paragraph format. Each
line is a maximum of 80 characters long. Lines of text can be copied, moved, and
deleted, just as in other applications that use SEU.

Exit with F3 and use 14 (compile) to create the panel group. Obviously, check
your messages for errors, then correct and recompile until you reach a normal completion of the compile.

Exercise 6.1G Computers Are US Inventory Project

Purpose
To modify existing code to incorporate Help method HELP3.

General Program Specifications
Create maintenance program INV016G and display file INVD016G to provide general Help on the entire screen and specific Help on the fields SELPN and D1PN.

13. Create the panel group INVP016G of type PNLGRP based on the sample in Figure 6.22. Compile the panel group.
14. Copy display-file member INVD016F to new member INVD016G. Modify INVD016G to add the file-level and record-level Help keywords as shown in Figure 6.21 and change all Help record keywords to Help panel group keywords. Remove the display-file records GENERAL, HLPSPN, and HLPDPN.
15. Copy RPG program source member INV016F to new member INV016G.

Exercise 6.2G Purchase Order Line Project

Purpose
To develop Help screens using the HELP3 method.

General Program Specifications
Create RPG program ORDL26G to provide general Help on the entire screen, as well as Help on each field displayed and on the footer record.

13. Create panel group ORDLP26F of type PNLGRP to hold Help definitions for the general Help, for each field on the display, and for the footer area. Compile the definition.
14. Copy display-file source member ORDD026F to new member ORDD026G. Make the necessary modifications to use a panel group to provide general Help on the entire screen, Help on each field, and Help on the footer record.
15. Copy RPG source member ORDL26F to new member ORDL26G.

Review

1. Discuss the problems associated with letting the user change the value in the key field.
2. What does the CHANGE keyword do?
3. How do you add a hidden field to a display-file description and why would you do it?
4. Describe how you determine which field users are "pointing" to when they press F4 for prompt.
5. Describe how you can determine the RRN of the subfile record where your cursor is positioned.
6. Describe how you can control the positioning of the cursor.
7. Why do you need to know the subfile RRN when the prompt is requested on a subfile field, how is this number determined, and how is it used?
8. Which of the Help options would require changes to the RPG code? What changes?
9. A display-file record displays the field EMPNAM. EMPNAM is not a subfile field. You are to provide Help on this field based on the HELP2 method described in this chapter. Write the Help specifications necessary to display the format HLPENM when F1 is pressed and the cursor is positioned on that field.
10. A display file contains a subfile field named EMPNM2. This field is defined in the subfile record SFLR1, which is controlled by the subfile control record SFLCR1. This field is 15 characters long and begins in column 19. The first record of the subfile is displayed on row 9 and the subfile page value is 10. You are to provide Help on this field based on the HELP2 method described in this chapter. Write the Help specifications necessary to display the format HLPENM when F1 is pressed and the cursor is on that field.
11. A display-file record displays the field EMPNAM. (EMPNAM is not a subfile field.) You are to provide Help on this field based on the HELP3 method described in this chapter. Write the Help specifications necessary to display the panel-group record HLPENM in panel group EMPHELP when F1 is pressed and the cursor is on that field.
12. Write the panel-group code for the Help record HLPENM in panel group EMPHELP. This should display the employee's last name. It must be the name that is on the employee's birth certificate, driver's license, or another legal document. If the name is longer than 25 characters, use the first 25 characters.

Chapter 7

Creating Window-Based Subfiles

Chapter Overview

When you complete Chapter 7, you will be able to create subfiles in windows that offer users an opportunity to make selections

✓ using the prompt option

✓ using the point-and-shoot feature

Subfiles in Windows

Windows are a great way to present pop-up information on a display screen and prompt users to make a choice. When the information to be presented is a list, subfiles are required. You will learn to display a subfile in a window and prompt users to make a selection among the options offered.

In the display-file description, the subfile record for a window is defined like any other subfile record. The width of the window, which is defined in the control record, must be enough to accommodate the left and right window borders. The subfile control record contains the window definition as well as optional window border commands. Adding a footer to a window containing a subfile is discussed later in this chapter. For now, the definition of function keys will appear *above* the subfile display. Remember to reserve one line at the bottom of the window as a message line as well as two rows, one for the top border and one for the bottom border, and two columns, one for the left border and the other for the right border.

In Chapter 6, you developed prompts for many fields, including the warehouse code (Figure 7.1). As you may recall, the warehouse code prompt window used in Chapter 6 had the valid values STL, DLS, and FTW hard-coded in it.

Warehouse Code: STL

Enter Warehouse
Correct Values are:
STL, DLS, FTW

Figure 7.1
Prompt for Warehouse Field with Hard-Coded Values

Although Computers Are US has a certain number of warehouses at present, the company may add more later. Therefore, instead of hard-coding the warehouse codes in the display, it would be better to load the values from a data file that contains up-to-date warehouse data. The warehouse file is shown in Figure 7.2.

Figure 7.2
Warehouse File

```
*...1....+....2....+....3....+....4....+....5....+....6

************************************************************
* Phil Levinson   Jefferson College  11/16/98  WHPF
* Warehouse Physical File
************************************************************
A                                       UNIQUE
A          R WHPFR
A            WHPWH         3A            TEXT ('WAREHOUSE ID')
A            WHPA1        20A            TEXT ('WH ADDRESS LINE 1')
A            WHPA2  .     20A            TEXT ('WH ADDRESS LINE 2')
A            WHPCT        20A            TEXT ('WH CITY')
A            WHPST         2A            TEXT ('WH STATE')
A            WHPZIP       11A            TEXT ('WH ZIP')
A          K WHPWH
```

Because Computers Are US has three warehouses at present, the warehouse files would contain the data shown in Figure 7.3.

Figure 7.3
Warehouse Data

```
WHPWH:  DLS
WHPA1:  2100 W 4TH STREET
WHPA2:
WHPCT:  DALLAS
WHPST:  TX
WHPZIP: 51233-1234

WHPWH:  FTW
WHPA1:  789 FIFTH STREET
WHPA2:
WHPCT:  FORT WORTH
WHPST:  TX
WHPZIP: 59191-1123

WHPWH:  STL
WHPA1:  9004 STATE STREET
WHPA2:
WHPCT:  SAINT LOUIS
WHPST:  MO
WHPZIP: 63511-1241
```

Two new records will replace the current warehouse prompt window in the display file: 1) the warehouse subfile record WHSF, shown in Figure 7.4, and 2) the subfile control record WINPWH, which contains the WINDOW definition, shown in Figure 7.5.

Figure 7.4
Warehouse Subfile

```
*...1....+....2....+....3....+....4....+....5....+....6

A*********************************************
A*** WHSF - WAREHOUSE SUBFILE
A     TO BE DISPLAYED IN WINPWH
A*********************************************
A          R WHSF                       SFL
A            WHWH          3A 0    4  5
A            WHCTY        20A 0    4  9
A            WHAD1        20A 0    4 30
A            WHST          2A 0    4 51
A            WHZIP        11A 0    4 54
```

```
*...1....+....2....+....3....+....4....+....5....+....6

*******************************************************
***    WINDOW subfile control record - WINPWH    ***
***    DISPLAYS WAREHOUSE SUBFILE    - WHSF       ***
*******************************************************
A
A            R WINPWH                    SFLCTL(WHSF)
A
     **** W I N D O W    C O N T R O L S     ***
A                                         WINDOW(8 6 12 70)
A                                         WDWBORDER((*COLOR RED)-
A                                         (*DSPATR HI -
A                                         RI) (*CHAR '          '))
     **** S U B F I L E    C O N T R O L S     ***
A                                         SFLSIZ(07)
A                                         SFLPAG(06)
A                                         OVERLAY
A  53                                     SFLDSP
A  53                                     SFLDSPCTL
A N53                                     SFLCLR
A  54                                     SFLEND(*MORE)
A
     **** S C R E E N    H E A D E R     *****
A                                       1 05'WAREHOUSE INFORMATION'
A                        .              2 5'Enter=Exit Screen'
A                                       3 5'WHs'
A                                       3 9'City'
A                                       3 30'Address'
A                                       3 51'St'
A                                       3 54'Zip'
```

Figure 7.5
Warehouse Subfile
Control Record

Let's suppose that users have indicated that a display of all of the warehouse fields except Address 2 would help them select the correct warehouse. Figure 7.4 shows the subfile record definition. Although we will not need it in this example, subfile drop or subfile fold (covered in Chapter 4) can be used in window-based subfiles, just as in other subfiles.

The control record (Figure 7.5) is slightly more complex than previous control records because it contains the WINDOW (Window) and WDWBORDER (Window Border) keywords as well as subfile control keywords. The number of columns (70) in the window must be wide enough for all the fields of the subfile, and the number of rows (12) must accommodate the subfile, which starts at line 4 and continues for the number of lines defined in the SLFPAG keyword (6).

Conditioning indicator 53 controls the SFLDSP (Subfile Display), SFLDSPCTL (Subfile Control Display), and SFLCLR (Subfile Clear) keywords. Indicator 54 is used to indicate the End of File (EOF) of the warehouse file.

The changes required in the RPG program are also familiar. The F-spec for the display file needs another continuation record for the new subfile, as is shown in the shaded line in Figure 7.6.

```
*...1....+....2....+....3....+....4....+....5....+....6

      FINVD017ACF  E              WORKSTN
16E F                                    KINFDS FILDS
    F                              RRN   KSFILE DSP01
15F F                              RRN   KSFILE DSP03
17A F                              WHRRN KSFILE WHSF
```

Figure 7.6
F-Specs for the
Display File with the
Warehouse Subfile

The program also requires an F-spec for the warehouse file, WHPF. This specification (not shown) would access the file for input as a keyed file.

Because the warehouse file is a short file that probably will remain relatively short, it is appropriate to use subfile load option 1, loading the entire file before it is displayed. The subroutine to load and display the warehouse window, WINWH, is called from the PROMPT subroutine, developed in Chapter 6, whenever the F4 key is pressed while the cursor points to a warehouse code. The WINWH subroutine is shown in Figure 7.7.

Figure 7.7

Subroutine WINWH
Loads and Displays the
Warehouse Window

```
*...1....+....2....+....3....+....4....+....5....+....6

************************************************
*   WINWH - LOADS AND DISPLAYS THE WAREHOUSE FILE
************************************************
C           WINWH     BEGSR
 *
C                     MOVE *OFF      *IN53
C                     WRITEWINPWH
C                     MOVE *ON       *IN53
C                     Z-ADD*ZERO     WHRRN     90
C           *LOVAL    SETLLWHPF
 *
C                     READ WHPF                      54
 *
C           *IN54     DOWEQ*OFF
C           WHRRN     ANDLT9999
C                     MOVE WHPWH     WHWH
C                     MOVE WHPCT     WHCTY
C                     MOVE WHPA1     WHAD1
C                     MOVE WHPST     WHST
C                     MOVE WHPZIP    WHZIP
C                     ADD  1         WHRRN
C                     WRITEWHSF
C                     READ WHPF                      54
C                     ENDDO
C           WHRRN     IFEQ *ZERO
C                     MOVE 'NO WHS ' WHCTY
C                     ADD  1         WHRRN
C                     WRITEWHSF
C                     ENDIF
C                     EXFMTWINPWH
C                     ENDSR
```

Exercise 7.1A Computers Are US Inventory Project

Purpose
To develop a program to display a subfile in a window.

General Program Specifications
Create maintenance program INV017A and display file INVD017A. When users prompt on the Warehouse field, the program displays the warehouse list in a subfile in a window.

1. Create warehouse file WHPF (Figure 7.2).
2. Use Data File Utility (DFU) to add the records shown in Figure 7.3 to the warehouse file.
3. Copy display-file member INVD016G to new member INVD017A. Modify INVD017A to add the subfile record shown in Figure 7.4 and the subfile control record shown in Figure 7.5.
4. Copy RPG program source member INV016G to new member INV017A. Modify this program by adding the F-spec for the new file (WHPF) and the continuation F-spec for subfile WHSF (Figure 7.6). Modify the program to call the WINWH subroutine when F4 is pressed while the cursor points to the Warehouse field, and add subroutine WINWH (Figure 7.7).

Exercise 7.2A Purchase Order Line Project

Purpose
To develop a program to display a subfile in a window.

General Program Specifications
Create RPG program ORDL27A, which will display a subfile in a window when the user presses F4 while the cursor points to the Part Number field in the subfile display.

1. Create the physical file called Parts Master Physical file (PMPF) with two fields: the Part Number field (PMPN 11 A) and the Part Description field (PMDS 30 A).

2. Use DFU to enter the data in Figure 7.8 into the file PMPF.

Figure 7.8
Product Data

PMPN	PMDS
A123	COMPUTER X486
A124	COMPUTER PENT
A125	PRINTER — LASER
A213	PRINTER — INK JET
A214	PRINTER — DOT MATRIX
A215	SCANNER — HAND
A216	SCANNER — FLAT BED
A217	SCANNER/KEYBOARD
A319	CD-ROM
A320	CD-ROM 4X

3. Copy display-file source member ORDD026G to new member ORDD027A. Make the necessary modifications to add a subfile and a control record with a window definition to display the data in file PMPF.

4. Copy RPG source member ORDL26G to new member ORDL27A. Modify the member to display the subfile with the part numbers when F4 is pressed while the cursor is in either the part-number or the part-description area of the subfile.

Selection in a Window Subfile Using the Prompt Option

Although we've done well to *show* users our prompt window subfile, prompt screens are intended to let users add or change a value. To make our prompt screen really useful, we need to let the user pick one of the entries and update the main display subfile. In this section, we'll explore adding a pick field to the subfile. The pick field is much like the option column that was added to the display in Chapter 2. When a user makes an entry in this column, the RPG program uses a READC operation to locate the warehouse record that the user has selected. With the warehouse value from the subfile in the prompt window, the program can update the main display and the physical file INVPF.

Changes to the display file are minor: We will need to add a new field to the subfile record WHSF (Figure 7.9). We will also modify the control record to activate F12 for cancel, add the display F12=Cancel to the heading, and add the text **SL** (for selection) to be displayed above the new column.

```
*...1....+....2....+....3....+....4....+....5....+....6
A          WHPIC          1A  I   4   2
```

Figure 7.9

Pick Field to be Added to the Subfile Record WHSF

The changes to the RPG code are a little more significant, as is shown in Figure 7.10 (page 140). After displaying the subfile/window, if IN12 is off, the processing continues. The program will use the READC operation to read the record selected in the warehouse prompt window. Use the cursor relative record number (CSRRRN) in the main subfile to retrieve the subfile record to be updated. Update the field in the subfile record from the warehouse value in the record selected in the warehouse prompt. Retrieve the matching record in the inventory physical file and update it.

Figure 7.10

Additions to Subroutine WINWH

```
*...1....+....2....+....3....+....4....+....5....+....6
        C                       EXFMTWINPWH
A17B    *
A17B    C           *IN12       IFEQ *OFF
A17B    C                       READCWHSF                        56
A17B    C           *IN56       IFEQ *OFF
A17B    *-- UPDATE THE MAIN SUBFILE
A17B    C           DESFLG      IFEQ *OFF
A17B    C           CSRRRN      CHAINDSP01                94
A17B    C                       MOVELWHWH    D1WH
A17B    C                       UPDATDSP01
A17B    C                       ELSE
A17B    C           CSRRRN      CHAINDSP03                94
A17B    C                       MOVELWHWH    D1WH
A17B    C                       UPDATDSP03
A17B    C                       ENDIF
A17B    *-- UPDATE THE PHYSICAL FILE
A17B    C           D1PN        CHAININVPF                93
A17B    C           *IN93       IFEQ *OFF
A17B    C                       MOVE D1PN    INPN
A17B    C                       MOVE D1DESC  INDESC
A17B    C                       Z-ADDD1QOH   INQOH
A17B    C                       Z-ADDD1UCST  INUCST
A17B    C                       MOVE WHWH    INWH
A17B    C                       MOVE D1WHL   INWHL
A17B    C                       UPDATINVPFR
A17B    C                       ENDIF
A17B    C                       ENDIF
A17B    C                       ENDIF
        *
        C                       ENDSR
```

Exercise 7.1B Computers Are US Inventory Project

Purpose

To develop code to display a subfile in a prompt window and use the user's response to update the display and the physical file.

General Program Specifications

Create maintenance program INV017B and display file INVD017B. When users prompt on the Warehouse field, this program displays the warehouse list in a subfile in a window. When the user makes a selection, both the display and the physical files are automatically updated.

5. Copy display-file member INVD017A to new member INVD017B. Modify INVD017B to add a pick field to the subfile record, as shown in Figure 7.9.

6. Copy RPG program source member INV017A to new member INV017B. Modify this program by adding the changes (shown in Figure 7.10) to the WINWH subroutine to update the display and the physical file with the value selected from the prompt window.

Exercise 7.2B Purchase Order Line Project

Purpose
To develop a prompt using a subfile in a window.

General Program Specifications
Create RPG program ORDL27B to display a subfile in a window when users press F4 while the cursor points to either the Part Number field or the Description field in the subfile display. When users select a value from the prompt window, the program then updates both the Part Number field and the Description field on the subfile display and in the physical file.

5. Copy display-file source member ORDD027A to new member ORDD027B. Make the necessary modifications to add a selection field to the part number prompt subfile.
6. Copy RPG source member ORDL27A to new member ORDL27B. Modify the member so that it uses the selected record on the prompt screen to update the display and the physical file. Both the Part Number and Description fields should be updated.

Selection in a Window Subfile Using Point and Shoot

The inventory maintenance system we've been developing is becoming quite user friendly. Our new prompt screens, however, still require that the user type a letter and then press Enter to make a selection. We can save users a keystroke by adding what are often called point-and-shoot capabilities. Such capabilities let users select a subfile record, such as a warehouse record, on the prompt screen by simply placing the cursor anywhere on the record and pressing Enter. This technique does not require a selection column in the subfile record.

The subfile cursor RRN keyword, SFLCSRRRN (Figure 7.11), is added to the subfile control record of the prompt window. The field associated with this keyword returns the RRN of the record that the cursor was pointing to when the display returned control to the RPG program. If the return from this keyword is zero, the cursor was not pointing to any record in that subfile.

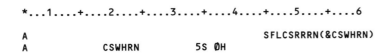

```
*...1....+....2....+....3....+....4....+....5....+....6
A                                     SFLCSRRRN(&CSWHRN)
A          CSWHRN       5S ØH
```

Figure 7.11
Additional Keyword
Control Record for
Prompt Window

Notice that a different variable (CSWHRN) is used to return the cursor position in the subfile because the WINWH subroutine needs to use the RRN in both the prompt window to retrieve the selection and the main subfile to retrieve the inventory record that is to be updated.

We have been using the value of SFLCSRRRN in our PROMPT subroutine to determine which record was active when F4 was pressed. The value of CSWHRN tells us which record the user pointed to in the prompt subfile. To use it, we replace the READC operation on the prompt subfile with a CHAIN (Random Retrieval from a

File) operation into the prompt subfile using the field CSWHRN (note the shaded lines in Figure 7.12).

Figure 7.12
New Code to
Replace READC in
WINWH Subroutine

```
*...1....+....2....+....3....+....4....+....5....+....6
      C                         EXFMTWINPWH
A17C  C           *IN12         IFEQ *OFF
A17C  C           CSWHRN        ANDNE*ZERO
A17E  C           CSWHRN        CHAINWHSF              56
A17C  C           *IN56         IFEQ *OFF
```

Exercise 7.1C Computers Are US Inventory Project

Purpose
To develop code to display a subfile in a prompt window and use the user's point-and-shoot response to update both the display and the physical file.

General Program Specifications
Create maintenance program INV017C and display file INVD017C. When users prompt on the Warehouse field, this program displays the warehouse list in a subfile in a window. After the user makes a selection using point and shoot, both the display and the physical file are updated.

7. Copy display-file member INVD017B to new member INVD017C. Modify INVD017C to delete the selection field from the prompt window, and add the subfile cursor RRN to the prompt subfile control record (Figure 7.11).
8. Copy RPG program source member INV017B to new member INV017C. Modify this program based on the code in Figure 7.12 to use the RRN of the record in the warehouse prompt window subfile to locate that record and update both the display and the physical files with the warehouse value.

Exercise 7.2C Purchase Order Line Project

Purpose
To develop a prompt in a subfile in a window using the point-and-shoot technique.

General Program Specifications
Create RPG program ORDL27C, which displays a subfile in a window if the user presses F4 while the cursor points to the Part Number or the Description field in the subfile display. When the user selects a value from the prompt window using the point-and-shoot method, the program then updates both the Part Number and the Description fields in the subfile display and the physical file.

7. Copy display-file source member ORDD027B to new member ORDD027C. Make the necessary modifications to remove the selection field in the part-number prompt subfile. Add the subfile RRN keyword SFLRRN to the control record for the window that prompts on part number.
8. Copy RPG source member ORDL27B to new member ORDL27C. Modify the member to use the RRN of the selected record on the prompt screen to update the display and the physical file. Both the Part Number and the Description fields should be updated.

Creating and Using a Window Definition Record

A window definition record contains the keywords that define a window and its border. Once the window definition record is written to the display, any number of display records can be overlayed in the window. Records to be displayed in the window reference the window definition record instead of containing detailed window and window border descriptions. Both subfiles and simple display records can be shown in a window defined by the window definition record.

Display records referencing the same window definition record and the OVERLAY keyword can be displayed simultaneously in the same window, provided they do not attempt to write in the same territory. This capability lets you design more complex and flexible displays within the window. The capability to display multiple records in the same window can also be used to add footer information displaying the text definitions of the function keys at the bottom of a window that contains a subfile.

Figure 7.13 shows the window definition record WDR1, which contains the WINDOW (Window) and WDBORDER (Window Border) definitions.

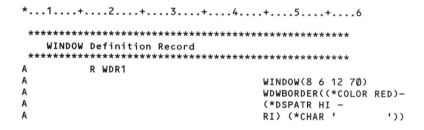

```
*...1....+....2....+....3....+....4....+....5....+....6

****************************************************
     WINDOW Definition Record
****************************************************
A          R WDR1
A                                    WINDOW(8 6 12 70)
A                                    WDWBORDER((*COLOR RED)-
A                                    (*DSPATR HI -
A                                    RI) (*CHAR '       '))
```

Figure 7.13
Window Definition Record

Figure 7.14 shows window reference record FOOTW1, which contains footer information.

```
*...1....+....2....+....3....+....4....+....5....+....6

****************************************************
     WINDOW Footer Record
****************************************************

A          R FOOTW1
A                                    WINDOW(WDR1)
A                                9   5'F12=CANCEL'
```

Figure 7.14
Window Reference
Record FOOTW1

Figure 7.15 is the subfile control record for the prompt window. It is a window reference record that contains the OVERLAY keyword so that its information can be added to the window display without erasing the existing footer record.

Figure 7.15
Warehouse Subfile
Control Record
Defined as a Window
Reference Record

```
*...1....+....2....+....3....+....4....+....5....+....6

*******************************************************
***     subfile control record - WINPWH          ***
***       DISPLAYS WAREHOUSE SUBFILE    - WHSF    ***
*******************************************************
A          R WINPWH                      SFLCTL(WHSF)
     **** W I N D O W    R E F E R E N C E  ***
A                                        WINDOW(WDR1)
     **** S U B F I L E    C O N T R O L S  ***
A                                        SFLSIZ(07)
A                                        SFLPAG(06)
A                                        OVERLAY
A 53                                     SFLDSP
A 53                                     SFLDSPCTL
A N53                                    SFLCLR
A 54                                     SFLEND(*MORE)
A                                        SFLCSRRRN(&CSWHRN)
A            CSWHRN         5S 0H
 **** S C R E E N    H E A D E R         *****
A                                      1 05'WAREHOUSE INFORMATION'
A                                      3  5'WHs'
A                                      3  9'City'
A                                      3 30'Address'
A                                      3 51'St'
A                                      3 54'Zip'
```

Before a program can write or execute a window reference record, the window that is referenced must be on the display. As shown in Figure 7.16, the RPG program writes the window definition record, WDR1, then writes the footer record, FOOTW1, and then executes the format of the subfile control record, WINPWH.

Figure 7.16
RPG Code with Window
Definition Record

```
*...1....+....2....+....3....+....4....+....5....+....6

    *-- Activate the window WDR1
A17D C                      WRITEWDR1
A17D C                      WRITEFOOTW1
     C                      EXFMTWINPWH
```

Exercise 7.1D Computers Are US Inventory Project

Purpose
To display a subfile in a prompt window using a window definition record.

General Program Specifications
Create maintenance program INV017D and display file INVD017D. When prompted on the Warehouse field, this program displays the warehouse list in a subfile in a window. When the user makes a selection using point and shoot, the display and the physical file are automatically updated. The prompt window will be a window definition record and the footer and subfile will be window reference records.

9. Copy display-file member INVD017C to new member INVD017D. Modify member INVD017D as follows:

    • Add the window definition record, WDR1 (Figure 7.13).
    • Add the window reference record, FOOTW1 (Figure 7.14).
    • Modify the record WINPWH to be a window reference record (Figure 7.15).

10. Copy RPG program source member INV017C to new member INV017D. Modify this program based on the code in Figure 7.16 to write the window definition record, WDR1, and the window reference record, FOOTW1, before executing the window reference record, WINPWH.

Exercise 7.2D Purchase Order Line Project

Purpose
To develop prompt windows using window definition records and window reference records.

General Program Specifications
Create RPG program ORDL27D, which displays a subfile in a window when the user presses F4 while pointing to the Part Number field or the Description field in the subfile display. When the user selects a value from the prompt window using the point-and-shoot method, the program automatically updates both the Part Number and Description fields in the subfile display and the physical file. The prompt window should use window definition records and window reference records.

9. Copy display-file source member ORDD027C to new member ORDD027D. Add a window definition record and a footer record that is a window reference record. Modify the prompt subfile control to be a window reference record.

10. Copy the RPG source member ORDL27C to new member ORDL27D. Modify the member so that it will write the window definition record and the footer record before executing the subfile control record for the prompt window.

Review

1. If a window is defined as 10 6 10 50 and the subfile to be put in the window is defined for row 3, what is the maximum value for the SFLPAG? What would be the maximum value if the subfile provided FOLD onto row 4?

2. How do you define a footer record in a window that displays a subfile?

3. With the point-and-shoot technique, how can you tell which record the cursor was pointing to when Enter was pressed?

4. Why do you need to update both the subfile display and the physical file when you return from a prompt?

Subfile Bookstore Order Project 2

Project Overview

To further demonstrate that you can design, code, test, and debug a system with two subfiles.

The Bookstore Order System (Continued)

12. Modify SCREEN2 from the earlier Subfile Bookstore Order Project 1 (page 103), so that the header information (except for the order number) is input capable (Use=B). Upon returning to your program from that screen, if you find that these fields have been changed, update the record in the physical file.

13. Modify SCREEN2 so that the subfile fields (except for the line number) are also input capable (Use=B). If you find that these fields have changed when you do your READCs, update them in the physical file.

14. Use panel group technology to create Help text for all the fields on Screen 1 and Screen 2.

15. Create a prompt window for selecting a shipping method. First, create a physical file that contains shipping options, including the following data:

Ship By	Description
UPS	United Parcel Service
US-POSTAL	United States Postal Service
FED X	Federal Express
FASTEST WAY	
CHEAPEST	

Provide a prompt capability on Screen 1 and Screen 2 for the Shipping Instructions field. The prompt is to display the prompt window for selecting shipping method. Users will point and shoot to select a method or press F12 to cancel the request.

16. Provide a prompt capability on Screen 2 for the Ship To fields. First, create a physical file to contain the shipping information — the data that is shown in the Ship To area of the screen.

Put the following data in the shipping file to test the window:

```
BOOKSTORE
JEFFERSON COLLEGE
1000 VIKING ROAD
HILLSBORO, MO 63050

MAIL ROOM
JEFFERSON COLLEGE
1000 VIKING ROAD
HILLSBORO, MO 63050
```

continued

Subfile Project 2 *Continued*

MAINTENANCE DEPARTMENT
JEFFERSON COLLEGE
1000 VIKING ROAD
HILLSBORO, MO 63050

The prompt is to display a window containing the list of Ship To addresses from the shipping file. User will point and shoot to select the Ship To address or press F12 to cancel the request.

Section 2

Advanced Topics in RPG

Section 2 (Chapters 8 through 12) of *Essentials of Subfile Programming and Advanced Topics in RPG* covers selected advanced programming techniques and tools.

Chapter 8 introduces advanced concepts in linking RPG programs and database files. It explores access paths and teaches you to use the record format level identifier, the OVRDBF (Override with Database File) command, the OPNQRYF (Open Query File) command, and file and record locks, as well as file security with RPG programs.

Chapter 9 presents an in-depth study of the file-information and program-status data structures that are used in normal processing and error handling. You will learn to use the file-information data structure to extract file status and other file-related data and the program-status data structure to extract program status and other program-related data.

Chapter 10 then explores error handling in greater depth. When you have completed Chapter 10, you will be able to use the *PSSR subroutine to capture general program errors and the INFSR keyword and LO indicators to capture file errors. You will also learn to use the file-information data structure for error information, send an error message, and develop an error log.

Chapter 11 examines journaling and commitment control, which provide both Control Language (CL) and RPG tools to improve data integrity. You will learn to create a journal and a journal receiver, start and stop the journaling of physical files, change a journal, and add commitment control at the program and transaction levels.

Finally, Chapter 12 explores program-to-program communication, then focuses on data queues, a powerful AS/400 tool for program-to-program communication.

As in Section 1, frequent exercises and summary reviews strengthen your knowledge of the concepts presented. After reading the Section 2 chapters and successfully completing the exercises in these advanced topic areas, you will be prepared for a solid launch into the world of AS/400 programming.

Chapter 8

The RPG Program and the Data File

Chapter Overview

In your previous studies, you have written RPG programs that access physical files, identifying the file by name in the F-spec and having the system search your library list for the specific file. You have also written RPG programs that access data in a physical file via a logical file. Chapter 8 expands your understanding of how programs and files are linked and of the Control Language (CL) tools that can redirect the link to create the equivalent of a logical file whenever needed. You will also be introduced to how RPG programs react to file and record locks and file security. Chapter 8 explores

✓ the importance of the record format level identifier

✓ the concept of access paths

✓ the concept and use of the OVRDBF (Override with Database File) command

✓ the concept and use of the OPNQRYF (Open Query File) command

✓ the impact and use of file and record locks with RPG programs

✓ the impact and use of file security with RPG programs

Programming Perspectives

A good programmer should to be able to look at a process or problem from a number of different perspectives, including those of the user, the programmer, the program, and the database. The range of perspectives that programmers can encompass will, in part, determine their effectiveness.

In an interactive system, users see certain screens and data, make certain entries, and then see new screens and data. One example of a design tool that helps programmers understand the *users' perspective* is storyboarding. Storyboarding uses sketches of screens and descriptions of what leads from one screen to the next to provide the users' view of what occurs. Understanding the users' perspective helps you design screens that are clear and easy to use.

The *programmer's perspective* includes multiple elements, such as sets of programs, database files, programming tools such as RPG and CL, and utilities. When that perspective is broad, it includes the whole "system" — the group of tools that meets enterprise-wide challenges. When it is focused, it might be concentrated on a single process, program, or data file.

In your programming courses, you have most likely been developing a *program perspective*. The program takes in data, manipulates data, and outputs data. The program may display screens and wait for a user response to determine its next action. From this perspective, you will look at the processes of a single program, a single subroutine, or a single statement and its effect on the data. You may think about one statement as various data flows by it, or about one data set as it flows through a section of code.

However, you can also view a computer process from the perspective of the *database* itself. The database management system (DBMS) is a set of programs that receives requests from a program, such as an RPG program, and attempts to fulfill the requests. The database perspective provides a distinctly different and useful view.

In this chapter, we will explore how the database and the operating system combine to meet your programs' data requests. You will be introduced to CL program commands that affect how the operating system and DBMS react to a program's data request. I will also introduce the **OPNQRYF** (Open Query File) command. Although a complete study of this powerful and complex tool is beyond the scope of this book, you should understand its effect on RPG programs. Elsewhere in your studies, you should gain a broader knowledge of the OPNQRYF command.

Connecting RPG Programs and Data Files

When an RPG program starts, it attempts to open all files listed in the F-specs except those that are under user control. The program demands access to these files by file name and access requirements, such as input, output, or update. OS/400 receives these requests and attempts to fill them. Unless otherwise directed, OS/400 searches the job's library list for each named file and uses the first type *FILE object with that name that it finds within this list. The search for each file occurs in the following sequence:

- the system section of the library list
- the product section of the library list
- the current library
- the user section of the library list

You can see your interactive job's library list with the **DSPLIBL** (Display Library List) command. The system and product portions of the library list are the same for every user and job.

The **CHGCURLIB** (Change Current Library) command changes your job's current library. The **EDTLIBL** (Edit Library List), **ADDLIBLE** (Add Library List Entry), and **DLTLIBLE** (Delete Library List Entry) commands change the job's user section of the library list. A permanent change to the user section of the library list requires a change to the job description that is being used by that job.

The **DSPOBJD** (Display Object Description) command provides a method to find the objects in your library list that have a specific name and a type of *FILE. To respond to this command, the system must make the same search through the library list for the object that it will make when the file is opened. If the system finds more than one file with the requested name, the DSPOBJD command reports that the screen will allow access to detailed information about the first file and the number of files found. When you press Enter, you will see the screen that provides access to information about the second, and so on. When your RPG program runs, it will access the first file it finds in the library list that has the requested name.

A batch job will start with the library list of the interactive job that submitted it — unless it has a particular library list specified in that job's job description.

Exercise 8.1 Learning to Use Files and Library Lists

Purpose

To experiment with library lists, particularly to see how a library list behaves when a program searches for a file.

Instructions

1. Display your library list with the DSPLIBL command and print it. Most CL display commands, including DSPLIBL, provide a neatly formatted printout that is available if you type the command name, press F4 (for prompt), and select *PRINT as the output type.
2. Copy one of your files to library QTEMP. (Every job, including your current interactive job, has a temporary library named QTEMP.)
3. Use the DSPOBJD command to find the file you copied. The command will probably find two copies of the object. (If it doesn't find two copies, use EDTLIBL to add the original library that the file was in as well as QTEMP to your job's library list.) Make note of the order of the two libraries that the file is in. Remember that your program will use the first occurrence of the file.
4. In seeking objects such as our experimental file, OS/400 will search your current library before it searches the libraries listed in your library list. This experiment on the effect of the position of libraries in the library list will not work if you have QTEMP or your library designated as the current library. To ensure that the current library doesn't impact this experiment, remove the category of current library from your library list by issuing the CL command CHGCURLIB *CRTDFT (Change Current Library) with the predefined value of *CRTDFT (Create Default), which removes the current library entry from your library list. (The value *CRTDFT lets OS/400 use the default library QGPL as the current library if necessary.) Now use EDTLIBL to put QTEMP at the "top" of your user list. Make sure that the original library of the file that you copied is below QTEMP. Use WRKOBJ to see the order of the two files.
5. Use EDTLIBL to move QTEMP below the other library. Now use WRKOBJ to look at the order.

Review

1. What control does the RPG program have over what files are used?
2. What control does the library list have over what files are used?
3. How can you test a program using data in a test library named TESTLIB, and, once it's operating correctly, have the same program use the data in another library named PRODLIB?

Record Format Level Identifier

The format information for externally defined files is critical to the correct operation of RPG programs. This information provides the record length, as well as the names, sizes, and types of the fields in the file. When RPG programs are compiled, the compiler incorporates structural information for files identified as externally defined. The RPG compiler obtains the necessary information on the file and fields directly from the data file. (Because the RPG compiler does not access the source member used to create the data file, the source member of the physical file does not need to exist on the system when the program is compiled.)

If an RPG program were allowed to open a file that has the wrong format, the input or output data to the file would almost certainly be wrong. Because this is critical, the system checks each file when it is opened.

Whenever a file is compiled, a record format level identifier is computed for each record format. The record format level identifier is a number that corresponds to the structure of a record format. It is computed using the record length and the sizes and types of all of the fields in the file. If you were to add a field, change a field, or change the record length, the system would generate a different record format level identifier.

When an RPG program is compiled, it saves the record format level identifiers of the record formats of externally defined files used in the program. As noted above, if a field is changed in length or type or is added to a record format, the identifier changes. A physical file has only one record format and, therefore, only one identifier. A multiformat logical file has one record format level identifier for each record format. For example, if the multiformat logical file defines a record format for the order header file, another record for the order detail file, and a third record for the order comments file, it will have three record format level identifiers, one for each record format.

A display file or a print file has an identifier for each record format. Typically, display files and print files define a number of record formats, and, like logical files, each record format will have a record format level identifier.

As the RPG program starts, it requests that the system open each file described in the F-specs except those that are user controlled. The system checks the record format level identifier of each record in each file with the identifiers that are stored with the program object. The program will abort if the values do not match. You can get a list of the files and the record format level identifiers that a program needs with the **DSPPGMREF** (Display Program References) command. You can obtain a file's record format level identifier (along with a wealth of other information) with the **DSPFD** (Display File Description) command.

By checking the level identifiers of a program against the level identifiers of the files to be used, you can determine whether a change to the file requires that the program be recompiled. This comparative information will also be useful in tracking down the cause if a program aborts due to a difference in the record format level identifier.

Exercise 8.2 Learning to Use Record Format Level Identifiers

Purpose
To examine the record format level identifier of physical files, logical files, and display files, and to compare these values to the identifiers an RPG program needs.

Instructions
1. Use the DSPPGMREF command on one of your subfile programs, directing the output to the printer (use F4 to fill in the command information). Note that even the display-file record identifiers are included and must match those from the display file. Circle or highlight the record format level identifiers for each record.

Review

4. What happens if the system attempts to open a version of a file that has a different record structure from the one that was used when it was compiled?

Access Paths

An access path is a map that connects your program to the data. Physical data files can have two access paths — arrival sequence and keyed sequence. With arrival sequence access paths, READ operations access the records in the sequence of the relative record number (RRN). The CHAIN, SETLL, and SETGT operations use RRN values to position the file.

With keyed sequence access paths (i.e., if the physical file has been keyed), READ operations access data based on a map or index that the key defines. The access path used is based on the value in the access method field of the RPG program's F-specs. Logical files provide a single-access path. With a simple logical file, the access path connects the program to some or all of the records in a single physical file. The key values of the logical file define the map or index used to access these records.

Multiformat logical files provide a single-access path that splits to map or index records from all of the physical files included in the logical file.

Join-logical files provide a map of composite records comprising fields from different physical files. Join-logical files are input only.

In the case of a multirecord logical file, the key or index is based on the composite key value. In multirecord logical files in which the READ operation specifies the logical file name, the DBMS delivers the next record based on the composite key from any of the physical files. However, if the READ operation specifies a record format name, the database reads through the file until it finds the next record with that format name.

The SETGT and SETLL operations reposition the access path pointer based on the value in factor 1.

All of the access paths except join-logical files support input, update, delete, and write operations.

Alternative Access: OVRDBF (Override with Database File)

CL commands that precede the file OPEN operation in the job stream can alert the system to present an alternative access path when an RPG program demands file access. File opens generally occur immediately after the program is called, except in the case of user-controlled files. With user-controlled files, an OPEN operation must be performed to open the file, and the file can be closed with a **CLOSE** operation or when the last record indicator is set on at the program end. You can "trick" the system into attaching your program to a different physical or logical file than the one that it would normally choose. You also can force the program to use a specific member of a multimember file instead of using the data from all members. The command to make this happen is OVRDBF (Override with Database File).

With the OVRDBF command, you can direct the system to use a file of the same or a different name in the library list or from a specific library.

Figure 8.1 shows a short CL program. The OVRDBF command redirects file operations targeted for FILEA to FILEB in the library MYLIB3. Whenever the program RPGPGM1 does a file operation on FILEA, the operating system redirects the operation to FILEB in the library MYLIB3. The program will, of course, immediately abort if the record format level identifier of FILEB does not match the record format level identifier that was used when the program was compiled.

Figure 8.1
Override Database
File Command

```
PGM
    OVRDBF   FILEA    MYLIB3/FILEB    SHARE(*YES)
      Call RPGPGM1
ENDPGM
```

The SHARE(*YES) causes that one path to remain open throughout this job stream or until the override is deleted with **DLTOVR** (Delete Override), shown in the shaded area in Figure 8.2.

Figure 8.2
Delete Override
Command

```
PGM
    OVRDBF    FILEA    MYLIB3/FILEB    SHARE(*YES)
      Call RPGPGM1
      DLTOVR FILEA
ENDPGM
```

As long as the override is in effect, the same access path and pointer are used. This can sometimes create a problem if the CL program calls two RPG programs while the OVRDBF command is in effect (Figure 8.3A). If the first program processes FILEB to the end of the file (EOF), the second program opens the file with the record pointer at the same point that the first program left it, at the EOF. The **POSDBF** (Position Database File) command can be used to reposition the file pointer to the top or bottom of a file (Figure 8.3B).

```
PGM
      OVRDBF    FILEA    MYLIB3/FILEB      SHARE(*YES)
      Call RPGPGM1
      Call RPGPGM2
      DLTOVR FILEA
ENDPGM
```

Figure 8.3A
A CL Program Calling Two Programs with a File Override in Effect for Both Programs

```
PGM
      OVRDBF    FILEA    MYLIB3/FILEB      SHARE(*YES)
      Call RPGPGM1
      POSDBF FILEA *TOF
      Call RPGPGM2
      DLTOVR FILEA
ENDPGM
```

Figure 8.3B
Position Database File Command Used to Reposition the Pointer to FILEA Before It Is Used by RPGPGM2

Exercise 8.3 Learning to Use the OVRDBF Command

Purpose
To experiment with the OVRDBF command.

Instructions
1. Select a program that you know works.
2. Copy one of the data files for this program to QTEMP, giving it the name TEMP1.
3. Use the command UPDDTA TEMP1 to modify the data so that you can verify that your program is using TEMP1 instead of the original file.
4. Use OVRDBF to redirect calls to the original file to QTEMP/TEMP1.
5. Call the program. Which file did it use?
6. Issue the command DSPJOB. Use option 15 to see what overrides are in effect for this job.
7. Use the DLTOVR command to eliminate the override of this file.
8. Repeat step 6 to make sure that the override has been removed.
9. Run your RPG program again. Which file did it use this time?

Review

5. Your RPG program PAYROLL opens the files TIMEKP and EMPLOY for input and PAY for output. A CL program contains the following commands:

```
OVRDBF TIMEKP      COMPANYA/TIME03      SHARE(*YES)
OVRDBF EMPLOY      COMPANYA/EMPLOY      SHARE(*YES)
OVRDBF PAY         COMPANYA/PAY03       SHARE(*YES)
CALL PAYROLL
DLTOVR TIMEKP
DLTOVR EMPLOY
DLTOVR PAY
```

What files does the program PAYROLL actually use?

The OPNQRYF (Open Query File) Command

This section provides a brief introduction to the OPNQRYF command and explores the impact of this command on RPG programs. More complete discussions of this command are available in the *Desktop Guide to CL Programming* (Duke Press, 1994), by Bryan Meyers; the *Starter Kit for the AS/400* (Duke Press, 1994), by Wayne Madden; *Database Design and Programming for DB2/400* (Duke Press, 1996), by Paul Conte; and *Control Language Programming for the AS/400* (Duke Press, Second edition, 1997), by Bryan Meyers and Dan Riehl.

Using the OPNQRYF (Open Query File) command, a CL program can create the on-the-fly equivalent of logical files (Figure 8.5). Just as you can with a logical file, you can use the OPNQRYF command to provide an alternative key structure and/or select records by specific rules. The OPNQRYF command is particularly powerful because the key fields, selection rules, and other features can be altered programmatically. For example, if we have a receivables file with a due date, you can use OPNQRYF to select only those records with due date < today's date and status = OPEN and with the primary key field as Due Date and secondary key field as Amount Due. The RPG program to print the aged receivables report would be a simple reporting program because the OPNQRYF command has done most of the work.

Figure 8.5
CL Program with
Open Query File

```
PGM
   DCL &VALUE1 *CHAR 100
   DCL &TODAY   *CHAR 6
   RTVJOBD DATE(&TODAY)
   CHGVAR &VALUE1 ('DUEDTE <= ' *CAT &TODAY)
   OVRDBF   RECP      SHARE(*YES)
   OPNQRYF RECP QRYSLT(&VALUE1) KEYFLD( DUEDTE, AMTDUE)
   CALL RPGPGM1
   DLTOVR RECP
ENDPGM
```

Exercise 8.4 Learning to Use the OPNQRYF Command

Purpose
To experiment with the OPNQRYF command.

Instructions
1. Create a short CL program that uses the commands that you used in Exercise 8.3. The CL program should include the OVRDBF command, the CALL (Call Program) command (to call an RPG program), and the DLTOVR command. Run the program.
2. Add an OPNQRYF command to select only specific records and rerun the program.

Review

6. Your RPG program PAYROLL opens the files TIMEKP and EMPLOY for input and PAY for output. A CL program contains the following commands.

```
OVRDBF  TIMEKP        COMPANYA/TIME03      SHARE(*YES)
OVRDBF  EMPLOY        COMPANYA/EMPLOY      SHARE(*YES)
OVRDBF  PAY           COMPANYA/PAY03       SHARE(*YES)
OPNQRYF TIMEKP QRYSLT('EMPST = "A" *AND EMPTY = "HOURLY"')
CALL PAYROLL
DLTOVR TIMEKP
DLTOVR EMPLOY
DLTOVR PAY
```

What records will be available to the program PAYROLL?

File and Record Locks

When the system links the RPG program and file together, it checks to see whether that file is locked by another job at a level that prevents the request from linking with the file. For example, the request will fail if another job has an exclusive lock on the file.

The commands used to detect and control locks can be found on the menu CMDLCK. To view this menu, type **GO CMDLCK.**

The CL command ALCOBJ (Allocate Object) is used to lock objects, including, of course, files. The object then remains locked until the job ends or the DLCOBJ (Deallocate Object) command is issued.

If the job has not previously locked the file, the file will be locked when the RPG program establishes its link to the file with access rights of Shared Read, for an input-capable file, or Shared Update, for an update- or add-capable file. If the RPG program locks the file, the lock ends when the RPG program turns on the last record indicator, *INLR.

The CL command WRKOBJLCK (Work with Object Locks) displays all of the jobs that currently lock a specific object (or file) and provides the option of working with any specific job. By working with specific jobs, you can determine the user, status, start time, and date of that job — and you can end that job (if you have job control authority). Ending a job will, of course, remove its locks from the object file of interest.

The DSPRCDLCK (Display Record Locks) CL command can be used to determine which job has a specific record locked. Remember, if an RPG program executes any of the READ operations (including READ, READP, READE, and READPE) or CHAINs into an update-capable file, it normally locks that record until an update or delete changes the record, the program reads or chains into another record, or the program closes the file.

The record can also be unlocked with an UNLOCK command or by adding an N (Not Locked) in the Operation Extender field (column 53 of the CHAIN or READ operation).

Exercise 8.5 Learning to Use Object Locks on Files

Purpose
To experiment with object locks on files.

Instructions
1. Sign on to two sessions on your AS/400 (this may require two terminals). Remember that each session is a separate job.
2. In session 1, issue the command to acquire an exclusive lock on a file in your library.
3. In session 2, issue the same command on the same file and note the error message.
4. Use the CL command WRKOBJLCK to determine which job has a lock on the file.
5. In session 1, deallocate the lock on the file.
6. In session 2, use the WRKOBJLCK to determine whether the object is unlocked.

Review

7. When does an RPG programmer need to be concerned about file locks?

8. When does an RPG programmer need to be concerned about record locks?

9. Attempting to lock all resources needed for a multiple-program job before beginning the first program is a common feature of many job-controlling CL programs. Why? What would happen if the first program ran successfully and the second one crashed because of a locked file?

10. Exclusive locks guarantee that no other jobs can lock records within a file. When the lock level is Exclusive Allow Read, other jobs can lock the file in shared read mode, which allows the file to be read but not updated. But when the lock level is Exclusive, no other job can access the file for any purpose. When would each lock level be important?

File Security

When the system links the file to the program, the system does not check to make certain that the user has authority to perform the update, add, and delete processes on that file. Instead, the system sends a file error condition to the program if it attempts to actually perform a process on a record for which it lacks authority. To determine the authorization necessary to access a file, use the **DSPOBJAUT** (Display Object Authority) command. To change the authorization required to access an object, use the **EDTOBJAUT** (Edit Object Authority) command.

The job that controls your program can only do things that the job's USER is authorized to do. The profile of the user may be tied to a group profile. (You can use the **DSPUSRPRF** (Display User Profile) and **CHGUSRPRF** (Change User Profile) commands to determine or change the group profile.) To determine a user's authority to an object, the security system uses the specific authority granted to that user. If no specific authority to the object is granted to the user, then the security system will use the authority granted to that user's group profile. If no specific authority to the object is granted to the user or the user's group profile, then the security system will use the authority granted to *PUBLIC (all other users).

To run a program, the user must have *USE authority to the program object. The description of the program object identifies whether that program will run with the user's authority or the program object owner's authority. If the owner authority is used, the security system will test the owner's authority or the owner's group authority to subsequent objects that the program needs. The owner's authority can be set so that it is used by the program at the time of compile or accessed via the CHGPGM command. Only the program object owner or security officer has the authority to change a program to use the owner's authority.

Exercise 8.6 Learning to Use File Security

Purpose
To experiment with file security.

Instructions
1. Use the EDTOBJAUT command to give a fellow student *ALL authority to your library and the program and files of one of your subfile projects that includes update, add, and delete options.
2. Let your fellow student experiment with your program, including doing adds, deletes, and updates.
3. Now remove your fellow student's authority to delete records from the file and have him or her attempt all the program options again.
4. Now remove your fellow student's authority to add records to the file and have him or her attempt all the program options again.
5. Now remove your fellow student's authority to change records in the file and repeat the test.
6. Now remove your fellow student's authority to read records in the file and repeat the test.
7. Now use the CHGPGM command to change the program to use the user profile *OWNER and test it again. Use the DSPOBJAUT to determine who is the owner of the program and the file.

Review
11. If a file has the following authorities

```
User
MIS          *ALL
*PUBLIC      *EXCLUDE
```

name two ways that an individual could run a program that uses this file without changing the object authorities.

Chapter 9

File-Information and Program-Status Data Structures

Chapter Overview

Chapter 9 helps you understand and use the file-information data structure and the program-status data structure, including

✓ accessing the data in the file-information data structure

✓ extracting and using file-status and other file-related data

✓ accessing the data in the program-status data structure

✓ extracting and using program-status and other program-related data

---

What Is the File-Information Data Structure?

Every file that an RPG program accesses has a buffer of critical data that is "handed" to the RPG program. This file-information buffer is available for all file types, including physical files, logical files, display files, and printer files. The data in this file-information buffer (also called the Open Feedback Area or I/O Feedback Area) is updated whenever the RPG program accesses the file. RPG programs use this data internally in many ways. For example, when the RPG program executes a READ operation, the associated indicator is turned *ON or *OFF, based on the value in a specific location in the file-information buffer.

The data in the file-information buffer is also used when a formatted dump is requested. A formatted dump can be requested at the time of a runtime error or requested via a DUMP operation in the RPG program. The formatted dump contains file-status information, program-status information, and the values of all variables. It is valuable in debugging a program with a runtime error. (The formatted dump is discussed further in Chapter 10.)

With the additional information available in this buffer, you can take more control of your program. The following list offers just a few examples of how the information can be used:

- To determine the cursor position in a display file.
- To determine the current line number on a print file.
- To determine the number of the current page on a print file.
- To determine the record name when accessing a multiformat logical file.
- To determine the number of records in a file.
- To determine why an input or output process failed.

- To ensure that an update or delete is not attempted unless the program has a record from that file locked by a previous successful READ or CHAIN operation. (If such an update or delete is attempted, the program issues the following message: *Program name* issued update or delete in *file name* without prior READ or CHAIN.)
- To create an error-handling routine that can determine the cause of the error, report an error, and, in some cases, correct an error and continue, so the program can continue. (For further discussion of error handling, see Chapter 10.)

Figure 9.1 shows an example of the file-information buffer for the file INVPF. In Exercise 9.1, you will learn how to retrieve this data.

Figure 9.1
528-Byte
File-Information
Buffer for File
INVPF after a
READ Operation

```
Column    1         2         3         4         5         6         7         8
12345678901234567890123456789012345678901234567890123456789012345678901234567890
INVPF     1000000READ F*DETC   605      INVPFR                          0000000000
DBINVPF      A300C1_BOK                          INVPF
UUNs                                 0                         _
                        INVPFR

D511        0                                  0      $ §              ny h   aa
                   £E                        0
```

```
Column    4       5       5       5       5
BottomRow9        0       1       2       2
12345678901234567890123456789012345678901234567 8
```

This file-information buffer contains 528 bytes of data. To use this information, you will need to 1) provide a link within your program to the file-information buffer and 2) structure this data into subfields of the correct types and lengths. It is obvious that without some division of the data shown in Figure 9.1 into subfields of the correct type, the buffer will be fairly useless. The result of the restructuring is the file-information data structure.

We provide a link to the file-information buffer with a continuation F-spec (Figure 9.2), which uses the option for INFormation Data Structure (INFDS). This statement links the file-information buffer for the file INVPF to the data structure name entered into the ENTRY field, INVDS. A separate data structure must be defined for each file about which that program needs information.

Figure 9.2
F-Spec for File INVPF
and Continuation
Defining the INFDS

```
*...1....+....2....+....3....+....4....+....5....+....6

FINVPF    IF  E          K         DISK
F                                                    KINFDS INVDS
 *
FINVDSP   CF  E                    WORKSTN
F                                                    KINFDS DSPDS
```

Applying a Data Structure to the File-Information Buffer

The data structure defines the structure (comprising subfields) that is mapped over the file-information buffer. You define this structure in the I-specs. The subfields are defined in the following sections of this chapter.

Positions 1 through 8 of the buffer contain the "internal" file name that the RPG program uses to refer to the file. The internal file name is also the actual file name unless a CL program redirects the file selection with an OVRDBF (Override with Database File) command. Later, we will find where the file-information buffer defines the actual file that is being used.

The continuation F-spec shown in Figure 9.2 links the file-information buffer for the file INVPF with the data structure INVDS. Figure 9.3 shows the I-specs that define the data structure INVDS. This definition maps the subfield FILNM1 over the first 8 bytes of the file-information buffer. These 8 bytes contain the name — known as the internal file name — that the RPG program uses for the file throughout the program. This name could differ from the actual file name if an OVRDBF command is in effect. (See Chapter 8 for more information on the OVRDBF command).

```
*...1....+....2....+....3....+....4....+....5....+....6

IINVDS      DS
I                            1     8 FILNM1
```

Figure 9.3
I-Specs that Map the Subfield FILNM1 over the First 8 Bytes of Data Structure INVDS

Figure 9.4 shows the result of the data structure definition. FILNM1 is mapped over the first 8 bytes of the buffer. The value currently in this location is INVPF; therefore, the value in FILNM1 is INVPF.

```
Column   1        2        3        4        5        6        7        8
12345678901234567890123456789012345678901234567890123456789012345678901234567890
INVPF   1000000READ F*DETC   605     INVPFR                      0000000000

|FILNM1|
```

Figure 9.4
Data Structure Applied to the File Data Buffer of the File INVPF that Maps the Subfield FILNM1

Positions 11 through 15 of the file-information buffer contain the file status. In the example in Figure 9.1, the status value is 00000. Figure 9.5 lists many of the file status values and their descriptions. Status 00000, for example, indicates that no exception or error has occurred.

Figure 9.5
File Status Codes
with Descriptions

Status	Description
00000	No exception/error occurred
00011	End of file
00012	No record found in a CHAIN operation
00013	A WRITE operation to a subfile resulted in subfile full; no record was added
00099	Error
01021	Attempt to write a record with a duplicate key
01211	Input or output operation attempted on a closed file
01215	Open operation attempted on file that was already open
01216	Error on implicit file open — file is not under user control (UC) Open occurs automatically based on RPG cycle File may not exist, may be locked, may exceed user authority
01217	Error on explicit file open — file is under user control (UC) Open attempt occurs at OPEN opcode
01218	Unable to allocate record (record is locked by another program)
01221	Update attempted without prior successful read
01299	Miscellaneous input/output error detected
01331	Wait-for-record time exceeded for READ or EXFMT operation

In Figure 9.6, you see the data structure INVDS with the subfield STAT1 mapped over the file status bytes.

Figure 9.6
I-Specs to Map
Subfields over the
Data Structure INVDS

```
*...1....+....2....+....3....+....4....+....5....+....6

IINVDS         DS
I                                        1    8 FILNM1
I                                       11  150STAT1
I                                       16   21 OPCD1
I                                       38   45 FILRC1
```

Figure 9.7 shows the buffer and the mapping of the subfields FILNM1, STAT1, OPCD1, and FILRC1, defined in Figure 9.6.

Figure 9.7
Data Structure Applied
to File Data Buffer of
the File INVPF

```
Column    1         2         3         4         5         6         7         8
12345678901234567890123456789012345678901234567890123456789012345678901234567890
INVPF   1000000READ F*DETC   605      INVPFR                            0000000000

|FILNM1|  |STAT1|OPCD1|                    |-FILRC1|
```

Positions 16 through 21 contain the last operation executed on the file. In Figure 9.1, the value in positions 16 through 21 is READ F, which indicates that the last operation on this file was a read of the file. Figures 9.6 and 9.7 show this value mapped into the subfield OPCD1. The subfield that shows the last operation executed will contain values such as OPEN F, READ F, and WRITE F.

The internal record name is the name that our program will use for the record. It is occasionally different from the actual record name because internal record names must be unique. A program that accesses the same file via two or more access paths (e.g., via logical files) will have to rename the record for all but one access path using a continuation F-spec rename operation.

Being able to determine the internal record name proves especially useful when a program reads from a multiformat logical file. Once the READ operation is accomplished, the program can use the value from the data structure to determine which record was accessed and therefore select the appropriate processing. The internal record name is in positions 38 through 45 of the file-information buffer; in Figures 9.6 and 9.7, this subfield is named FILRC1.

Notice that I have used 1 as the last digit of all of the file's data structure variables. In the data structure of the next file, I would use the same subfield names, but the names would end in the suffix 2. If there were third and fourth files, the subfields would end in 3 and 4, respectively.

The four parts of the data structure that we've mapped into our program are used so frequently that IBM has provided the keywords *FILE, *STATUS, *OPCODE, and *RECORD to represent the positions of these items in the file-information buffer. Figure 9.8 uses these keywords to define the equivalent structure (as was defined in Figure 9.6 with field positions).

```
*...1....+....2....+....3....+....4....+....5....+....6

IINVDS      DS
I                               *FILE     FILNM1
I                               *STATUS   STAT1
I                               *OPCODE   OPCD1
I                               *RECORD   FILRC1
```

Figure 9.8
I-Specs to Map Variables over the Data Structure INVDS Using Keywords

Exercise 9.1 Accessing the File-Information Data Structure

Purpose
To develop an understanding of data structures in general and the file-information data structure in particular. You will experiment with extracting the data from the file information and with mapping subfields for the file's internal name, status, operation code, and record name, using position and keyword definitions.

Instructions

1. Write the program CHAP9A to READ each record in INVPF. It should map the 528 bytes of data in the file-information buffer into seven fields; each of the first six should be 80 characters long (the seventh should comprise the remaining 48 characters). Before the program performs the initial READ operation, as well as after each READ, it should print out the contents of the seven fields. Each time it prints, the output should look similar (but it won't be identical) to the data in Figure 9.1. We'll discuss the differences later in this chapter.

2. Create the program CHAP9B to READ each record from the file INVPF. Before it performs a READ operation on the first record and after each READ, it should print out a line that contains the file name, status, operation code, and record name. Use the actual locations for these fields in the I-specs.

3. Create program CHAP9C to READ each record from the file INVPF. Before it performs a READ operation on the first record and after each READ, it should print out a line that contains the file name, status, operation code, and record name. Use the keywords for these fields in the I-specs.

Review

1. Write a segment of code that would delete a record only if the last operation on that file was a successful CHAIN or READ. This code will use the value of the operation code and the file status to ensure that the last process on that file was a READ or CHAIN operation and that it was successful. The delete takes place if these conditions are true (and fails if they are not).

2. Write a Select statement to follow a read from a multiformat logical file. If the READ operation is successful, your code should call the ORDH subroutine if the record name is ORDER, the ORDL subroutine if the record name is ORDLINE, and the ORDC subroutine if the record name is ORDCMT.

More on the File-Information Data Structure

In the previous section of this chapter, you learned about four subfields of the file-information data structure. There are, in fact, a large number of values that can be extracted from the file-information buffer. In Figure 9.9, a more complete list of available subfields is defined. As you see in the figure, some of the subfields apply exclusively to printer or workstation files.

To use any of these values, subfields are defined in the file-information data structure over the correct location. You can see the data type: C indicates character, N indicates numeric, and B indicates binary data. Most of the subfields should be defined as character type. The status field can be defined as either character or numeric. When you create the I-specs, binary fields must be identified with a B in the type field.

Type	From	To	Dec	Description	Values	Keyword	Type of File
C	1	8		Internal file name		*FILE	PF
C	9	9		Open	1=Open		PF
C	10	10		EOF	1=EOF		PF
N	11	15	0	Status		*STATUS	PF
C	16	21		Opcode		*OPCODE	PF
C	22	29		Routine — What part of RPG cycle was access in (meaningful for RPGII)			PF
C	30	37		Statement number of last access			PF
C	38	45		Internal record name		*RECORD	PF, DSPF
C	81	82		Type of open data path — DS=display file, DB=database file, SP=spool file			ALL
C	83	92		External file name — up to 10 characters long			PF
C	93	102		External file library name			PF
C	103	112		SPNAME — spool file name			Printer
C	113	122		SPLIBR — spool file library			Printer
B	123	124	0	SPNBR — spool number			Printer
B	125	126	0	Record length			PF
C	120	138		Member name of external file. This can be really useful when processing multimember files.			PF
B	147	148	0	File type			
B	152	153	0	Number of lines per page (page length)			Printer Workstn
B	154	155	0	Number of columns			Printer Workstn
B	156	159	0	Number of records in file when it was open			PF
C	160	161		Type of database file access	KU=Keyed Unique, KF=Keyed FIFO, KL=Keyed LIFO, AR=Arrival sequence		PF
C	162	162		Duplicate keys allowed	D=Yes U = No (Unique)		PF
C	163	163		Is file a source physical file?	Y=Yes		PF
B	188	189	0	Overflow line			Printer
B	367	368	0	Current line number			Printer
B	370	371	0	Workstation cursor position	Z-ADDCURPOS CURSA DIV 256 MVR CURSA 50 ROWPOS COLPOS		Workstn

Figure 9.9

Subfield Definitions for the File-Information Data Structure

Figure 9.10 shows the data structure for the display file. In Figure 9.2, the file-information data structure DSPDS was linked to the file-information buffer of the display file INVDSP. (The cursor position subfield was introduced in Chapter 6.) Because the value is binary, the type is shown as binary.

Figure 9.10

I-Specs to Map Variables over the Display-File Data Structure DSPDS

```
*...1....+....2....+....3....+....4....+....5....+....6

IDSPDS          DS
I                                          *FILE    FILNM2
I                                          *STATUS  STAT2
I                                          *RECORD  FILRC2
I                                          *OPCODE  OPCD2
I                                          B 370 3710CURPS2
```

Exercise 9.2 Using Subfields in File-Information Data Structures

Purpose

To develop a further understanding of the file-information data structure, as well as of data structures in general. You will experiment with extracting the data from the file-information buffer and mapping subfields.

Instructions

1. Copy and modify CHAP9C and call the new program CHAP9D. Make the file opens user controlled. Add the open, end of file (EOF), record count, statement number, external file name, external file library name, external member name, file type, type of database file access, and duplicate key allowed to the file structure. Print out the values in these subfields before you open the file, after you open the file, after every read, and before and after you close the file. Modify the F-specs in one run to use the keyed access to INVPF and in another to use arrival sequence.

Exercise 9.3 Accessing a Printer File's File Information

Purpose

To develop a further understanding of the file-information data structure and data structures in general. You will experiment with extracting the data from the file-information buffer and mapping subfields for a printer file.

Instructions

1. Copy CHAP9D to CHAP9E. Modify CHAP9E if necessary to use a printer file. Add a data structure to the printer file F-specs. You will want to capture the spool file name, spool file library, spool file number, the external file and external library names, as well as the number of lines per page, number of columns per page, the overflow line number, and the current line number. Output this data to a second printer file. Print a detailed line every time a line is written to the first printer file.

Exercise 9.4 Accessing a Display File's File Information

Purpose

To develop a further understanding of the file-information data structure, as well as of data structures in general. You will experiment with extracting data from the file-information buffer and mapping subfields for a display file.

Instructions

1. Modify one of your subfile programs to print a line of file-information data structure to a report after every EXFMT. Use a file-information data structure to capture information about the display file, including the file name, the record name, status, operation code, statement number, external file name, external file library, file type, and workstation cursor position (row and column).

Review

3. Go through the list of data structure subfields and identify what value each would have during normal and abnormal operations of a program.

4. Go through the list of status codes and identify how each could be of value during normal operations (and whether each could occur then) and during abnormal operations.

5. The order form shown in Figure 9.11 should print detail lines until all the lines of the order have been printed. Detail lines should be printed only between lines 10 and 14 of the order form. If more lines are needed, then the program must print another page. The overflow line number is 17 — the line on which the totals print. Although the overflow indicator will come on when the line number is greater than 17, this is of little value when you print detail lines because you need to know whether the printer is positioned beyond line number 14. Your program should use the line number from the file-information data structure to determine whether the line number is greater than 14. If it is, the headings and the next detail will print on the following page. Write the F-spec, the data structure, and the C-specs to test for the need to print a new page.

Figure 9.11
Order Form

Order Form	Order: 12345		Page 1

TO:	Duke Press	FROM:	Jefferson College
	221 E. 29th Street		1000 Viking Road
	Loveland, CO 80538		Hillsboro, MO 63050

Quantity	Item	Unit Cost	Extended Price
50	Subfile Programming Essentials	60.00	3,000.00
100	RPG/400	60.00	6,000.00
		Total	**9,000.00**

What Is the Program-Status Data Structure?

While an RPG program is running, OS/400 maintains 333 bytes of data about the job and the program. This data is available to the program through a special data structure called the program-status data structure. This data structure provides some useful data during normal program operations and a wealth of information if the program fails.

The complete data structure is shown in Figure 9.12. The program-status data structure is declared with an option value of S in column 18. Usually, programmers define only the subfields of the program-status data structure that apply to their specific needs. The program-status data structure contains a wealth of information that will be valuable if the program encounters an error. It also contains information that can be useful during normal operations. Job and user information can be used, for example, in sending messages and controlling spool files; program information can be printed on reports and shown on display screens.

Figure 9.12
Program-Status
Data Structure

```
*...1....+....2....+....3....+....4....+....5....+....6

*-------------PROGRAM DATA STRUCTURE
*--------  SDS -- DECLARES THIS AS THE PROGRAM DATA STRUCTURE
IPROGDS    SDS
I                                          1  10 PRGNAM
I                                        *STATUS PSTAT
I                                         16  200PRVSTS
I                                         21  28 LINNUM
I                                         29  36 SUBRUT
I                                         37  390PARMS
I                                         40  42 ERRTYP
I                                         43  46 ERRCOD
I                                         47  50 INSNBR
I                                         51  80 MSGWRK
I                                         81  90 PGMLIB
I                                         91 170 MSGTXT
I                                        171 174 EXCMBR
I                                        201 208 ERRFIL
I                                        209 243 ERRINF
I                                        244 253 JOBNAM
I                                        254 263 USER
I                                        264 2690JOBNUM
I                                        270 2750JOBDAT
I                                        276 2810SYSDAT
I                                        282 2870SYSTIM
I                                        288 2930PGMDAT
I                                        294 2990PGMTIM
I                                        300 303 CMPLVL
I                                        304 313 SRCFIL
I                                        314 323 SRCLIB
I                                        324 333 SRCMBR
```

Operational Data in the Program-Status Data Structure

Figure 9.13 defines the subfields of the program-status data structure that are most frequently used to gather data that is valuable during normal program operation.

Type of data	Typical Operational Uses
User ID	Can be used to route reports to the correct queue or printer.
	Can be used to send messages to the user.
	Can be used on displays, and so forth.
Job name	For a batch job, the job name is the line ID or terminal ID and is sometimes shown on displays and printed in reports. It can be used in sending break messages.
	Can be shown on displays or printed on reports.
	Can be used to send break messages.
System century date & time	Can be used on reports, displays, and messages. Century is in CC format and date in YYMMDD format for the time when the program started running.
Job date	In YYMMDD format, gives the date when the job became active.
Program name	Can be placed on reports and displays.
Program library	Can be placed on reports and displays.
Program date & time	Date in YYMMDD format.
	Time when program was compiled.
Program source	The library, file, and member names of the program source.
Compiler level	Revision of the compiler that was used to compile code.

Figure 9.13
Operational Data Available in the Program-Status Data Structure

Exercise 9.5 Getting Operational Data from the Program-Status Data Structure

Purpose
To access the program-status data structure to obtain operational data.

Instructions
1. Write the program PGM101, which uses a program-status data structure and outputs all the available operational data with appropriate headings to a spool file.

Review

6. Why do many AS/400 systems include the user ID, display ID, and time and date on all the DSPF displays?

7. When would the program library, compile date and time, and source data be particularly important?

Error-Related Data in the Program-Status Data Structure

The program-status data structure contains all of the operational information plus the error-related data shown in Figure 9.14. If a program fails, this information is often invaluable in discovering the cause.

Figure 9.14
Error-Related Data in the Program-Status Data Structure

Type of Data	Typical Operational Uses
Status Code	Defines the type of error that occurred (see the program status code table, Figure 9.15)
Previous Status	Shows the status prior to the error
Source Statement	Identifies the source line number that caused the error
MSGID	Shows system error message ID
MSGTXT	Contains an error message if the status code is 09999
ERRFIL	Identifies the last file accessed
ERRINF	Shows the status of last file accessed + operation code + RPG

Figure 9.15 contains the values of the program-status codes, which are located in columns 11 through 15 of the program-status data structure. As shown in Figure 9.12, the status can be defined using the keyword *STATUS.

Figure 9.15
Program Status Codes

Status	Description
00000	No exception/error
00001	Called program ended with LR indicator on
00101	Square root of a negative number attempted
00102	Divide by zero attempted
00121	Invalid array index
00122	OCCUR operation outside of data-structure occurrence range
00211	Program specified in CALL or FREE operations not found
00221	Program accessed a parameter that was not passed to it
00401	Data area specified in IN or OUT operation code not found
00411	Attributes of data area specified in IN or OUT operation do not match those of the actual data area
00412	Data area specified in the OUT operation was not locked
00413	Error occurred during IN or OUT operation to the data area
00414	Security violation while attempting to read a data area
00415	Security violation while attempting to write to a data area
00421	Error occurred during UNLCK operation to a data area
00431	Data area lock detected by another process while attempting to access a data area in this program

continued

Status	Description
00432	Data area lock detected by another program in this job stream while attempting to process a data area in this program
00907	Decimal data error; packed or zoned field is blank or corrupt
09998	Internal failure in RPG
09999	Program exception in an operating system routine

Figure 9.15
Continued

Review

8. Describe at least three scenarios in which the error status and other program-status data structure error-related fields could be of use.

Chapter 10

Error Handling

Chapter Overview

Chapter 10 explores RPG tools and methods used to capture errors and determine their cause. A useful subroutine — *PSSR — will execute whenever errors occur. File errors can be captured by a subroutine that runs automatically if access to that specific file encounters an error. Errors in file input/output operations can be monitored with an indicator in the LO indicator column and used to branch to error-handling code. Further, the chapter will demonstrate how to use a single file-information structure for multiple files, how to send error messages, and how to keep an error log. Finally, you'll learn how to avoid the endless-error condition.

When you have completed Chapter 10, you will be able to

✓ describe when the *PSSR subroutine will run and use it to capture general program errors

✓ link error-handling subroutines to files using the INFSR keyword

✓ use the Input/Output operation error indicator to detect I/O errors

✓ use the file-information data structure with multiple files

✓ send an error message from an RPG program

✓ log errors to an error log

✓ avoid the endless-error condition in *PSSR

General Error-Handling Concepts

Without special error-handling code, your programs will eventually "crash." When a program crash occurs, the operators and/or users will be left with cryptic error messages. They may have to respond to these messages with a response such as G(o), I(gnore), R(etry), C(ancel), or D(ump). Unless you have given instructions on how to respond to a particular message for a specific job or program, they may choose any of the above — or call you at home at 2 a.m. for clarification.

The error might not have a serious impact, or it might wreak havoc with the data. But without special error-handling code, you may never even know that an error occurred — or you may not know about the error until it is too late to easily correct whatever problems it created.

Error-handling tools in RPG let your program detect an error and determine its cause. The program-status data structure will contain the type of error and the RPG statement number that was in error. If the error is a file-related error, the file-information data structure for that file will contain a wealth of information about the file and the error.

Error-handling subroutines in RPG programs can include code for dealing with frequently encountered errors. These error-handling subroutines can send messages to system operators or users informing them of the error, can log the error to an error log or execute an RPG-formatted DUMP, and can print every file's status and every variable's value at the time of the error.

Program Errors

There are two basic types of errors — syntax errors and runtime errors. Syntax errors, violations of the of RPG grammar rules, are detected by the compiler and must be corrected before a program object can be created. Therefore, a program cannot be run until all syntax errors have been corrected. Runtime errors occur when the program is running.

Runtime errors can be divided into two types: A program with logic errors will run but not produce the correct results. An example of a logic error is a program that *adds* pay rate to hours worked to compute gross pay. The program runs, but the results are wrong. Fatal runtime errors will, unless a program contains error-handling code, cause the program to terminate (see the sidebar "Avoidable Program Errors").

Any program can encounter an error. Errors can occur when the program is requested to perform in ways outside its design parameters or when it receives bad data. Errors can also occur when the program attempts to call or use an object that is not in the job's library list or when the program or user does not have the necessary authority to the object.

Using the *PSSR Subroutine to Capture Program Errors

Fatal errors caused by file operations require specific file error-handling tools introduced in the next section of this chapter. All other fatal errors can be captured with a special subroutine called the *PSSR subroutine. This subroutine does not have to be called; it is called automatically whenever a non-file error occurs. The *PSSR subroutine can include all of your non-file error-handling code, or it can call other subroutines to handle specific types of errors. Many programmers also put their file error code in the *PSSR subroutine. If you want the program to terminate at the end of the *PSSR subroutine, it should end with the Last Record indicator on.

Figure 10.1 shows the simplest *PSSR subroutine. The H-spec is required with the DUMP operation code. The H-spec has a 1 in the debug field, and it must be the first specification in your program.

Figure 10.1

H-Spec with DEBUG=1 and *PSSR Subroutine That Creates a Formatted RPG DUMP and Ends the Program

```
*...1....+....2....+....3....+....4....+....5....+....6
H          1
.
.
.
C          *PSSR     BEGSR
C                    DUMP
C                    MOVE *ON    *INLR
C                    RETURN
C                    ENDSR
```

Avoidable Program Errors

Three common runtime errors that can be avoided by adding preventive code follow:

- 00102 Divide by zero — Every divide operation involving a denominator that is a variable can end in a divide-by-zero situation. This common error can be avoided with the sample code in Figure 10.2.

```
*...1....+....2....+....3....+....4....+....5....+....6
* The never-divide-by-zero code --
C           DIV2    IFEQ *ZERO
C                   Z-ADD*LOVAL    RES1
C                   ELSE
C           DIV1    DIV  DIV2      RES1
C                   ENDIF
```

Figure 10.2
Code to Avoid
the Divide-by-
Zero Error

You can avoid the divide-by-zero error by performing the division only when the denominator is not equal to zero.

- 00101 Square root of a negative number — In business processing, we don't get much call for the SQRT (Square Root) operation code. But you can avoid the square-root-of-a-negative-number error by using code similar to the code used to avoid the divide-by-zero problem. In this case, the SQRT operation would not be used if the variable contains a negative number.

- 00907 Decimal data error — A decimal data error occurs when a decimal field is blank or corrupt. This error crops up most often when you move data to decimal fields from other decimal or character fields. This type of error can be eliminated by the use of the TESTN operation code to confirm that the character string contains a true numeric before it is moved to a numeric field. Remember: you should always use the Z-ADD operation to move values from one numeric field to another.

When a non-file error occurs, the program will terminate after it creates a program dump. The termination of this program will not appear to be abnormal. Users and the calling program may not realize that the program "abended" (ended abnormally).

Exercise 10.1 Error Handling Using *PSSR and the DUMP Operation

Purpose

To demonstrate file error handling using the *PSSR subroutine and the DUMP operation.

Instructions

Create program PGM101, which initiates a dump when an error occurs.

1. Create the program PGM101, which contains the DUMP - *PSSR subroutine as shown in Figure 10.1.

2. The program should contain the following C-specs, which will create a runtime error by attempting to divide by zero.

```
*...1....+....2....+....3....+....4....+....5....+....6

C                     Z-ADD*ZERO     FLD1      20
C          10         DIV  FLD1      RSLT      20
```

Note: This program error occurs because FDL1 is equal to zero when it is used as a denominator for division. The sidebar "Avoidable Program Errors" presents the code to avoid divide-by-zero errors.

Exercise 10.2 Using the *PSSR Subroutine to Print Program Information to a Spool File

Purpose
To develop a program that demonstrates error handling using the *PSSR subroutine to extract error status code, program name, job, and user from the program-status data structure and print it to a spool file.

Instructions
Create program PGM102, which will print the line number of the error, the program name, the program status code, the job name, and the user ID when an error occurs.

1. Copy PGM101 to PGM102.
2. Add the program-status data structure from Chapter 9, including error-related fields.
3. Add O-specs or a print file to print the fields from the program-status data structure.
4. Remove the H-Spec and the DUMP.
5. Add output operations to the *PSSR subroutine to print the fields of the program-status data structure.
6. Run the program. What is the program-status code? Is it consistent with what you would expect according to the list of program-status codes shown in Figure 9.15?
7. Copy PGM102 to PGM103. Replace the operations that cause the program to divide by zero with the operations that cause it to take the square root of a negative number. Run the program. What is the program-status code? Is it consistent with what you would expect according to the list of program-status codes shown in Figure 9.15?
8. Copy PGM102 to PGM104. Replace the operations that cause the program to divide by zero with code that will cause it to call a nonexistent program. Run the program. What is the program-status code? Is it consistent with what you would expect according to the list of program-status codes shown in Figure 9.15?

Review

1. What advantages are there to using the DUMP code in the *PSSR subroutine?
2. What advantages are there to using formatted output in the *PSSR subroutine?
3. What problems do you anticipate if the program ends without an error message?

File Errors

File errors include

- an attempt to update, delete, or add a record to a file without authority
- an attempt to access a record locked by another job
- an attempt to delete or update a record when the program does not have a current record lock on that file

File errors can be trapped in two ways. First, all file errors for a specific file can be trapped by assigning a subroutine to be used if any access to that file encounters an error.

Using the INFSR Keyword

The INFSR keyword is coded by adding another continuation F-spec to the file with the keyword INFSR and the name of the subroutine to be run in case of error. In Figure 10.3, the subroutine FILSR1 will be run if a file error is encountered when the program accesses the file EMP3. The file-information data structure (FILDS1) will contain information about that file and its status at the time of the error. The file-information data structure was defined in Chapter 9 and contains

- the internal file name
- the actual file, library, and member accessed; the file status; the last operation performed
- the RPG statement number of the last operation that accessed the file
- the record name of the last record accessed

Figure 10.3
File EMP3 Opened with Informational Data Structure FILDS1 and Error Routine FILSR1

```
*...1....+....2....+....3....+....4....+....5....+....6

FEMP3      UF  E          K          DISK          KINFDS FILDS1
                                                   KINFSR FILSR1
```

Using the Input/Output Operation Error Indicator

File errors can be trapped as specific file operations occur. This method is coded by putting an indicator in the LO position of the specific file operation for which you want to catch errors (Figure 10.4). (This indicator position was the LO/Minus/Less Than/Error indicator position on old RPG II coding sheets.)

Figure 10.4
Using an Indicator in the LO Position to Trap an Operational File Error (Program Code Then Tests the Value of the Indicator and Executes the BADR3 Subroutine)

```
*...1....+....2....+....3....+....4....+....5....+....6

C                          READ EMP3                     4090
C             *IN40        IFEQ *ON
C                          EXSR BADR3
C                          ENDIF
```

If a file operation with an indicator identified in the LO position fails, the indicator is turned on and no other response to the error occurs. In this case, the program does not abort, the *PSSR (if it exists) is not automatically called, and the INFSR subroutine for the file (if it exists) is not automatically called. Code should be added to the program to test the indicator and process the error as shown in Figure 10.4.

Exercise 10.3 Using the Keyword INFSR and a Subroutine to Capture File Input/Output Errors

Purpose
To demonstrate file error-handling techniques.

Instructions
Create program PGM105, which will open a file, read a record from it, and issue an update of the record. If the user does not have the authority to update the file, the program prints error information from the file-information data structure.

1. Create a simple program, PGM105, that opens the file INVPF for update, reads a record from the file, and then issues an update on it.
2. Run your program. It should run without error.
3. Use the EDTOBJAUT command to remove your update authority to the file.
4. Run your program again and dump the results.
5. Add a file description continuation line to associate the subroutine FILSR with the file. This subroutine should run only if an error occurs during file access. The FILSR subroutine should contain the code to display the value 'ERR BADU'.

```
*...1....+....2....+....3....+....4....+....5....+....6

C          FILSR     BEGSR
C          'ERR BADU'DSPLY
C                    ENDSR
```

6. Run the program again; it should display the error message whenever an error occurs.
7. Add the file-information data structure from Chapter 9. When an error occurs, print out the relevant status data.
8. Add the program-status data structure from Chapter 9. When an error occurs, print out the relevant status data.

Exercise 10.4 Using the LO Indicator to Detect File Errors

Purpose
To demonstrate file error handling using the LO indicator to detect file access errors.

Instructions
Create program PGM106, which will detect file operation errors via the LO indicator.

1. Copy PGM105 to PGM106.
2. Add an indicator in the LO indicator field of the UPDAT operation.
3. Run the program. What happened? Why?
4. After the UPDAT operation, add code to test the value of the new indicator and if it is on, call the subroutine BADUPD. BADUPD should print the file-information and program-status data structures.
5. Change the object authority on the file to what it was originally.

Review

4. If you were to route all errors to the *PSSR subroutine instead of to individual subroutines, how could you determine whether the error was file-based as well as which file was in error?
5. What would happen if you coded an indicator in the LO field of every I/O operation but did not check the indicator status?

Reusing the File-Information Data Structure

If you code the file-information data structure with subfields for every file, you discover the following:

- Your code is really long.
- The data structure subfields for each file must have unique names, which makes subsequent reporting cumbersome because it would require a separate set of O-specs for each file-information data structure.

Figure 10.5 demonstrates how error handling with multiple files can be simplified by using a general file-information data structure, and, at the time of error, moving the specific data structure of the file in error to the general data structure. The compiler will only recognize the keywords *FILE, *STATUS, *OPCODE, and *RECORD for a data structure that is associated with a file, and, because the data structure FILEDS is not associated with any specific file, all field definitions must be coded with the field's positional values.

In the *PSSR subroutine shown in Figure 10.5, the file that caused the error is determined from the program-status data structure subfield ERRFIL. The data structure of the file in error is moved to the general file data structure FILEDS, then the subfields within that structure can be used to report the error.

The printer file for error reporting — ERRRPG — is identified in the F-specs as user controlled because it is needed only when an error occurs. Before writing to the error printer file in the *PSSR subroutine, the printer file must be opened with the OPEN operation code. Making the error-reporting printer file user controlled will save the program the overhead of opening this printer file except on the occasions when it is needed.

Figure 10.5

Using a General File Data Structure and a Printer File (ERRRPG) Designed to Handle the Reporting of All Errors from All Files

```
*...1....+....2....+....3....+....4....+....5....+....6

FEMP3    UF  E          K         DISK           KINFDS FILED1
F                                                KINFSR *PSSR
FQSYSPRT O   F     132     OF      PRINTER
 * Standard Error Print File
FERRRPG  O   E          39         PRINTER                        UC
 * No need to identify the subfields of the actual file data structure
IFILED1     DS
 * Subfields of the general information data structure
 * cannot use *Keyword, must specify positions of all subfields used
IFILEDS     DS
I                                      1   8 FILNAM
I                                     38  45 RECNAM
I                                     11  15 FSTAT
I                                     16  21 OPCODE
 *------------ PROGRAM STATUS STRUCTURE SDS ---- *
IPROGDS     SDS
I                                      1  10 PRGNAM
I                                  *STATUS  PSTAT
I                                     16  200PRVSTS
I                                     21  28 LINNUM
I                                     29  36 SUBRUT
I                                     37  390PARMS
I                                     40  42 ERRTYP
I                                     43  46 ERRCOD
I                                     47  50 INSNBR
I                                     51  80 MSGWRK
I                                     81  90 PGMLIB
I                                     91 170 MSGTXT
I                                    171 174 EXCMBR
I                                    201 208 ERRFIL
I                                    209 243 ERRINF
I                                    244 253 JOBNAM
I                                    254 263 USER
I                                    264 2690JOBNUM
I                                    270 2750JOBDAT
I                                    276 2810SYSDAT
I                                    282 2870SYSTIM
I                                    288 2930PGMDAT
I                                    294 2990PGMTIM
I                                    300 303 CMPLVL
I                                    304 313 SRCFIL
I                                    314 323 SRCLIB
I                                    324 333 SRCMBR
 *-------------------------------------------------------
C               READ EMP3                      90
C               UPDATEMPREC
C               MOVE *ON     *INLR
C               RETRN
 *---------------------------
```

continued

Figure 10.5
Continued

```
*...1....+....2....+....3....+....4....+....5....+....6
C           *PSSR      BEGSR
* -- Move the data structure of the file in error to the General File
*    Data Structure
C           ERRFIL     IFEQ 'EMP3'
C                      MOVE FILED1    FILEDS
C                      ENDIF
C                      OPEN ERRRPG
C                      WRITEHEADS
C                      WRITEDETAIL
C                      CLOSEERRRPG
C                      MOVE *ON        *INLR
C                      RETRN
C                      ENDSR
```

Exercise 10.5 Reusing the File-Information Data Structure

Purpose
To demonstrate file error handling that incorporates the code to reuse the file-information data structure.

Instructions
Create program PGM107, which will detect file operation errors through the use of the LO indicator and utilizes the concept of a reusable file-information data structure.

1. Copy PGM106 to PGM107. Modify your code to change the error handling to use the general file-information data structure.
2. Open and use the external printer file ERRRPG. This printer file should create the report shown in Figure 10.6

Figure 10.6
Output from ERRRPG Printer File (Lowercase/Shaded Denotes Where Values Are To Be Provided from the Program-Status or File-Information Data Structure)

```
RPG ERROR REPORT                                    DATE: mm/dd/yy
PROGRAM: pgmlib/pgmname                             TIME: 00:00:00

JOB: jobname   USER: user              JOBNUM: jobnum
JOBDATE: mm/dd/yy

PROGRAM HISTORY: SOURCE: pgmsrclib / pgmscrfil ( pgmsrcmbr )
        COMPILE: pgmdat pgmtim cmplvl


PROGRAM ENDED WITH STATUS program status
AT STATEMENT # 031001 error type/code
MESSAGE: msgwrk
         msgtxt


FILE: File name from program data structure WAS IN ERROR.
FILE STATUS: 000000   OPERATION: opcode
```

Review

6. What is the advantage of using a printer file over O-specs for error reporting? How many programs could use this printer file?

7. What is the advantage of using a single data structure when you develop the report?

Sending an Error Message

Sometimes you'll need to send the operator or user a message that clearly defines the problem and resolution. Perhaps the easiest way to manage this is to write a short CL program that sends an inquiry message to the specified message queue.

```
/****************************************************************/
/* PHIL LEVINSON    5/17/98   ADVANCED RPG                     */
/* PROGRAM: SMSG                                              */
/* THIS PROGRAM SENDS A BREAK MESSAGE TO THE DISPLAY          */
/* or a message to the user or messageQ                       */
/****************************************************************/
PGM PARM(&WRKSTNQ &USER &MSGQ &MESSAGE)
DCL &USER    *CHAR 10
DCL &MSGQ    *CHAR 10
DCL &WRKSTNQ *CHAR 10
DCL &MESSAGE *CHAR 180
    IF (&WRKSTNQ > ' ') then( SNDBRKMSG  MSG(&MESSAGE) TOMSGQ(&MSGQ))
    IF (&USER > ' '  ) then( SNDUSRMSG  MSG(&MESSAGE) TOUSR(&USER ))
    IF (&MSGQ > ' '  ) then( SNDUSRMSG  MSG(&MESSAGE) TOMSGQ(&MSGQ))
ENDPGM
```

Figure 10.7
CL Program to
Send a Message

The CL program shown in Figure 10.7 will

- send a break message to the specified workstation
- send a message to the specified user
- send a message to the specified message queue

It will only send the message to each of these locations if the appropriate variable — &WRKSTNQ, &USER, or &MSGQ, respectively — contains a value. The message destinations are passed to the program when it is called in the first three parameters.

The message to be sent is passed to the program as the fourth parameter.

The RPG program that sends a message would either compose the message from data collected from the program-status data structure and/or the file-information data structure (or it could use this data to access a record in a data file that contains a list of errors and related message text). The program would call the CL program shown in Figure 10.7 and pass it the necessary parameters, including at least one destination for the message and the message text. If the RPG program passes a workstation message queue to the CL program in Figure 10.7, the CL program sends a break message to that queue. A break message appears immediately on the display station to which it is sent, temporarily interrupting other processes on that screen.

Break messages can be sent only to display stations' message queues, not to other message queues.

Exercise 10.6 Sending an Error Message

Purpose
To develop a program that demonstrates file error handling, including sending an error message.

Instructions
Create program PGM108, which will send the user an error message.

1. Copy PGM107 to PGM108.
2. Create the CL program in Figure 10.7.
3. Add the necessary code to your error-handling subroutine to call the CL program that sends a message to your display with the program name and a message to check the spool file for further data if the program has failed. The call to the CL program should pass four variables with widths of 10, 10, 10, and 180. The value of the first variable should be the job name as indicated in the program-status data structure. The second and third variables should be blank. The fourth should contain the desired message.

Review

8. If you are creating a spool file that reports the problem, why is it necessary to send a message?

Logging Errors to a Data File

An excellent way to keep a record of errors is to create an error log, which is a database file that is written to every time that any program encounters an error. The error log contains fields for the program name, job name, time, date, program status code, statement in error, file name (if one was in error), last operation on the file and file status code, and job user. The error log should be checked periodically or when errors are suspected.

Additional fields in the error log can be used to manage problem resolution. These fields would identify to whom the problem was assigned, when it was assigned, when it was resolved, and how it was resolved. With this additional information, the error log becomes a resource that records past problems and their solutions.

Exercise 10.7 Logging Errors to a Data File

Purpose
To demonstrate file error handling that incorporates logging errors to a data file.

Instructions
Create program PGM109, which will log errors to a data file.

1. Copy PGM108 to PGM109.
2. Create a data file named ERRFILE with the correct structure to hold all the field data reported on the error report. The field names and structures should be the names you use in your data structures.
3. Add the F-specs to make ERRFILE user controlled.
4. In the error-handling subroutine add code to
   - open ERRFILE
   - write a record to the file
   - close the file

Review

9. Describe how the IS manager would make use of the error log.

Using *PSSR to Avoid the Endless-Error Condition

When a program that contains the *PSSR subroutine detects an error, the *PSSR subroutine is executed. If an error is detected while the *PSSR subroutine is executing, the subroutine is called again. If the error is encountered again, the subroutine is called again. You can see that an error in the error-handling subroutine can lead to an endless series of calls to it.

In the *PSSR subroutine as shown in Figure 10.8 (page 190), the variable ERRTST is *OFF when the program begins. The first time that the error subroutine *PSSR is reached, ERRTST is still off. Therefore, the test is true — ERRTST is changed to *ON, and the operational code is processed. If an error occurs in the error-handling code, *PSSR is called a second time; because ERRTST is now on, the operational code is skipped, the last record indicator is turned on, and processing returns to the parent program.

Figure 10.8
Error-Handling Code
That Avoids the
Endless Loop Error

```
*...1....+....2....+....3....+....4....+....5....+....6
C           *PSSR     BEGSR
*
C           ERRTST    IFEQ *OFF
C                     MOVE *ON      ERRTST

.           OPERATIONAL CODE FOR ERROR HANDLING GOES HERE

C                     ENDIF
C                     MOVE *ON      *INLR
C                     RETRN
C                     ENDSR
```

Exercise 10.8 Avoiding the Endless-Error Condition

Purpose
To demonstrate file error handling that incorporates the code to avoid the endless-error condition.

Instructions
Create program PGM1010, which incorporates the code to avoid the endless-error condition.

1. Copy PGM102 to PGM1010.

> **Note:** The following experiment will lock up your terminal. To end the request, press ALT-SysRq. A line should appear at the bottom of your display. Press 2 to "End the Previous Request."

2. Modify your *PSSR subroutine to include a divide-by-zero situation after the call to the CL program.
3. Run your program. Your program will keep sending you messages and printing reports until the cows come home. Abort the job using the system request key.
4. Add code to avoid the endless-error condition and retest.

Review

10. Why is it necessary to include code to avoid the endless-error condition in your *PSSR subroutine?

Chapter 11

Journaling and Commitment Control

Chapter Overview

When you have completed Chapter 11's exploration of journaling and commitment control — two tools that help you protect the integrity of your database and recover from abnormal system termination — you will be able to

✓ describe journaling and understand its purposes

✓ describe commitment control and understand its purposes

✓ create a journal receiver and a journal

✓ start and stop the journaling of physical files

✓ change a journal

✓ add commitment control at the program level

✓ add commitment control at the transaction level

Introduction to Journaling and Commitment Control

This chapter introduces two tools that are used to maintain the integrity of the data in data files — that is, to ensure that stored data is valid.

Programs that update, add, or delete records from data files can corrupt the records if

- bad data is supplied to the program
- operations errors cause the program to run at the wrong time or in the wrong way
- programming errors cause the program to execute improper changes
- the program ends without completing all of the required processes

The first tool, **journaling**, can record all changes to a file or files. The database of the AS/400 contains built-in journaling tools, including tools to

- record all changes to the data file or files
- back out selected changes from the data file or files
- apply selected changes to an earlier version of the data file

Journaling is a database function, not a programming function. It requires no special techniques when you program the application. Journaling is introduced in this book because it is the basis for the second tool, **commitment control**, which *is* a programming tool.

Commitment control is a programming tool that holds a series of updates, deletes, and adds until the program issues a command related to these changes. The set of changes is held until

- the program issues a command to commit, which causes the current set of changes to become permanent
- the program issues a command to roll back, which causes the current set of changes to be removed from the database
- the program ends or aborts without issuing a commit, which causes the current set of changes to be removed from the database

Commitment control can protect a set of database files from an incomplete update, add, or delete. Exercise 11.1 demonstrates what can happen to a set of data files if an update program without commitment control ends abnormally.

Exercise 11.1 The Inherent Risks of Update Programs

Purpose
To develop an appreciation for the risks inherent in updating data and demonstrate the need for commitment control.

Instructions
You will analyze how data changes under different scenarios that use the logic in the pseudocode shown in Figure 11.1A and the data files shown in Figure 11.1B for a program to post shipments to inventory and to order detail.

The program posts shipments to our customers. It will update the inventory file by subtracting the quantity shipped and update the order detail by adding date and quantity shipped.

continued

Exercise 11.1 *Continued*

Read the first record from the shipping file (step 1)
Do until end of file (EOF)
    If shipping record has not been posted (Posted = 'N') do
        Find the correct inventory record based on product number (step 2)
        Subtract the quantity shipped from the quantity on hand and update
        the inventory record (step 3)
        Find the order detail (line) record (step 4)
        Update the customer's order record to reflect the shipment date and
        shipment quantity (step 5)
        Create a record in the billing file for the billing program (step 6)
        Mark the shipping record as posted (step 7)
    End if
Read next record from the shipping file (step 8)
End do

Figure 11.1A
Pseudocode for a Program to Post Shipments to Inventory and to Order Detail

Shipping File

Date	Ord No	Ord Ln	ProdNo	Quantity	Posted
971207	100140	3	A154	15	N
971207	100140	4	A155	7	Y
971207	100140	5	A156	11	N
971207	100140	6	A157	15	N

Figure 11.1B
The Shipping, Inventory, Order Line, and Billing Files

Inventory File

Prod No	QOnH
A153	250
A154	17
A155	3
A156	15
A157	19
A158	150
A159	300

Order Line File

Ord No	Ord Line	Prod No	QOrd	QShip	QNet
100140	1	B1201	430	215	215
100140	2	C1501	3	3	0
100140	3	A154	15	0	15
100140	4	A155	13	6	7
100140	5	A156	21	10	11
100140	6	A157	15	0	15
100141	1	A155	17	0	17

Billing File

OrderN	LineN	Date	Quantity

continued

Exercise 11.1 *Continued*

Case 1 — Program runs successfully. Create a copy of these files as they should appear after the Post Shipments program finishes, using the shipping records above. Remember: post only records with an N in the posted flag.

Case 2 — Program ends before completion.

1. Beginning with the original data, the operator makes an error and stops the program when it is processing the third shipping record (order 100140, line 5). Just before it is stopped, the program executes pseudocode step 6 for this record. Show the files as they would look at this point.

2. When you realize what has happened, you restart the program (step 1). Show how the files look after processing completes.

If you do this exercise correctly, the third record has been posted twice. This transaction was partially processed in the first run (Case 2, step 1) and posted a second time in the second run (Case 2, step 2).

This kind of error is unacceptable. I might be happy about this error if it were made when deposits were being posted to my checking account but not when withdrawals were being posted. Bank examiners take a dim view of any error.

A program can abort for a number of different reasons, including system problems, security problems, file contention problems, operator errors (as in our example), data errors, and programmer errors. The system may also halt (this is extremely unlikely with an AS/400, but it can happen).

When a program is changing one or more files and failure will make recovery difficult, special controls have to be put in place. The program's design can be altered to remove some of the possible problems. For each transaction, for example, we could lock all the necessary records before the first file change is done. Although this ensures that we have access to all the records that we need for the transaction before we begin it, it increases the length of time that the records are locked — potentially causing problems for other programs.

We can add a *PSSR subroutine (see Chapter 10) to avoid the program crashing. However, its subsequent recovery or soft ending would leave the transaction partially posted. The *PSSR subroutine can detect a great deal about the program at the time of error and could be designed to back out the steps that were completed before the error, but this would be a difficult program to develop. You can imagine the difficulties if the records that you changed and need to revert to their former status were changed in the interim or deleted by another process. (Interim changes are possible because as your program changes a record, it is unlocked and therefore available to other processes.)

There is also potential for logical errors. Inventory should never be negative, the quantity shipped should not exceed the quantity ordered, and so forth. Each of these rules would require more checks before beginning the processing.

Commitment control keeps all the steps of the transaction in limbo — a state of near completion with all the updated records locked — until the transaction is either committed or rolled back. If the program aborts, the transaction is rolled back. If a rollback occurs, all the changes in the "protected" files revert to their status before the transaction and are then unlocked.

The whole process takes only a few lines of code in RPG and a few lines in CL. However, commitment control considerably increases the work that the system has to do, and this causes the program to run slower. The additional load may also slow down other processes on the system. Therefore, commitment control should be used only when

- files are being changed
- recovery will be difficult or impossible if the process fails
- the quality of the data is critical

About half the work load that commitment control puts on the system is actually created by a function that operates at a level below commitment control: journaling. Before we continue our discussion of commitment control, let's discuss journaling.

Journaling

It is relatively simple to imagine a system that records changes to many database files. In this system, if any records are written to the database, a copy of each record would be added to another database. To ensure that all changes were recorded, the implementation of this system would have to be a part of the database management system (DBMS) software. We might want the system to capture the type of change, before and after images of the data, the date and time a change occurred, who authorized the change, and what program made the change.

With such a system, it would be rather simple to find a specific change to a record and undo it, in effect removing a change to the database file. Further, if a backup of the database file were restored to the system, selective changes could be applied to the database to bring it up to the exact date and time desired — perhaps just before a program ran that destroyed data. The system could audit who used or updated the files and what changes were made.

The journaling tools on the AS/400 contain all the features of our imagined system. Every AS/400 includes a complete set of journaling tools as part of the built-in database, DB2/400. Journaling isn't "free," however. Its two "costs" are system overhead and disk consumption. Because the system writes the data twice — to the file and to the journal — the programs that use journaled files run slower and use more system resources. Because we will be in effect keeping the copy of the database file plus the copy of the changes, we will need more disk. Of course, we don't need to keep the record of the changes forever. We can move them to tape. But until we do, they take up disk space.

Exercise 11.2 Experiments in Journaling

Purpose
To experiment with AS/400 journaling tools toward a clear understanding of the why and how of journaling.

Instructions
Journal the file INVPF, make changes to the file, view the history of the changes, then remove the changes.

   This project requires that each student have a separate library that is the first library in the student's library list containing the file INVPF. (Each student's library must have a copy of the file INVPF that contains records.) In the following instructions, wherever I specify YOURLIB, substitute the name of your data library.

continued

Exercise 11.2 *Continued*

Issue the CL commands described in the eight steps that follow at any command line.

1. Create a journal receiver. The command CRTJRNRCV (Create Journal Receiver) creates an object much like a physical file. When it is full, you can tell the system to "roll" to the next receiver. The system will compute that the next receiver should be INVJRN0002.

    CRTJRNRCV   yourlib/INVJRN0001

2. Create a journal. A second object, created with the command CRTJRN (Create Journal), contains the journaling rules, including which files are journaled, what data is captured for each file, and what journal receiver is in use. These rules will be defined after the journal is started with the STRJRNPF (Start Journal Physical File) command (step 3).

    CRTJRN   and press F4 for prompting

    The prompt screen for CRTJRN is shown in Figure 11.2.

    Fill in journal, journal library, journal receiver, and journal receiver library, as shown in Figure 11.2.

Figure 11.2
Create Journal
Command
Prompt Screen

```
                              Create Journal (CRTJRN)

Type choices, press Enter.

Journal . . . . . . . . . . . .   INVJRN        Name
   Library . . . . . . . . . .      yourlib     Name, *CURLIB
Journal receiver . . . . . . .    INVJRN0001    Name
   Library . . . . . . . . . .      yourlib     Name, *LIBL, *CURLIB
                                  *LIBL
Auxiliary storage pool ID  . . .  *LIBASP       1-16, *LIBASP
Journal message queue  . . . . .  QSYSOPR       Name
   Library . . . . . . . . . .    *LIBL         Name, *LIBL, *CURLIB
Manage receivers . . . . . . .    *USER         *USER, *SYSTEM
Delete receivers . . . . . . .    *NO           *NO, *YES
Receiver size options  . . . . .  *NONE         *NONE, *RMVINTENT
Text 'description' . . . . . . .  *BLANK

                                                                  Bottom
F3=Exit   F4=Prompt   F5=Refresh   F10=Additional parameters   F12=Cancel
F13=How to use this display        F24=More keys
Parameter JRN required.                                              +
```

The CRTJRN prompt screen also defines which set of disks (called an auxiliary storage pool or ASP) is to be used for the journal receivers. For insurance, it makes sense to locate the receiver in a different storage pool from the physical file. If the disk with the physical file fails, the journal receiver, which is on a different disk, will probably be available with a history of all the lost changes.

When you create the journal, you can define the journal message queue. You can define whether the user or the system should generate and attach the journal to the new receiver via the Manage Receivers option (see Figure 11.2). The *USER value indicates that the user must generate and attach new receivers to the journal when the receivers are full. The *SYSTEM indicates that OS/400 will generate and attach new receivers when receivers are full.

continued

Exercise 11.2 *Continued*

If the value for the Manage Receivers option is *SYSTEM and the value for the Delete Receivers option is *YES, the system will delete the old receiver as soon as it generates and attaches the journal to a new receiver.

3. Start journaling the file. The STRJRNPF command identifies a data file that will be journaled to a specific journal as well as what data should be collected for that file. The command itself will be journaled along with any other activity to that physical file until and including the ENDJRNPF (End Journaling Physical File) command. Any number of files can be journaled to the same journal. All files in a commitment control set *must* be journaled to the same journal.

   STRJRNPF   and press F4 for prompting

   Fill in the name and library of the file to be journaled, as well as the journal and the images to be captured, as shown in Figure 11.3. Set the image value to *BOTH, which captures what a record looks like both before and after a change. Both images will be required for commitment control.

```
                    Start Journal Physical File (STRJRNPF)
 Type choices, press Enter.

 Physical file to be journaled  .   INVPF       Name
    Library . . . . . . . . . . .     YOURLIB   Name, *LIBL, *CURLIB
                  + for more values
                                    *LIBL
 Journal . . . . . . . . . . . .    INVJRN      Name
    Library . . . . . . . . . . .     *LIBL     Name, *LIBL, *CURLIB
 Record images  . . . . . . . . .   *BOTH       *AFTER, *BOTH
 Journal entries to be omitted  .   *NONE       *NONE, *OPNCLO



                                                                     Bottom
 F3=Exit    F4=Prompt    F5=Refresh    F12=Cancel    F13=How to use this display
 F24=More keys
```

Figure 11.3
Start Journal Physical File Command Prompt Screen

Other frequently used journaling commands include ENDJRNPF, mentioned above, and CHGJRN (Change Journal). You can get a complete list of journaling commands by entering the command GO CMDJRN and a list of journal receiver commands by entering the command GO CMDJRNRCV.

4. Use the DSPFD (Display File Description) command to determine whether a file is journaled as well as to which journal.

   DSPFD INVPF

   Figure 11.4 shows part of the DSPFD display. The Page down key should be pressed until the journaling information is displayed.

```
 File is currently journaled . . . . . . . . :        Yes
 Current or last journal . . . . . . . . . . :        INVJRN
    Library . . . . . . . . . . . . . . . . . :        YOURLIB
 Journal images  . . . . . . . . . . . . . . : IMAGES   *BOTH
 Journal entries to be omitted . . . . . . . : OMTJRNE  *NONE
 Last journal start date/time  . . . . . . . :        12/14/98  10:51:50
```

Figure 11.4
Part of the DSPFD Display Showing Journaling Status

continued

Exercise 11.2 *Continued*

The information in Figure 11.4 shows that the file is journaled to the journal INVJRN in the library YOURLIB. Both images are captured. The value *NONE in the option Journal Entries to be Omitted causes the journal to include a record of every file open and file close as well as all changes to the data. (There is a value that would omit the record of the file opens and closes.)

5. Display journal entries. Journal entries can be viewed by using the DSPJRN (Display Journal) command, which includes the option of seeing journal entries based on time and date, physical file being journaled, job, and so forth. So far, there are only a few entries to the journal, as shown in Figure 11.5.

   DSPJRN INVJRN

Figure 11.5
Display Journal
Entries for the
Journal INVJRN

```
                           Display Journal Entries

Journal  . . . . . . :    INVJRN          Library  . . . . . . :      YOURLIB

Type options, press Enter.
  5=Display entire entry


Opt    Sequence  Code  Type  Object    Library     Job          Time
          1       J     PR                          BL0566S1     10:50:41
          3       F     JM    INVPF     YOURLIB      BL0566S1     10:51:50
```

The first entry notes that the journal was created, and the second notes that the file INVPF was added to the journal.

6. Delete records from the file INVPF. Use Data File Utility (DFU) to delete some of the records in the file. An easy way to start DFU is with the UPDDTA command:

   UPDDTA INVPF

Press the Page down key to advance to the first record and press F23 twice to delete it. Repeat this process five times, deleting the first five records. Press F3 twice to exit DFU.

7. View the journal entries (Figure 11.6), including the deleted records, using the following command:

   DSPJRN INVJRN

Now our journal contains a copy of each deleted record. The F code records the file opens and closes; the R code records any changes to records. DL is delete. Use option 5, Display Entire Entry, to view the details. You will find that the journal contains the "image" of the record before it was deleted along with the time, date, user, program, and job that deleted it.

8. Recover the deleted records. To recover the five deleted records, we will back out the changes that were made to the file, which were recorded by the journal. The command for backing out the changes to a file is RMVJRNCHG (Remove Journal Changes).

   RMVJRNCHG JRN(INVJRN) FILE((INVPF))

We've just asked the journal to remove the effects of all the entries that it had against INVPF, and the system responded with the following message: Remove failed. 5 entries removed from member INVPF. (Even though this message indicates that the remove request failed, it failed after five entries were removed because the remaining entries did not contain any file changes that could be removed. These entries indicated the start of

continued

Exercise 11.2 *Continued*

```
                    Display Journal Entries
Journal  . . . . . . :    INVJRN        Library  . . . . . . :     YOURLIB

Type options, press Enter.
  5=Display entire entry


Opt    Sequence   Code   Type   Object     Library     Job          Time
           1       J     PR                            BL0566S1     11:22:31
           3       F     JM     INVPF      YOURLIB     BL0566S1     11:22:51
           4       F     OP     INVPF      YOURLIB     BL0566S1     11:25:15
           5       F     OP     INVPF      YOURLIB     BL0566S1     11:25:15
           7       R     DL     INVPF      YOURLIB     BL0566S1     11:25:34
           8       R     DL     INVPF      YOURLIB     BL0566S1     11:25:38
           9       R     DL     INVPF      YOURLIB     BL0566S1     11:25:40
          10       R     DL     INVPF      YOURLIB     BL0566S1     11:25:42
          16       R     DL     INVPF      YOURLIB     BL0566S1     11:25:57
          13       F     OP     INVPF      YOURLIB     BL0566S1     11:25:52
          14       F     OP     INVPF      YOURLIB     BL0566S1     11:25:52    +
F3=Exit    F12=Cancel
```

Figure 11.6

Display Journal INVPF After Deleting Five Records

journaling.) We can find out more details about the remove journal changes process by displaying our job log, using the command DSPJOBLOG. To see the detailed log, press F10, and to see previous messages, press Page up. One of the messages that you will find in your job log is

Cannot perform operation beyond journal entry 3.

Our command was supposed to back out the changes to the file INVPF from the very last change all the way back to entry #2. Our request to remove journal changes started with the most recent change, the journal entry with the highest number, and worked backward, removing each change until it removed journal entry 3. Five of the entries indicated changes to the data, and these were changed back to their previous values. (When the process reached journal entry 2, it stopped because the first and second entries were not removable — those entries indicated that this file would be journaled.)

We could have been more explicit about which entries to remove by typing RMVJRNCHG and pressing F4 (Prompt). We could identify all the files from which to remove the entries — using the entry number range or the dates and times range. Because the removal works backward, the start would be the most recent time or the highest entry number and the end would be the earliest time or lowest entry number.

9. Check the file to see the effect of the RMVJRNCHG command. Use the command UPDDTA INVPF to verify that the records deleted in step 7 were actually restored.

   Use the DSPJRN command to see how the journal recorded the RMVJRNCHG command. You will see that it didn't remove the record of the deletions; rather, it added new records to the bottom that record the RMVJRNCHG process.

In our previous discussion and experiments, only a single physical file was journaled. The next experiment demonstrates that multiple files can be journaled to a single journal. Journaling more than one file to the same journal will be necessary when you use commitment control with multiple files as discussed later in this chapter.

Exercise 11.3 Further Experiments in Journaling

Purpose

To use journaling tools to remove specific changes to a database.

Instructions

Changes to the file INVPF will be made using the inventory maintenance program. Once these changes have been made, they will then be backed out using the RMVJRNCHG command. This project requires that the file INVPF is journaled.

1. Add the file ORDLNP to the journal INVJRN, recording *BOTH images.
2. Add two new records to INVPF.
3. Delete two records from INVPF.
4. Change two records from INVPF.
5. Use DSPJRN to determine the entry numbers that represent these changes.
6. Remove the last change by entry number.
7. View the file and confirm that the change has been removed.
8. Remove the range of changes that have not yet been removed.
9. View the file and confirm that the change has been removed.

   Using your Order Line Maintenance program,

10. Add two new records to ORDLNP.
11. Delete two records from ORDLNP.
12. Change two records in ORDLNP.
13. Use DSPJRN command to display the journal INVJRN. Your are now viewing all changes to both files. Now exit the display and use the DSPJRN command again, but this time use prompting (by pressing F4) to display the journal INVJRN but only for file ORDLNP. Not only could you restrict the display to one or more files, but you could also restrict the display to a time/date range or entry number range, so you can find the specific entries that you're seeking.
14. Remove the last change by entry number.
15. View the file and confirm that the change has been removed.
16. Remove the range of changes that have not been removed.
17. View the file and confirm that the change has been removed.

Closing Words on Journaling

More than one file can be journaled to a single journal. Journals record all changes to the file. Journals can also record all opens and closes to the file. Journals can provide a way to back out one or a group of changes to one or more files. Journals can be used from the other direction by restoring an earlier backup and then using the command APPJRNCHG (Apply Journal Changes) up to the point at which a disaster occurred.

Exercise 11.4 Using Journaling to Reduce the Risk Inherent in Update Programs

Purpose

To demonstrate how to use journaling to reduce the risk inherent in updating data.

Instructions

You will analyze the changes to the data that occur under a number of different scenarios that use logic to post shipments to inventory and order detail.

Case 3 — All the files in Exercise 11.1 are journaled to the journal FAROUT. Both the before and after images are captured for all files. Our operator makes the same mistake that was made in Exercise 11.1, Case 2, and aborts the job before the third transaction is complete. The job name is POSTSHP.

1. Describe how you could remove the effects of the entire job POSTSHP. Take the image of the files at the time of the abort and "roll" them back until all the journal entries have been removed.

2. Starting with the files as they are at the completion of step 1, we run the shipment posting program again. What is the image of the files after it runs? How does it compare to the image after Exercise 11.1, Case 1?

Case 4 — As in Case 3, all files are journaled and the operator aborts the program.

1. Describe how you could determine what range of entries comprises the transaction that was aborted. Describe how to remove just these changes. Create an image of the file after these changes are removed.

2. Start with the file as it appears at the end of Case 3, step 2. Run the program to post shipments. How do the results of this run compare to the results from Case 1?

If you followed the path of bread crumbs properly, you are either a) at the witch's house, or b) at the same place that you reached in Exercise 11.1, Case 1. You found two ways to get there: by removing the entire process (Case 3) or by removing just the single corrupt transaction (Case 4).

In these exercises, both solutions yield the same results and with nearly the same amount of effort on the part of humans and machines. Commitment control provides both options — to roll back the entire job or just a single transaction. The best choice is primarily dependent on the nature of the application, as we will discuss.

Commitment Control

As you have seen in the preceding exercises, journaling contains the essence of the solution to improper or incomplete changes to a data file or a set of data files. However, to use it, you have had to discover that when the program aborts, you need to know the range of journal entries to remove and issue the commands to make the corrections. Until the journal entries are actually removed, the files are in error; and any processes that access these files can produce bad results. If any further changes occur to the affected records between the time of the aborted process and the attempt to remove the journal entries, those journal entries cannot be removed. The system compares the after image of the record to the current image of the record at the time the removal of the journal entry is attempted. This prevents the system from losing subsequent changes.

Commitment control adds to journaling in two ways:

1. It locks all records from the commitment boundary until either a commit or rollback request occurs. (Program abort is assumed to be a rollback.)

2. If a rollback is requested or the program aborts, commitment control automatically removes the journal entries back to the commitment boundary (defined in the next section).

Commitment Control Boundary

The commitment control boundary is the point at which the current commitment transaction begins. The first commitment transaction begins at the CL command STRCMTCTL (Start Commitment Control) and continues until the first commit, rollback, or program abort. Subsequently, the boundary's beginning is moved to the end of the last transaction — the last commit or rollback.

To provide the "all-or-nothing" option (all or no records are updated), the commit or rollback is done at the end of either the CL program or the RPG program.

In transaction-level commitment control, the commit operation will be placed just before the read of the first record of the next transaction. This commit will make the completed transaction permanent and move the commit boundary to the beginning of the new transaction. If a problem condition is detected that indicates that the transaction should not be carried out, a rollback is issued that backs out the changes and moves the boundary. Then the first record of the next transaction is read.

Commitment Control: Rules and Restriction

Commitment control will work only if the three following rules are observed:

- All files that are to be put under commitment control must be journaled to the same journal and must have Record Image = *BOTH.
- The RPG update programs must be called by a CL program, which must issue the command to start commitment control before calling the RPG program. This must be a call, not a submit job, because the CL program that starts commitment control must be in the same job stream as the subsequent processing.
- The total number of record changes that can be contained within the commitment control boundary was limited to about 32,000 in OS/400 Version 2. Although that is not likely to be a problem for commitment on the single transaction level, it has proven to be a problem for the all-or-nothing option. In subsequent versions of OS/400, the commitment boundary has been changed to 2 billion record changes.

Commitment Control: CL Commands

To establish commitment control, the job stream must contain a CL program that issues the CL command STRCMTCTL (Start Commitment Control). The CL program must then call the RPG program, which contains special F-specs that identify the files that will be protected by commitment control. On completion of the RPG program, processing returns to the CL program, which issues a command to end commitment control. Commands to commit or roll back can be located at the RPG program level and/or in the CL program. Transaction level commitment, in which each transaction is committed or rolled back before the next transaction, requires a commit or rollback operation in the RPG program.

The CL commands to start, end, commit, and roll back will be described in this section. The RPG F-specs and operations for commitment control will be described thereafter.

Remember, the RPG update program must be called by a CL program that has already issued the command to start commitment control.

STRCMTCTL initiates the commitment control process. This command requires a value for the LCKLVL (Lock Level) parameter to define which records remain locked until they are committed or released with a rollback.

Without commitment control, records accessed from a file with update status will be locked until unlocked, updated, deleted, or released when the program accesses another record from the same file.

Commitment control must lock all of the records that are changed until the commit or rollback is issued to prevent other processes from changing or deleting these records before that program has ascertained that the change can be committed. The lock applies to records accessed from files designated as under commitment control in RPG F-specs. There are three different levels of lock:

- *ALL — All records that have been accessed are locked until the commit or rollback occurs even if they are not changed and would be unlocked if commitment control were not used.

- *CHG — All records that have been changed (updated, added, or deleted) are locked. Also the records that would be locked if commitment control were not used are locked (records which have been accessed but have not yet been released). Records can be released with the RPG UNLOK (Unlock) command, with the unlock value on the access specification, or by accessing another record from the file.

- *CS — All records that have been accessed are locked unless a record is released by accessing another record from the file without changing (updating or deleting) the record.

ENDCMTCTL (End Commitment Control) terminates commitment control. If you try to issue this command while records are still in limbo, an error occurs.

ROLLBACK (Roll Back) rolls back any records that have not been committed at the time the command is issued.

COMMIT (Commit the Pending Changes) commits the changes to any records that have not been committed at the time the command is issued.

The CL program shown in Figure 11.7 starts commitment control and calls the RPG program PGMRPG11A.

```
/* Program PGMCLP11A   */
PGM
    STRCMTCTL *CS
    CALL PGMRPG11A
      /*Program will rollback */
      /*  uncommitted changes */
    ROLLBACK
    ENDCMTCTL
END:    ENDPGM
```

Figure 11.7
CL Program with Commitment Control

After the RPG program has completed, all uncommitted changes are rolled back and commitment control is ended.

Commitment Control and RPG

Commitment control requires CL commands to start the commitment process described in the previous section of this chapter. Each file that will be protected by commitment control requires a continuation F-spec to declare that it will be protected by the commitment control process. Only files that are opened for update, output, or input with addition capabilities can be protected.

Two operation codes control the commitment process. The COMIT (Commit Group) operation makes the current file changes permanent; the ROLBK (Roll Back) operation removes the current file changes.

F-Specs for Commitment Control

We identify the files to be protected by commitment control by adding an F-spec continuation line (input with prompt format type FK). Remember: only files for update, output, or input with addition allowed can be under commitment control, and all files that are committed must be currently journaled to the same journal with Image=*BOTH. The continuation line that declares that a file is to be put under commitment control has a K in column 53 to indicate that it is a continuation line and a COMIT in columns 54 through 58. Thus the F-specs shown in Figure 11.8 place the file INVPF under commitment control.

Figure 11.8

F-Specs for a File Under
Commitment Control

```
*...1....+....2....+....3....+....4....+....5....+....6

FINVPF   UF  E         K        DISK
F                                              KCOMIT
```

The C-spec operation COMIT will cause commitment control to commit the changed records, and the records are unlocked. The commitment boundary (the previous COMIT or ROLBK) is restarted at this point. The changes are now permanent.

The C-spec operation ROLBK will cause commitment control to roll back records to the commitment boundary (the previous COMIT or ROLBK). The changes are removed and the records are unlocked. The commitment boundary is restarted at this point.

Exercise 11.5 Commitment Control: Rollback at the Process Level

Purpose

To gain an understanding and appreciation of commitment control. This exercise will demonstrate how rollbacks can be implemented to control all of the changes in a process.

Instructions

The following sentences describe a situation that you will be asked to verify: An RPG program deletes all of the records of a file under commitment control but fails to issue either a commit or rollback command. The CL program that established commitment control and called the RPG program issues a rollback when the RPG program ends. The database file should be unchanged by the process.

1. Copy file INVPF to INVPF2 with the following command:

    CPYF INVPF INVPF2 MBROPT(*REPLACE) CRTFILE(*YES)

2. Display the contents of the file with the following command:

    DSPPFM INVPF2

3. Enter and compile the CL program shown in Figure 11.7.

4. Enter and compile the RPG program shown in Figure 11.9. This program deletes all the records in INVPF, but it places INVPF under commitment control and doesn't contain a COMIT operation.

```
           *...1....+....2....+....3....+....4....+....5....+....6
          *************** Beginning of data ********************************
0001.00    FINVPF2  UF  E                     DISK
0002.00    F                                              KCOMIT
0003.00    C                        READ INVPF2           90
0004.00    C          *IN90         DOWEQ*OFF
0005.00    C                        DELETINVPFR
0006.00    C                        READ INVPF2           90
0007.00    C                        ENDDO
0008.00    C                        MOVE *ON      *INLR
0009.00    C                        RETRN
          ***************** End of data ********************************
```

Figure 11.9
Sample
Program
PGMRPG11A

5. Call the CL program you created in step 3.
6. Display the contents of the file INVPF2 with the following command:

    DSPPFM INVPF2

    The file should be the same as it was at step 2.

Exercise 11.6 Commitment Control: Commit at the Process Level

Purpose
To gain an understanding of and appreciation for commitment control. This exercise will demonstrate how commitment control can be implemented to control all of the changes in a process.

Instructions
The following sentences describe a situation that you will be asked to verify: An RPG program under commitment control deletes all the records of a file. Just before it ends, the RPG program issues a commit operation. If the RPG program runs to completion, all of the records should be deleted. If it fails, none of the records will be deleted.

1. Modify program PGMRPG11A. Add a COMIT operation after the ENDDO. This is one way to commit at the all-or-nothing level. If this program fails, it doesn't reach the COMIT. And because the calling CL program has a rollback command immediately after the CALL to the RPG program, it will roll back any uncommitted records. Call the CL program you created in Exercise 11.5, step 3.
2. Display the records in file INVPF2 with the following command:

DSPPFM INVPF2

The member should not contain any records.

Placing Commit and Rollback
The commit and rollback commands could be placed in the CL program or the RPG program. In the RPG program, the COMIT operation can be placed in the processing loop or at the end of processing. The ROLBK operation can be located in error-handling subroutines and called when aborting a partially executed transaction. This section provides guidelines on the placement of these commands.

    All-or-Nothing Case 1 — Put a commit in the RPG program just before the Move *On to *INLR.

    All-or-Nothing Case 2 — In this case, there is no commit/rollback in the RPG code. The CL code is modified as shown in Figure 11.10 so that the program will commit the changes unless the RPG program ends in error. If the program ends in

Figure 11.10
CL Program with a Commit If the RPG Program Ends Normally and a Rollback If It Ends Abnormally

```
/* Simple CL program will roll back uncommitted changes */
PGM
              STRCMTCTL *CS
              CALL PGMRPG11A
              MONMSG CPF0000 RPG0000 MCH0000 EXEC( ERROR )
              COMMIT
              ENDCMTCTL
              GOTO END
ERROR:        ROLLBACK
              ENDCMTCTL
END:          ENDPGM
```

error, the MONMSG (Monitor Message) command causes the program to skip down to the error: label and execute the ROLLBACK.

Commit at the Transaction Level — The commit should be placed in the code as soon as the transaction is complete, as shown in the screened line in Figure 11.11.

```
   *...1....+....2....+....3....+....4....+....5....+....6
           ************** Beginning of data *********************************
0001.00    FINVPF   UF  E                        DISK
0002.00    F                                                    KCOMIT
0003.00    C                          READ INVPF                    90
0004.00    C            *IN90          DOWEQ*OFF
0005.00    C                          DELETINVPFR
0005.01    C                          COMIT
0006.00    C                          READ INVPF                    90
0007.00    C                          ENDDO
0008.00    C                          MOVE *ON      *INLR
0009.00    C                          RETRN
           **************** End of data *********************************
```

Figure 11.11
RPG Program with Transaction Level Commitment

Rollback and *PSSR — If your program contains a *PSSR subroutine, the MONMSG and ROLLBACK commands in the CL program will not work; the *PSSR subroutine ensures that the RPG program will not abort. Therefore, the CL program won't skip to the ERROR label. Instead, the ROLBK operation must be included in the RPG *PSSR subroutine, as shown in the screened lines in Figure 11.12.

```
   *...1....+....2....+....3....+....4....+....5....+....6
0001.00    FINVPF   UF  E                        DISK
0002.00    F                                                    KCOMIT
0003.00    C                          READ INVPF                    90
0004.00    C            *IN90          DOWEQ*OFF
0005.00    C                          DELETINVPFR
0005.01    C                          COMIT
0006.00    C                          READ INVPF                    90
0007.00    C                          ENDDO
0008.00    C                          MOVE *ON      *INLR
0009.00    C                          RETRN
0010.00    C            *PSSR          BEGSR
0011.00    C                          ROLBK
0012.00    C                          MOVE *ON      *INLR
0013.00    C                          RETRN
0014.00    C                          ENDSR
           **************** End of data *********************************
```

Figure 11.12
RPG Program with Rollback in Error Handling Subroutine

Exercise 11.7 Adding Commitment Control to an Interactive Program

Purpose
To understand how to add commitment control to an interactive program.

Instructions
Add commitment control to the inventory maintenance program.

1. Modify your most recent inventory maintenance program to add transaction-level commitment control.
2. Create a CL program to start commitment control and call the RPG program.
3. Test the program.
4. Modify the program from step 1 so that it makes the changes to the file and shows the operator a window that displays the changes and asks for user approval. (If the user approves, the changes will be committed; if the user rejects, the changes will be rolled back.)

Review

1. For each of the following examples, describe why you would either back out all transactions and start the job over or back out only the corrupted transactions and start the job over.

   • The shipment posting program contains 2 million shipping records to post and aborts halfway through.

   • The home-shopping order entry system crashes.

   • Everyone in your company gets a 5 percent raise. You write a program to read each record, multiply the pay rate by 1.05, put the result in the pay rate field, and update the record. It crashes after updating about a million records.

2. Describe why commitment control is an important tool for RPG programmers.
3. What is the commitment control boundary and how does it restrict the effect of an RPG rollback operation or CL command?
4. A typical RPG program loops each time that a transaction is completed. Where should you locate the commit operation to

   a. establish transaction-level commitment

   b. establish program-level commitment

5. If a program has an error-handling subroutine *PSSR, would you expect to find a commitment control statement there? If so, which one? Why?
6. What are the CL commands required to support commitment control?

Chapter 12

Program-to-Program Communication and Data Queues

Chapter Overview

When you have completed Chapter 12, you will be able to

- ✓ define the types of program-to-program communication
- ✓ decide when each type of program-to-program communication is required
- ✓ describe data queues, a powerful AS/400 tool for program-to-program communication
- ✓ create programs using FIFO and LIFO data queues
- ✓ create programs using keyed data queues

Program-to-Program Communication

The first two sections of this chapter discuss, compare, and contrast the range of tools for program-to-program communication. The remainder of the chapter will explore the nature and applications of one of those tools: data queues. Unique to the AS/400, data queues comprise an extremely fast and powerful way to transmit data between programs.

Program-to-program communication techniques provide tools to address a range of system design challenges. Table 12.1 shows the basic uses for program-to-program communication.

Table 12.1
Uses for Program-to-Program Communication

Purpose	Timing	Issues
Program modularity	Synchronous	Simpler programs Reusable code
Subsequent processes	Asynchronous	Completion of a transaction lets a subsequent process proceed

Synchronous processing occurs when programs perform in a controlled sequence: program A calls program B and waits for program B to finish before continuing. When program A calls program B, it can pass data to program B; when program B ends, it can pass back data to program A — one form of program-to-program communication.

Asynchronous processing occurs when two programs run independently. However, because one may still have to send requests for data or lists of completed transactions to the other program, some method of program-to-program communication is required.

Program-to-Program Communication Techniques

The program analyst or system designer on the AS/400 has four different program-to-program communication techniques available. These techniques vary in timing (synchronous, asynchronous, or both) and performance. Table 12.2 presents the various communication techniques.

Table 12.2
Communication Techniques

Technique	Timing	Comments
Passing data in call	Synchronous	Simple coding of synchronous processing
Data areas	Synchronous Asynchronous	Each data area can hold only one "record"
Trigger files	Asynchronous	File contains data or enough data to identify the records for subsequent processing
Data queues	Synchronous	Fastest transfer of data
	Asynchronous	Easy to make a program that waits for passed data

Program-to-Program Technique: Passing Data

RPG program A calls program B and passes parameters to it. Program A's processing is then suspended until program B is completed. The parameters "passed" or shared between the programs may include a value to indicate whether program B succeeded or failed. With this indicator or variable, program A can then continue processing based on the success or failure of program B. Synchronous processing is necessary when the primary processing must be delayed until the process in the called program has been completed.

RPG/400 offers two alternative forms of the CALL operation when parameters are passed or shared with the called program. Figure 12.1 shows a CALL operation followed by the parameter list.

Figure 12.1
Call to PROG12B
with Parameter List

```
*...1....+....2....+....3....+....4....+....5....+....6

                  CALL 'PROG12B
                  PARM              VAR1
                  PARM              VAR2
                  PARM              VAR3
```

Figure 12.2 shows the same CALL operation using a PLIST (a parameter list) that is defined in the program initialization subroutine. The PLIST presents a series of variables that will be passed to or shared with the called program.

```
*...1....+....2....+....3....+....4....+....5....+....6
C          PLST1    PLIST
C                   PARM            VAR1
C                   PARM            VAR2
C                   PARM            VAR3
C                   CALL  'PROG12B'
```

Figure 12.2
Call to PROG12B
with PLIST

Figure 12.3 shows a portion of a program that is called and receives (or more accurately shares) data. The called program identifies the internal field names of the shared fields in an *ENTRY PLIST that would be included in the called program in the initialization subroutine. The *ENTRY PLIST is a special PLIST that identifies the list of parameters shared with the calling program. A program can contain only one *ENTRY PLIST. This list should provide the same number of variables of the same types and sizes as the calling program passes.

```
*...1....+....2....+....3....+....4....+....5....+....6
C          INIT     BEGSR
C          *ENTRY   PLIST
C                   PARM            X1       155
C                   PARM            X2       32
C                   PARM            *IN10
```

Figure 12.3
PROG12B Receives the
"Passed" or Shared
Variables with an
*ENTRY PLIST

Table 12.3 shows various outcomes of mismatching the passed parameters and the *ENTRY PLIST.

Table 12.3
Outcomes of Calling a Program and Passing Parameters

Calling Program: Program A	Called Program: Program B	Results
Passes parameters	*ENTRY PLIST matches passed parameters	Programs run as designed
Passes parameters	Does not have a *ENTRY PLIST or does not have as many entries in *ENTRY PLIST as are passed	Call fails
Passes parameters	Variables in *ENTRY PLIST are not of the same type or size	Program B runs but values passed to or from it may be corrupt and may cause logic or runtime errors
Does not pass parameters	Has *ENTRY PLIST	Call works but any attempt in Program B to use the variables in the *ENTRY PLIST will cause an error
Does not pass parameters	Does not have an *ENTRY PLIST	Programs run as designed

The parameter lists of the calling and called programs must contain the same number of variables with identical variable structures in the same sequence. The structure of any numeric variable that is passed by the calling program or received by the called program should be 15 digits wide with 5 decimal positions in both programs. Character fields should be the same width in both programs. The variable names do not have to be the same in the calling and called programs.

RPG does not actually pass the values of the variables to the called program; it passes the addresses of the variables. These locations are shared by both programs. If the called program changes the value of any variable in its PLIST, that value is placed in the shared location. When the called program ends, the calling program resumes but with the new value of the shared variable. For example, Prog12A places the value 'Hi Prog12B' in the variable VAR2 and then calls PROGB (Figure 12.1 and Figure 12.2). The *ENTRY PLIST for Prog 12B can use the variable X2, which is 'Hi Prog12B'. Before Prog 12B ends, it changes the value in variable X2 to 'Right back at you'. When ProgA resumes, the value in VAR2 is 'Right back at you'.

Program-to-Program Technique: Data Areas

A data area is an object of type *DTAARA. It can contain one numeric or character value. If the data area is created in a library other than QTEMP, it will continue to exist and retain the data stored in it until it is deleted. If the data area is created in QTEMP, it will exist only until the job ends because QTEMP is a unique library created for each job and deleted at job end. Each job also has a local data area created at the beginning of the job and accessible to all programs that run in the job stream.

Data areas can be used in two ways. In synchronous processing, the data area can be used much like a passed parameter to convey data to and from a program within the job stream. Unlike the use of parameters in which data must be actively passed from program to program to program, you can use a data area to share data with any program or programs in the job stream that access it.

Data areas are also useful for asynchronous processing in which a program stores a single piece of data for use at a later time — either by itself or by another program. For example, a data area is an excellent place to keep the last invoice number issued. Any program that needs to issue an invoice can lock the data area, pick up the last number from the data area, add 1 to it, write it back to the data area, and then unlock the data area. Any number of programs could "share" this data area. The data area used in asynchronous processing is likely to be created in a permanent library so it will be available to other jobs and later executions of the same job.

Program-to-Program Technique: Trigger Files

Data files that contain data or transaction requests to be processed (sometimes referred to as trigger files) can be used as a method of passing data from one program to another. This method is most common in asynchronous processing in which the first program doesn't wait for the completion of the second program. The second program may in fact be processing a record from the shared file that was created several cycles ago by the creating program. Any number of programs could place data in this file, and any number of programs could be reading the records and carrying on their component of the subsequent processing.

A good example of this might occur in a grocery store system. Processing may be broken down into two stages. Stage one includes only the processing required at the check-out counter. Stage two is a batch program run once a day that updates the inventories from the day's sales and transmits restocking orders. Stage one has to be fast; the customer and check-out clerk are waiting. For each item rung up in stage one, the stage-one program writes a record to the inventory change file. Later, the stage-two inventory-update/restocking program reads each record from the inventory change file, subtracts the sales from the inventory quantity, and reorders stock if the quantity falls below the reorder value. As the stage-two program processes, it may either remove each record or change the value in a field on each record to record that the processing has taken place.

Program-to-Program Technique: Data Queues

Data queues can be used for synchronous processing in which one program puts a request for processing into one data queue and then waits for a response provided by a second program, typically in a second data queue. Data queues also can be used for asynchronous processing in which a program puts a request for processing into a data queue and continues without waiting for a response.

Data queues are much faster than data files in program-to-program communication. Whereas data files are structured with fields, each entry in a data queue is only a single numeric value or character value. Structure over the data queue element will have to be created internally in any program. The fields to be sent to a data queue are all included in a single data structure along with a single character field that is the combined width of all the fields of the data structure. Once data is loaded into the subfields of the data structure, the field the width of the data structure is sent. The fields to be received from a data queue are all included in a single data structure along with a single character field that is the combined width of all the fields in the data structure. The element is received into the wide field of the data structure and then is structured and available through the subfields.

Data queues are less flexible than data files. Data file records can be viewed, added, changed, and deleted, using programs or utilities such as Data File Utility (DFU). Data queue elements can only be sent to and received from the queue.

Records are deleted from a data file by a unique step in the program that issues a delete. Elements in a data queue, however, are deleted from the queue automatically whenever they are received into a program. The one-step access and deletion is fast, but the risk of potentially losing an element when the receiving program has a logical or runtime error must be considered when you design a system.

Chapter 11 presented two powerful tools — journaling and commitment control — that can be used to protect or recover data from a data file. *Neither* of these tools applies to a data queue. Therefore, if a program, even one under commitment control, accesses an element in a data queue and subsequently aborts, that element is lost.

Data queues grow over time. Every element added takes space in the data queue. Receiving an element from a data queue removes the element, but does not reclaim the space. For example, if, over time, a data queue of 100-byte elements has been sent 50,000 elements, it occupies 5,000,000 bytes. Even if all elements have been received by the time the next element is sent to the data queue, the data queue will be enlarged to 5,000,100 bytes. To reset the queue's size, you must periodically delete and re-create the queue.

Using Data Queues

You can use data queues through a combination of CL commands and calls to IBM-supplied programs. This section introduces those commands and calls and demonstrates how to use them in RPG programs.

CRTDTAQ — The CRTDTAQ (Create Data Queue) command shown in Figure 12.4 is used to create a data queue. The data queue is an object and therefore has an object name and a library in which it is stored. The queue can be a standard queue (on the local AS/400) or a distributed data management queue (on a remote AS/400). Each element of the queue can be from 1 to 64,512 characters long. Each entry in the queue can be stored to disk before processing continues. Although this reduces the chance of lost data if the system crashes, it slows the performance of the data queue.

Figure 12.4
CRTDTAQ with
Additional
Parameters (F10)
and Keyed
Information

```
                            Create Data Queue (CRTDTAQ)

 Type choices, press Enter.

 Data queue . . . . . . . . . . . . . . . . . . _____   Name
   Library . . . . . . . . . . . . . . .   *CURLIB___   Name, *CURLIB
 TYPE . . . . . . . . . . . . . . . . .   *STD         *STD, *DDM
 Maximum entry length . . . . . . . . .   _____ 1-64512
 Force to auxiliary storage . . . . . .   *No_         *NO, *YES
 Sequence . . . . . . . . . . . . . . .   *KEYED       *FIFO, *LIFO, *KEYED
 Key Length . . . . . . . . . . . . . .   _____        1-256
 Include sender ID . . . . . . . . . .   *NO_         *NO, *YES
 Text 'description'. . . . . . . . . .   *BLANK_____

                            Additional Parameters

 Authority . . . . . . . . . . . . . .   *LIBCRTAUT    NAME, *LIBCRTAUT, *CHANGE...
```

When you create a data queue, you must select the sequence that defines the order of retrieval of elements. Elements can be retrieved in first-in-first-out (FIFO) order, last-in-first-out (LIFO) order, or an order based on a key value.

A keyed data queue could contain data elements sent to the queue for a number of different programs. When each of those programs attempts to retrieve elements from the queue, the program would send the queue a key value and would receive only records that match that value.

Data is sent to the data queue by the IBM-supplied program QSNDDTAQ (Send to Data Queue). Because QSNDDTAQ is a program, it is called, and four required parameters must be passed to it:

- QNAME — The name of the queue.
- QLIB — The library containing the data queue or *LIBL or *CURLIB.
- FieldLen — The length of field that contains the value to send, which cannot exceed the data queue's element length. This field must be a packed-decimal field 5 digits wide with zero decimals.
- Field — The field that contains the value to send.

If you are using a keyed data queue, two additional parameters are required:

- Keylength — The length of the Keyvalue field, which cannot exceed the data queue's key field length. The field must be a packed-decimal field of 3 digits with zero decimals.
- Keyvalue — The actual key value.

Figure 12.5 shows a section of an RPG program that sends an element to the data queue DATQ1 in the job's library list (*LIBL). The value sent to the queue is stored in the variable SNDTOQ, and it is the value of the variable or data structure INVNUM. The value is 20 characters long.

```
*...1....+....2....+....3....+....4....+....5....+....6

C                    MOVEL'DATQ1'   QNAME  10
C                    MOVEL'*LIBL'   QLIB   10
C                    MOVELINVNUM    SNDTOQ 20        actual value
C                    Z-ADD20        FLEN    50        len of value
 *
C                    CALL 'QSNDDTAQ'
C                    PARM           QNAME
C                    PARM           QLIB
C                    PARM           FLEN
C                    PARM           SNDTOQ
```

Figure 12.5

RPG Call to QSNDDTAQ Without Key

Like Figure 12.5, Figure 12.6 sends an element to a data queue. Because queue DATAQ2 is keyed, two additional values are passed to program QSNDDTAQ. The key length is 5 characters and the key value is TYPE1. Later, to retrieve this element, the retrieval program will have to pass the same key value to the program to retrieve elements from the queue.

```
*...1....+....2....+....3....+....4....+....5....+....6

C                    MOVEL'DATQ2'   QNAME  10
C                    MOVEL'*LIBL'   QLIB   10
C                    MOVELINVNUM    SNDTOQ 20        actual value
C                    Z-ADD20        FLEN    50        len of value
C                    MOVEL'TYPE1'   KEYVAL  5
C                    Z-ADD5         KLEN    30
 *
C                    CALL 'QSNDDTAQ'
C                    PARM           QNAME
C                    PARM           QLIB
C                    PARM           FLEN
C                    PARM           SNDTOQ
 *
C                    PARM           KLEN
C                    PARM           KEYVAL
```

Figure 12.6

RPG Call to QSNDDTAQ with Key

Receiving data from the data queue is done with an IBM-supplied program called QRCVDTAQ, which requires the following five parameters:

- QNAME — The name of the data queue.
- QLIB — The library containing the data queue or *LIBL or *CURLIB.

- FieldLen — The length of the field that receives the value. This length cannot exceed the length of the data queue as defined in the CRTDTAQ command. This field must be packed decimal with a width of 5 digits and zero decimals.
- Field — The field to receive the value.
- Wait — The number of seconds to wait to receive an entry from the data queue. This field must be packed decimal, 5 digits wide, with zero decimals. The value of the Wait parameter controls how long the program waits for a data element to be returned from the data queue. (Caution: If the value of the Wait parameter is a negative number, the program will wait forever.)

  If the value of the wait parameter is zero, the program will not wait. If no entry is available to be received, QRCVDTAQ will set the field length value to zero. Your program can tell that no elements were available to be received by checking the returning value of the field length.

  If the wait parameter value is greater than zero, it represents the number of seconds that program can wait for element to be received. (Maximum value is 99999, which is about 28 hours).

These additional parameters are required if the data queue is keyed:

- KeyRule — 2-byte character. Values are 'GT', 'LT', 'NE', 'EQ', 'GE', 'LE'. This is the test used to determine whether an element should be received. In the example, 'GT' would cause QRCVDTAQ to return the next element with a key value greater than the Request Key Value.
- RequestKeyLength — Length of Request key value field, which cannot exceed the length of the data queue's key field. This value must be a packed decimal with 3 digits and zero decimal positions.
- RequestKeyValue — Value used to test elements to determine whether they qualify for receipt; for example, if KeyRule is 'GT' and RequestKeyValue is 'AB', the next element with a KeyValue greater than 'AB' will be received.

If the parameters for the key are included, then the next two parameters must also be included — although they will be meaningless if you did not specify Include Sender ID in the CRTDTAQ command:

- SenderLength — Length of the field to receive sender data. It must be a packed-decimal field 3 digits wide with zero decimal positions. It can have a value of zero (no data will be returned) or a value from 8 to 44.
- Sender — The name of a character field to receive element sender data. If the SenderLength is not zero, then the sender data will contain at least the first two fields defined below. The actual amount of data received to Sender is determined by the value of SenderLength.
- 4 bytes — The length of returned data (packed decimal, 7 digits, zero decimal positions).
- 4 bytes — The length of all sender data available (packed decimal, 7 digits, zero decimal positions).
- 26 bytes — Character field with job name, user, job number.
- 10 bytes — Character field with name of sender's user profile.

Figure 12.7 shows the RPG code to receive from a data queue without key or sender information.

```
*...1....+....2....+....3....+....4....+....5....+....6
C                    MOVEL'DATQ1'    QNAME      10
C                    MOVEL'*LIBL'    QLIB       10
C                    Z-ADD20         FLEN       50           len of value
 * negative wait value = wait for ever
 * zero wait value = do not wait but set FLEN to Zero if no element
 * positive number = wait that many seconds (up to 99999)
C                    Z-ADD-5         WAITQ      50           len of wait
 *
C                    CALL 'QRCVDTAQ'
C                    PARM            QNAME
C                    PARM            QLIB
C                    PARM            FLEN
C                    PARM            RCVFQ      20
C                    PARM            WAITQ
 *
C          FLEN      IFGT *ZERO
C                    MOVELRCVFQ      INVNUM     20           actual value
C                    ELSE
C                    EXSR NOELEM
C                    ENDIF
```

Figure 12.7
RPG Call to
QRCVDTAQ
without Key

Figure 12.8 is an example of the code that retrieves entries with the key 'TYPE1' from the data queue. The sender information is captured in SNDVAL, and the structure SNDR provides sender job name, sender user, and sender job number.

```
*...1....+....2....+....3....+....4....+....5....+....6
I          DS
I                                    1  44 SDRVAL
I                                 P  1  40LENRTV
I                                 P  5   80LENAVL
I                                    9  18 SJOBNM
I                                   19  28 SUSER
I                                   29  34 SJOBNM
I                                   35  44 SUSRPF
C                    MOVEL'DATQ2'    QNAME      10
C                    MOVEL'*LIBL'    QLIB       10
C                    MOVEL'TYPE1'    KEYVA       5
C                    Z-ADD5          KLEN       30
 *
C                    Z-ADD20         FLEN       50           len of value
C                    Z-ADD44         SDRLEN     30
 * negative wait value = wait for ever
 * zero wait value = do not wait but set FLEN to Zero if no element
 * positive number = wait that many seconds (up to 99999)
C                    Z-ADD-5         WAITQ      50           len of wait
 *
C                    CALL 'QRCVDTAQ'
C                    PARM            QNAME
C                    PARM            QLIB
C                    PARM            FLEN
C                    PARM            RCVFQ      20
C                    PARM            WAITQ
C                    PARM            KLEN
C                    PARM            KEYVAL
C                    PARM            SDRLEN
C                    PARM            SDRVAL
 *
C          FLEN      IFGT *ZERO
C                    MOVELRCVFQ      INVNUM 20               actual value
C                    ELSE
C                    EXSR NOELEM
C                    ENDIF
```

Figure 12.8
RPG Call to
QRCVDTAQ with
Key and Sender
Information

Program QCLRDTAQ clears the data queue. But remember: it doesn't reclaim the space. To reclaim the space, you will have to delete the data queue and re-create it. When QCLRDTAQ is called, it must be passed the Queue Name and Library Name (or *LIBL or *CURLIB).

The command DLTDTAQ (Delete Data Queue) deletes the data queue.

Exercise 12.1 Data Queue Exercise Without Key

Purpose
To develop a further understanding of passing values using data queues.

Instructions
Create data queue DQ1, send elements to the data queue, and retrieve elements from the data queue.

1. Create a data queue named DQ1, which is 60 bytes wide, unkeyed, and FIFO.

2. Copy and modify one of your interactive programs that updates the inventory file. Modify the program so that every time it adds a record to the file, it will send a copy of that record to the data queue. You cannot actually send a record to the data queue (only a field or data structure). Therefore, you will need to create a structure that is identical to your file structure. The easiest way to create a data structure identical to an externally defined file is to use an externally defined data structure. This is done via an I-spec for an externally defined data structure, as shown in Figure 12.9. This entry can be made in Source Entry Utility (SEU) with the prompt IPDS (Input with Prompt Data Structure). This structure, called SNDVAR in Figure 12.9, uses the external structure defined in file INVPF. If your program moves this data structure to a field of the correct length, your program can then pass that field to the program to send to the data queue.

Figure 12.9
Defining an Externally Defined Data Structure Identical to the Record Structure of File INVPF

```
*...1....+....2....+....3....+....4....+....5....+....6

ISNDVAR    E DSINVPF
```

3. Use your program to add records to the file. Each time you add a record, your program should send copies of each record to the data queue.

4. Write a second program to receive each value from the data queue and print out each entry. This program will read each entry from the data queue. Transfer the entry to a data structure as defined in Figure 12.9 and print the field data. The request to receive from the data queue will have a zero wait condition. When there are no more entries, the program will end. Remember, every time that you run this program, it will remove all entries from the data queue. If you want to run this program again, you will have to run the maintenance program that you created in step 2 to send new entries to the data queue.

Exercise 12.2 Data Queue Exercise with Key

Purpose

To develop a further understanding of passing values using data queues with keys.

Instructions

Create data queue DQ2, send elements to the data queue, and retrieve elements from the data queue.

1. Create a new data queue, DQ2, which includes a 1-byte key and sender information.
2. Copy and modify the program created in Exercise 12.1, step 2, to send records to DQ2 whenever a record is added, deleted, or changed. When a record is sent to the queue, the action taken should be keyed with A, D, or C.
3. Run your program and add, delete, and change inventory data.
4. Copy and modify your program from Exercise 12.1, step 4, so that it will loop three times. The first loop will receive entries keyed with a 'D' and write a report of all deleted records. The second will write a report of all added records. The third will write a report of all changed records.
5. Copy and modify your program from step 4. Change it to a single loop that retrieves only added entries. Change the wait value to a negative number, which will make it wait forever. Do not run the program until you read step 6.
6. Do not call the program that you created in step 5. Because it will run forever, it will lock up your terminal session. Instead, submit the Receiver program to run in batch with the SBMJOB (Submit Job) command.

    SBMJOB CMD(CALL yourpgmnm) JOB(YourLastName)

    Check to make sure that the job is running using the command

    DSPJOB YourLastName

7. Now add about 75 records to the inventory file using your modified inventory maintence program from step 2.
8. Check on your program with the DSPJOB option. It should still be active. Check option 14, Display Open Files, and select the option to display I/O details (either F10 or F11). Note how many records have been written to your output file. Press Enter and select option 4, Work with Spool Files. If your program is on the second page, you will be able to view the first page. If not, go back and add more inventory items and try again.
9. To end the job, issue the command

    WRKSBMJOB

    Move to your batch job and end it by pressing 4 (F4) *IMMED. Make sure that it ends. (You may have to press F5 to refresh the screen to make sure that the job has ended.)

Review

1. Describe how you could make synchronous processing occur between two programs using two data queues.
2. Describe how you could make synchronous processing occur between two programs using a single keyed data queue.
3. Describe the dangers of using data queues. In what ways are data files safer?
4. How can you "impose" a structure on a single element of a data queue?
5. Why might a daily job start by deleting a data queue and then re-creating it?

Appendix A

A Matter of Style

Standards and Style

An organization's IS department establishes its own standards. When you join a programming team, they will give you a copy of a standards document. That document will probably

- Identify test and production libraries
- Describe program- and object-naming conventions

It may also identify

- Standard subroutines
- Variable naming conventions
- Commands to use or avoid
- General programming methodology
- Standard program headers

You will want to study the standards and use them.

But beyond these standards, much about how your programs work is your decision. Where standards end, style takes over. Each individual must develop his or her own style. Style doesn't necessarily make a program better, but it can clearly make your work appear and be more professional. This appendix contains my opinions on some key matters of style, developed over years of working with many organizations.

Every program that you design, develop, or maintain reflects your skill and methodology. If you're in a rush or sloppy, those qualities will be reflected in your code — its appearance, performance, and maintainability. You should be proud of every line that you code and of the mark that your style leaves on every program.

Three areas where style can make a difference are program headings, subroutines, and program modifications.

Program Headings

Programs, data files, and other objects should be clearly identified with an introductory or heading section. This heading section comprises comments that could contain some or all of the following:

- Who wrote the program and when
- Why it was written
- What it does
- A short narrative that describes the program
- Pseudocode for the program
- A list of all files and how they are used
- A list of all variable names and how they are used
- A list of all indicators and how they are used

- A list of all modifications to the program, with the following information for each:
  - Who made a modification
  - When a modification was made
  - Why a modification was made
  - What was modified
  - The modification "mark" (if used) that identifies modified lines

That's a lot of information to include in every program. You will want to save time and keep the headings of all programs similar by laying out a heading once and then copying it into every program. An example of a program heading is shown in Figure A.1. Similar headings should be used for CL programs, physical and logical files, and any other source developed. The cost of these extra lines is that the compiler runs for an extra few fractions of a second and the source code takes a little more space on disk. The compiler does not transfer any of the comments to the object code, so the actual program is not affected by the number of comments included in the source code.

Figure A.1
Sample RPG Program
Heading

```
**************************************************************************
*      Jefferson College
*      PROGRAMMER:          - Professor Levinson
*      DATE:                - 12/15/97
*      APPLICATION NAME:    - Inventory System
*      PROGRAM NAME:        - INVR01
*
*  DESCRIPTION  - 1. Clears Subfile  2. Loads Subfile  3. Displays Footer
*                 4. Exercises the Screen Display with the Subfile
**************************************************************************
*  L O G   O F   M O D I F I C A T I O N S
*
*  DATE          PGMR         DESCRIPTION
*  ----------------------------------------------------------------------
*  /  /
**************************************************************************
*  F U N C T I O N   O F   I N D I C A T O R S
*  IND            FUNCTION
*  ----------------------------------------------------------------------
*  03             USED TO EXIT DISPLAY
*  50             USED TO DISPLAY/CLEAR SUBFILE
*  90             EOF FLAG FOR INVPF
*  LR             SET ON LAST RECORD
**************************************************************************
*  S U B R O U T I N E   I N D E X
**************************************************************************
*  INIT       - INITIALIZATION
*  LOAD       - CLEAR AND ACTIVATE SUBFILE DSP01
*  DISP       - DISPLAY SUBFILE
**************************************************************************
```

The header section becomes especially valuable when the program needs to be maintained. For example, the code may be very complex, and the pseudocode is crucial because it gives a clear picture of how the parts of the program fit together. The most recent modifications may point to the cause of the newest bug.

Subroutines

The basic organization of a program into subroutines may be specified by your company's standards. However, you will probably have some discretion about creating additional subroutines. Opinions vary about the number of subroutines that should be used in RPG/400 programs. Here are three opinions with rationales:

- None — RPG runs best with straight-line code. Every call to a subroutine wastes processing time.
- Few — RPG runs best with straight-line code. Every call to a subroutine wastes processing time.
- However many the program needs — Create one subroutine for each repeated task.

And the right answer is — one for each identifiable, repeated task. At least that's my opinion. Code that is easy to write, debug, understand, and modify will generally save more in programmer costs than will be saved in other ways by designing faster programs. Subroutines are the result of good modular design. Good code should, in fact, contain many short subroutines — because, as a rule of thumb, a subroutine should not be longer than 20 lines. If you cannot see an entire subroutine on the screen, you may overlook some important feature when you do the initial coding and debugging, when you perform program maintenance, or when you modify the program. Subroutines should always place the next level of nesting in a subordinate, or "child," subroutine.

Create as many subroutines as are necessary so that no subroutine contains nested code. Instead, subroutines should always place the next level of nesting in subordinate subroutines. With this methodology, each subroutine will do a clear and simple task.

I use modular design techniques and coding, which make more sense today than ever before. Modular design reduces time spent designing, coding, testing, and debugging. When you use modular design techniques, you create subroutines that are likely to be reusable in future programs. And with these techniques, you prepare your code to take advantage of the move to RPG IV. In particular, RPG IV lets your program efficiently call other programs and procedures. In RPG/400, the same task may be coded into hundreds of programs or included in a copy book that must be copied into hundreds of programs. In RPG IV, only one copy of the code to perform a task is necessary; it can be called from all other RPG programs.

The exact number of subroutines is dependent on the number of clear tasks or modules. However, anytime a module becomes complicated, it makes sense to divide its tasks further.

> **Note:** Complicated code, including code with multiple levels of nesting, is difficult to read and comprehend. Such code will, therefore, be hard to debug, maintain, and modify. Therefore, anytime a module becomes complicated, it makes sense to divide its tasks further, moving nested code into subroutines that are called by the controlling or "parent" subroutine.

Subroutine Sequence

Subroutine sequencing may be specified in your organization's standards. If it is not, it becomes a matter of style. Among the options for ordering your subroutine are

- using the sequence in which the subroutines are processed
- placing the subroutines that are used the most at the beginning and those used the least at the end of the source code (This puts the initialization, end of job, and error handling at the end of a program.)
- putting the subroutines in order by relationship
- putting the subroutines in alphabetical order

The performance impact of subroutine order is usually too small to measure. And by using the "find" capability in the editor, it is always easy to find a subroutine — wherever it's located. However, when I'm coding, I attempt to place subroutines in the sequence in which they are processed. The reason is this: if Subroutine A, which is located near the beginning of a large program, calls Subroutine B, which is located near the end of the program, system performance can be affected. The system might have to swap the page containing Subroutine B into memory and, when Subroutine B ends, swap the page containing Subroutine A back into memory if it has been swapped out. Swapping does slow a program and — if it occurs frequently — lead to a measurable drop in performance. If the two subroutines were in the same logical page, swapping would not occur. And in theory, the chances that the two would be in the same page are greater if they are near each other in the source code.

Subroutine Headings

Subroutines should be clearly identified with a subroutine heading that is easily visible when you read the subroutine on the screen or in printed form. It should contain the name of the subroutine (and because the subroutine name is only six characters long, the heading should also include a meaningful name). Some standards require that the subroutine heading include

- the pseudocode for the subroutine
- the subroutines that call this subroutine
- the subroutines called by this subroutine

Figure A.2 presents a sample subroutine heading. The source shown includes a /EJECT, a compiler directive to start a new page in the listing at that point. The use of /EJECT before each subroutine creates compiler listings that are easy to read.

```
*...1....+....2....+....3....+....4....+....5....+....6
/EJECT
 *
 ******************************************************************
 *   LOAD - LOADS 8 RECORDS INTO THE INVENTORY SUBFILE INVSF1
 *          FROM THE DATAFILE INVPF
 *
 *          CALLED BY: MAINLINE, RESPND
 *          CALLS:     NONE
 *
 ******************************************************************
 *
C           LOAD      BEGSR
 *
```

Figure A.2
Sample Subroutine
Heading

Modifications

Programs are modified for many reasons:

- to debug them
- to respond to specification changes
- to respond to system changes

Whenever a program is changed, the change should be recorded. The program heading should indicate who made the change, when, why, and what the change is. Although modification notes are often short, they can be invaluable in hunting down problems or when subsequent changes are needed.

Many organizations use modification marks (mod marks) to record the exact changes that are made. In this system, lines are not deleted or changed but rather converted to comments by adding an * in column 7. In the case of an addition or change, a new line is then inserted. The modified lines are "marked" in columns 2 through 6 with the mod mark beginning with the letter D for the deleted line or A for the added line. An example of a program modification is shown in Figure A.3. In this example, you can see that mod mark 101 replaced the addition with a division.

```
     *...1....+....2....+....3....+....4....+....5....+....6

     ************************************************************
     *   DEMONSTRATION ROUTINE
     *   SHOWS HOW MOD MARKS CAN BE USED
     ************************************************************
     *
     C           DEMO      BEGSR
     *
D101 C*          FLD1      ADD  FLD2      RSLTFD
A101 C           FLD1      DIV  FLD2      RSLTFD
     C                     ENDSR
```

Figure A.3
Code with Modification
Mark 101

In Figure A.4, you see that the division was replaced by multiplication, using the mod mark 102. Unfortunately, when a second modification occurs to the same line, the mod mark will tell the number of the last change but mask the origin of the line. In this case, it would be impossible to tell that the division was added in modification 101.

Figure A.4
Code with Modification
Mark 102

```
*...1....+....2....+....3....+....4....+....5....+....6

****************************************************************
*    DEMONSTRATION ROUTINE
*    SHOWS HOW MOD MARKS CAN BE USED
****************************************************************
*
C           DEMO      BEGSR
*
D101 C*          FLD1      ADD  FLD2     RSLTFD
D102 C*          FLD1      DIV  FLD2     RSLTFD
A102 C*          FLD1      MULT FLD2     RSLTFD
C                     ENDSR
```

Depending on the organization's standards, the modification number may be a number assigned to the request for program modification, a project number, or a number kept in a file that contains a record of all modifications.

As was stated at the beginning of this appendix, where standards end, style takes over. Style alone can't correct an incorrect program, but it may make it easier to find and fix an error. Style can't make a bad design better, but it may make its flaws obvious sooner. Style is worth "points" when it takes you beyond the minimal standards. Other programmers will see that you know clear and well-documented code is a pleasure to work on.

Appendix B

Testing and Debugging Programs

Testing and debugging programs is an essential element of programming. This appendix covers

- fast code vs. good code
- syntax, runtime, and logic errors
- resolving errors (finding the right suspects)
- debugging techniques: temporary print output lines, the DISPLAY operation, the DUMP operation, ISDB, the function keys, advanced breakpoint control, pull-down menus, and indented listings

Testing and Debugging: Part of the Job!

The old joke runs something like this: As the plane took off, a voice came over the intercom, announcing, "This airplane is totally computerized. Nothing can go wrong … go wrong … go wrong …"

In fact, things do go wrong. Your job, your challenge, and I hope your entertainment will be in testing to prevent errors and when they do occur, finding what's gone wrong and making it right. This appendix is devoted to helping you do that.

Fast Code vs. Good Code: The Importance of Testing

You probably would like to be a great programmer and to get the job rewards for being one — the raises and promotions you deserve. Although many programmers share these goals, there are differences in the way they try to achieve them. Some become "hackers" who turn out "fast and dirty" code that is often error prone and hard to maintain. They take pride in speed and cleverness. Other programmers produce fewer lines of code per day but also fewer errors. Their code is usually cleaner and easier to maintain — often because they take time to test their programs extensively.

There are times when speed is everything — usually in maintenance programming, when an essential production program is down and is needed immediately. However, I would prefer to manage a team of careful rather than fast programmers.

Careful programmers design extensive tests for any program, even a program to which they are making only minor changes. Testing procedures must run a program through all of its paces. The testing must work the program functions in all possible sequences. These tests are necessary to find instances in which one function may cause another function to perform improperly. A batch program can be run through a range of functions by providing it with enough variations in the data to exercise all functions of the program. Then, by providing the data records in all possible sequences, the effect of sequence can also be detected. Interactive programs generally require extensive testing using all the functions and variations of activities available to the user. In the modified program, this testing checks for unexpected "side-effects" of the changes. A program must run properly through these tests and produce the correct results every time. The tester must determine what the correct results should be and check each carefully. If an additional modification to a program results from the testing, the entire testing regimen should be repeated.

Many large IS shops have a quality control department that tests all code. Your goal is to become so dependable that the quality control department considers your code exemplary.

If the organization doesn't have an IS quality control department, users become the final step in quality control. If your users become frustrated by program errors, your organization will be impaired — and eventually your career may be in jeopardy.

Syntax, Logic, and Runtime Errors

There are three basic types of errors:

Syntax errors — Syntax errors are grammar errors — errors in your use of the programming language. They are easy to detect because the compiler finds them for you. Fix them, and your program will compile and, assuming there are no other errors, will be nearly perfect.

Logic errors — Logic errors are errors in program design. Because they are the hardest kind of error to detect, they are usually the hardest to correct. Logic errors do not create compiler errors nor do they cause the program to end abnormally (abend). On some or all conditions, logic errors simply produce the wrong results. The occurrence of an extremely unlikely situation or event could cause the wrong result. For example, when the first 10.0 was awarded in an Olympic gymnastics, the board showed 0.0. Because the score had not been anticipated, the scoreboard hardware and software had not been designed and tested to show it.

To detect logic errors, you must test every program extensively. The tests must give the program a thorough "workout" with a complete range of data and conditions. As a programmer, you will be expected to design, carry out, and evaluate tests. And keep in mind that programs do not pass tests with a C — any performance short of perfect is failure.

Runtime errors — Runtime errors are actually a kind of logic error that prevents your program from completing normally. Runtime errors occur when your program compiles and runs but at some point aborts. Whether the program aborts once in a thousand or once in a million records, the error is unacceptable. The program may abort for many reasons. It may have tried to divide a number by zero, access an array out of range, write a subfile with no records, or read a record that was locked. Fortunately, when a program aborts, a great deal of information is available to help you discover the error so you can correct it.

Among the tools that can help you analyze a runtime error are the job log, the error display, and the program dump.

- **Job log** — Job logs are saved as spooled files if the job ended abnormally and had a level of message logging greater than 0. Job logs will also be saved as a spooled file if the job ends normally, has a job level of message logging greater than 0, and the message logging text is not equal to *NOTEXT. All jobs that are active have job logs.

  If a program runs interactively, then messages from that process are included in the user's current job log. While the user is still logged on, these messages can be investigated by first finding the job with the command WRKUSRJOB (Work with User Job). If there are multiple jobs, the correct job must then be selected. You then use option 10, Display Job Log, to display the current job log. The most recent command or message is displayed. To see earlier commands or messages, press the F10 key and then press the Page up key. To see more information about any message or command in an active job log, point to the message or command and press F1. You can also reach the work with job menu if you know the job's name, using the WRKJOB command. If the job has the logging of CL commands value set to *YES, then the job log will contain all of the CL commands issued as well as the messages that were logged.

- **Error messages** — Depending on the message type, severity, and your job description, the system will convey error messages differently. It may display them, for example, on your screen or even interrupt your processing with a message screen requiring a response. In these cases, you can learn more about the message by pointing to it and pressing F1. In other cases, the messages will be sent to your session's message queue, with the command DSPMSG (Display Message). Finally, the message may be sent to the system operator (message queue QSYSOPR), and you can display these messages with the command DSPMSG QSYSOPR. If an error has occurred, the system will have sent a message somewhere, and you may learn what went wrong when you find the message. Remember, these messages were probably logged onto a job log.

- **Dump** — The error message may let you respond with a D to request a dump, a spooled file that you can view or print. The RPG- or CL-formatted dump contains a detailed picture of what the program was doing at the time of the error, the error message itself, and the values of every variable in the system. (Later, we will discuss how to get dumps of programs even when the system doesn't invite you to do so.)

Resolving Errors: The Right Suspects

Resolving runtime and logic errors is a little like solving a murder mystery. You can see the final results of the program: the reports, database changes, and screen displays. From these results and a knowledge of the program, you must deduce possible causes of the outcomes that occurred. The sequence of events by which you should collect and analyze errors is outlined in the three steps below.

1. You should perform runtime program tests during development, modification, and whenever you suspect a runtime error. During these tests, you should keep a log of the data or screen interactions and the results. Obviously, the conditions that lead to errors are of special interest, but the conditions under which the program performs correctly are also important.

    As an example, if the payroll program produces the wrong values for gross pay for hourly employees who work overtime but the correct gross pay for all other employees, then we would suspect that the problem is in the code that detects and computes gross pay for hourly employees working overtime. We could focus our attention first on that area of the code.

    Some of the errors that you detect may be the result of other errors. In the previous example, one would assume that an error in gross pay would result in subsequent errors in withholding and net pay. This does not, however, mean that the error causing the the wrong value for gross pay is the only error affecting the values of the withholding and net pay. When multiple errors are affecting the results, you may have to fix the most obvious, retest, reanalyze, fix the next error, and repeat the process until the results are correct.

2. For each error, identify the conditions under which it occurs. The conditions can be determined from the data processed that led to the error or the user interaction that led to the error. Detecting the conditions may require the use of display operations, program dumps, or a debugger (all discussed later in this appendix). Here is a list of typical key factors that you will need to analyze the error. However, in a specific situation, you will have to determine the best list of factors based on your program and the errors that occur.

- Does the error occur for every detailed record?
- Does the error occur only for records with a specific value or code?
- Does the error occur for every summary field at a specific level break?

3. Go back to your design armed with this list. Where did the records that failed fail? What conditions or what inherent qualities make the records that passed different from those that failed? All the places, actions, and differences in records are suspects.

If you pick the right suspect, you can now find the piece of code in which you think the error occurs. You now know what should be happening at that point. Do a walk-through of the code. A walk-through is a mental exercise in which you trace the program steps that will be executed and the values that will be computed or changed within the entire program or a specific part that is of immediate interest. Take a record that fails, and write down what happens at each step within the suspect segment of code. Keep a record of the values of each variable as each statement is processed. When you analyze IF statements, it is necessary to determine what code is actually executed and follow the effects of that code on the variables and on subsequent processing. Pretend that you are the data going through the program maze. Where do you go, and what happens to you along the way?

If you find the problem, fix it and test again.

If your analysis doesn't locate the problem, then you will need to use more sophisticated debugging tools that will help you determine the sequence of operations that is actually performed by the program and the values of variables as the program executes. These tools are described in the remainder of this appendix. They will provide results that can be compared with the sequence and variable values that you predicted as you did your walk-through of the code. Where the tools show that something happened that you didn't predict, you will need to return to the code and determine why the sequence or values aren't what you expected and whether the different sequence or values are, in fact, causing the error.

Using Temporary Print Output Lines

The simplest technique that is available, a technique that can be used with virtually every programming language, is to add temporary code to print intermediate results. You add WRITE (Write) or EXFMT (Execute Format) operations at critical locations in the program — points at which you've determined you should test to verify the values that you predicted manually would be warranted. In RPG, it's also necessary to add the appropriate O-specs for the EXFMT operations or the appropriate O-specs in the print file for the WRITE operations. The critical points at which these temporary operations are added are chosen to determine both values of critical variables and the sequence of statements actually performed when the program is processing a record or interaction that produces the wrong results. The output of these temporary print operations should indicate the route that the program takes by printing the subroutine name or the sequence number of the output operations. Figures B.1 and B.2 show how these temporary operations can be added. Figure B.1 contains some suspect code, and Figure B.2 shows the additional operations and the O-specs that would be added to report the variable values and the statement number, which can be used to trace the processing sequence.

```
        *...1....+....2....+....3....+....4....+....5....+....6
0003.00    C        FLD1    MULT FLD2    FLD3
0004.00    C        FLD1    ADD  FLD3    FLD4
```

Figure B.1
Suspect Code

If the values of intermediate variables are important to debugging the program, locate temporary output operations in the locations where the values of these variables are critical to the final results and print the variables along with the subroutine name or sequence number, as shown in the shaded lines of Figure B.2.

```
          *...1....+....2....+....3....+....4....+....5....+....6
0003.00      C          FLD1    MULT FLD2    FLD3
0004.00      C          FLD1    ADD  FLD3    FLD4
0004.01 TEMP C                  MOVE '000401'  SEQNO    4
0004.02 TEMP C                  EXFMTTEMP1

0150.01 O    E   1              TEMP1
0150.02 O                       SEQNO        15
0150.03 O                       FLD1         25
0150.03 O                       FLD2         35
0150.03 O                       FLD3         45
0150.03 O                       FLD4         55
```

Figure B.2
Suspect Code with
Temporary Output

When you are working with large data sets, this debugging technique is better than most others because you can run the program and then analyze the data at your leisure, comparing the intermediate results produced when records that lead to errors are processed and records that lead to the correct values are processed.

Using the DSPLY (Display) Operation

Another tool you can use to debug either interactive or interactively called jobs is the DSPLY operation, which can display a character variable or constant value. Batch jobs are submitted with the CL command SBMJOB (Submit Job) and cannot be debugged with this tool. The DSPLY operation can be used to debug code in a way similar to adding temporary print operations. As shown in Figure B.3, DSPLY operations are added temporarily to assist with debugging. The DSPLY operation uses Factor 1 for either a constant, such as the statement number '000401', or a variable name. When the program reaches a DSPLY operation, it displays the value and waits for the variable identified in the display operation, waits until the user presses the Enter key, and then continues processing. The DSPLY operation is good for tracing the flow of a program, as well as for tracing the intermediate results created during processing.

Figure B.3

Suspect Code with
DSPLY Operations

```
            *...1....+....2....+....3....+....4....+....5....+....6
0003.00        C              FLD1     MULT FLD2      FLD3
0004.00        C              FLD1     ADD  FLD3      FLD4
0004.01 TEMP   C              '000401' DSPLY
0004.02 TEMP   C              FLD1     DSPLY
0004.03 TEMP   C              FLD2     DSPLY
0004.04 TEMP   C              FLD3     DSPLY
0004.05 TEMP   C              FLD4     DSPLY
```

DSPLY is a quick and easy-to-use debugging tool. Every time the program encounters a DSPLY operation, it stops and displays the value. This tool is best suited to displaying a few data elements for a few records; it becomes cumbersome and slow for large data sets.

Using the DUMP Operation

If you want to know *everything* about a program at one point or at a few points during program execution, use the DUMP operation. The DUMP operation offers abundant information, including the values of every variable, the last processes performed on every file, and the outcome of those operations. Nothing matches a dump for its useful wealth of data; just as with murder mysteries, among the many, the guilty party may be the one least suspected.

To trigger a dump, add a C-spec with the DUMP operation at the point at which you want the dump to occur. To use the DUMP operation, your program must begin with an H-spec that has a 1 in the DEBUG field. Caution: if you put the DUMP in a section of the code that is exercised repeatedly, you get a dump every time the command is executed.

Using the Interactive Source Debugger (ISDB)

The AS/400 provides more advanced tools for debugging programs. On Versions 2 and 3 of OS/400, the DEBUG tool provided line-oriented debugging that is started with the STRDBG (Start Debug) command. This useful tool, described in many textbooks, will not be described here. In Version 3 of OS/400, IBM added the Interactive Source Debugger (ISDB). This debugger is great for RPG/400, COBOL/400, and CL code; however, it does not work with the ILE versions of the compilers. (The ILE versions are supported via a debugger similar to ISDB, which is started like the earlier debugger — with the STRDBG command.)

Debugging Source Code

The following sections of this appendix introduce you to the details of operating the source debugger. The source debugger is started by issuing the command STRISDB (Start Interactive Source Debugger) from a command line. Additional parameters can be issued as part of the call or by typing STRISDB and pressing F4.

```
STRISDB  ProgramName
STRISDB  INV017A      or      STRISDB  MYLIB/INV017A
```

The command STRSDB has a number of options that can be selected by typing STRSDB and pressing F4. The options are described in the next few lines.

- UPDPROD(*YES) (Update Production — Yes) — The program will run, provided it does not need to update any files in libraries of type *PROD.

- UPDPROD(*NO) (Update Production — No) — The program will update files in libraries of type *TEST, and it will simulate updating files in libraries of type *PROD.
- INVPGM(*YES) (Invoke Program — Yes) — There are three values for Invoke Program, but you will always want the *YES value.
- PARM (Parameters) — If the program would normally be called and passed parameters, you can fill in one parameter per line.

All of the following are valid calls to the debugger:

```
STRISDB INV017A
STRISDB INV017A UPDPROD(*YES)
STRISDB INV017X INVPGM(*YES) PARM(CUST)
STRISDB INV017X INVPGM(*CMD) CMD(CALL INV017X     +
         PARM('CUST' 351.12))
```

ISDB HELP is available by pointing to a desired item and pressing F1 or selecting the Help option from the menu bar.

To end an ISDB session, press F3 and then select the option to quit ISDB from the dialog window that pops up.

If your program ends and you are still in the session, you can restart your program with the RESTART command.

Using Function Keys

The ISDB function keys, summarized in Table B.1, offer a wealth of tools.

Table B.1
ISDB Function Key Definitions

Key	Description	Use
F1	Help	Displays Help about the item to which the cursor is pointing.
F3	Exit	Exits ISDN.
F4	Cur Line	Goes to currently executing line.
F5	STEP	Executes one line at a time.
F6	Add/Remove Break Points	Program runs (F17) until it encounters a break point. The debugger does not recognize comment lines because they don't exist in the compiled code; therefore, break points can be set only on active lines.
F7	Page up	Pages up.
F8	Page down	Pages down.
F9	Retrieve	Retrieves previous ISDB command line command.
F10	Go to Menu Bar	Moves cursor to the menu bar. You can then tab to any menu item and press Enter to open that menu.
F11	Display Variable	Displays the current value of the variable to which the cursor is pointing.

continued

Table B.1 *Continued*

Key	Description	Use
F13	Run to	Program runs to the cursor position. Put your cursor where you want the program to halt and press F13.
F14	Program List	Lets you include programs that are called by the initial program. Once the program is included, you can add break points and/or step through code in the initial program and the called program.
F15	DSP Screen	Displays the last screen used for interactive programs.
F16	Repeat Find	Lets you specify find conditions in your source.
F17	Run	Runs until end or breakpoint.
F19	Left	Shifts screen left. On the command line, L or Left will also shift the screen to the left.
F20	Right	Shifts screen right, also R or right will also shift the screen to the right.
F21	System Cmd	Lets you issue system commands at the command line.
F22	Var-Hex	Displays variable in hexadecimal.
F23	Chg Var	Changes the current value of the variable pointed at, then when you continue, you can see the impact of that change.

Figure B.4 shows the source display modified to show all function key definitions.

Figure B.4
ISDB Source Display

```
Debug          Goto          Program          Options          Help
A300C1_BOK/INV017A:/0001        ISDB/400                    More:  +   >
000100     ***************************************************************
000200     *    Jefferson College      Professor Levinson    12/15/98
000300     *      APPLICATION NAME         - Inventory System
000400     *      PROGRAM NAME             - INV017A
000500     *
000600     * DESCRIPTION - Loads entire subfile
000700     *               Displays grand total of total costs
000701     *               Better cursor positioning
000800     ***************************************************************
000900     * L O G    O F    M O D I F I C A T I O N S
001000     *
001100     * DATE          PGMR        DESCRIPTION
001200     * ------------------------------------------------------------
001300     *   /  /
001400     ***************************************************************
001500     * F U N C T I O N    O F    I N D I C A T O R S
001600     *   IND        FUNCTION
001700     * ------------------------------------------------------------
ISDB ===>
F15=User screen      F16=Repeat find   F19=Left   F20=Right
F21=System command   F22=Hexadecimal   F24=More keys

F3=Exit      F5=Step    F6=Break    F11=Display variable
F12=Cancel   F17=Run                F23=Change variable    F24=More keys

F4=Go to current      F9=Retrieve        F10=Actions
F13=Run to location   F14=Program list   F24=More keys

F15=User screen      F16=Repeat find   F19=Left   F20=Right
F21=System command   F22=Hexadecimal   F24=More keys
```

Exercise B.1 Using ISDB

Purpose
To learn how to use ISDB

Instructions
1. Start ISDB on any one of your interactive programs by issuing the CL command UPDPROD(*YES).
2. Use F5 to step about ten sets of data through the program.
3. Point at a statement in your main processing loop and set a break point.
4. Point at a variable in the source code and press F11 to get its current value.
5. Point at the ISDB command line and press F1 for Help. Page down and point at the highlighted word Break and press Enter. (Words that are highlighted and underlined have more detailed Help.) Use F12 to return to the ISDB screen.
6. Run the program to the next break point.
7. Issue the ISDB command DSP *RPGIND to see the values of indicators.
8. Use F3 to quit the debugger.

Using Advanced Breakpoint Control
To set a conditional breakpoint, you will type a BREAK command on the ISDB command line. The format of the command you type is **BREAK stmt WHEN var condition value**. In this command, *stmt* is replaced with a statement number at which the break will occur, *var* is replaced by a variable name, *condition* is replaced with a relational operator such as = or *EQ (equal), < or *LT (less than), or *CT (contains). Thus, a conditional break statement that looked like this — BREAK 7200 WHEN CNTCDE='CAN' — would stop the program at 7200 each time that the field CNTCDE was equal to the value 'CAN'.

You also can set a breakpoint that would stop the program after the break statement was executed a specific number of times. Thus, the statement BREAK 7300 SKIP 50 would stop the program after statement 7300 had been executed 50 times.

Using Watch Variables
If there are some variables that you want to watch closely, make them Watch variables. They will be displayed at the top of the screen with their current values. Up to 15 variables can be "watched." To make a variable a Watch variable, you type WATCH followed by the variable name on the ISDB command line. For example, WATCH RRN causes ISDB to display the variable name RRN and its value at the top of the screen. WATCH *IN40 causes ISDB to display the variable name *IN40 and its value at the top of the screen.

If you no longer want to watch a variable, you can Unwatch it by issuing the ISDB command UNWATCH followed by the variable name — for example, UNWATCH RRN or UNWATCH *IN40.

Exercise B.2 Using ISDB with Watch Variables

Purpose
To learn how to use ISDB with Watch variables.

Directions
1. Start ISDB on any one of your interactive programs — UPDPROD(*YES).
2. Set WATCH on five variables.
3. Step through the code until one of the variables changes.
4. Set a conditional breakpoint and run the program until it breaks.
5. Set a step breakpoint and run the program until it breaks.
6. Remove one of the Watch variables with the Unwatch command.
7. End the session.

Using Pull-Down Menus
ISDB provides five pull-down menus for the following purposes:

- Debug — Used to control the debugging process, display breakpoints, clear breakpoints, and add additional programs to the trace process.
- GoTo — Used to locate positions in the code.
- Program — Used to offer the commands DSPOBJD (Display Object Description), DSPPGMT (Display a Program Text), DSPPGMREF (Display Program Reference), and WRKJOB (Work with Current Job).
- Option — Used to set display options and find text.
- Help — Provides Help for command and function keys in ISDB.

To pull down one of these menus, press F10, tab to the desired menu, and press Enter.

Using Indented Listings

The compiler can provide an "indented listing," which is especially valuable when you are searching for missing END statements or when you are attempting to make sense out of complicated nested code. The indented listing indents each level of nesting by two characters and puts a character of your choosing (usually a vertical line) in the first position to indicate the level of nesting of the code. As shown in Figure B.5, the VAR1 IFGT VAR2 is itself nested one level, and that operation controls the lines that follow, which are nested two levels. It is easy to follow the vertical bars down to the ENDIF operation and to see which operations are nested within the specific structure.

```
*...1....+....2....+....3....+....4....+....5....+....6
C           *IN90      DOWEQ *OFF
C           VAR1       | IFGT VAR2
C                      | | MOVEL'GREATER' VARR
C           VAR3       | | IFGT VAR6
C                      | | | MOVEL'GREATER' VARS
C                      | | ELSE
C                      | | | MOVEL'LESS/EQ' VARS
C                      | | ENDIF
C                      | ENDIF
C                      ENDDO
```

Figure B.5

Example of Indented Listing

To request an indented listing from the WRKMBRPDM (Work with Members in PDM) screen, select 14 (compile) but don't press Enter. Press F4 (Prompt) and then use F10 (Page down) to move to the indented listing entry and type a vertical line (|).

Tracking down errors is a challenging task. If you've written a piece of code, it is difficult to believe in and/or find the error in the code. It is often easier for others to find the errors in your code (and for you to find the errors in theirs). Therefore, it often saves time to have someone else help you find code errors.

Getting familiar with techniques and tools introduced in this appendix will prove beneficial to your career. Many graduates find that their first assignments involve program maintenance. They are often asked to track down errors in complex code. This is not the simplest job in the department — just one that often no one wants or has time for. With the debugging techniques described in this appendix, you can succeed with these tough assignments.

Appendix C

Using Screen Design Aid (SDA)

One of the tools many AS/400 shops use to create a simple display is Screen Design Aid (SDA). This appendix covers the following elements of screen design using SDA:

- Creating a simple display
- Testing the display
- Editing the display
- Creating a window
- Creating a subfile record
- Creating a subfile control record
- Testing the subfile

What Is SDA?

SDA is a powerful tool that IBM provides with the AS/400. It is a screen painter, a screen editor, and a screen tester. It reads and writes display-file members and submits the compiles of the screen files. (It is also a menu builder, a feature not covered in this text.) SDA offers an easy way to develop and test screens for use with RPG, Cobol, and CL.

Some organizations do not use SDA because it does not add modification marks to changes in the display files. When you delete or change a field in SDA, SDA deletes or changes the line but doesn't keep any note of the old value. Even if you're in an organization that doesn't encourage the use of SDA for modification of screen designs, however, you will still find SDA useful to view and test screens.

Creating a Simple Display

SDA can be used to create simple display formats, window formats, and subfile formats. This section will demonstrate how to create the simple screen format shown in Figure C.1.

```
A300C1              COMPUTERS ARE US INV SYS          09/21/98
                    WORK WITH INVENTORY LIST

   Locate Part Number:_____



   ================================================================
   * F3=Exit Subsystem
```

Figure C.1
Simple Input Screen

Type **STRSDA** (Start Screen Design Aid) to bring up the initial SDA screen (Figure C.2).

Figure C.2
Start SDA Screen

```
                        AS/400 Screen Design Aid (SDA)

Select one of the following:

       1. Design screens
       2. Design menus
       3. Test display files


Selection or command
===>

F1=Help    F3=Exit    F4=Prompt    F9=Retrieve   F12=Cancel
                                    (C) COPYRIGHT IBM CORP. 1981, 1995
```

To design screens, select option 1. SDA displays the Design Screens screen shown in Figure C.3. This display is used to specify the name of the display-file member, the source file, and the library in which the display-file member will be stored.

Figure C.3
Design Screens
Screen

```
                              Design Screens
Type choices, press Enter.

     Source file . . . . . . .   QDDSSRC      Name, F4 for list

        Library . . . . . . .    PHILSLIB     Name, *LIBL, *CURLIB

     Member  . . . . . . . . .   APPENDIXC1   Name, F4 for list




  F3=Exit      F4=Prompt      F12=Cancel
```

Fill in the name of the file in which you want the source member to be stored, the library where that file is located, and the name of the screen member. If the screen exists, it will be brought into SDA for editing. If it doesn't exist, you will be starting a new member. Either way, the next screen to appear is the Work with Display Records screen (shown in Figure C.4). If the DDS previously existed, the list would contain the record names and types.

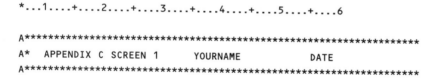

Figure C.4
Work with Display
Records Screen

```
                    Work with Display Records
     File . . . . . . . :    APPENDIXC          Member . . . . . . :   APPENDIXC1
        Library . . . . :    A300C1_BOK         Source type  . . . :   DSPF

     Type options, press Enter.
       1=Add                2=Edit comments        3=Copy              4=Delete
       7=Rename             8=Select keywords      12=Design image

     Opt   Order     Record          Type        Related Subfile    Date        DDS Error


        (No records in file)




                                                                         Bottom
        F3=Exit                   F12=Cancel       F14=File-level keywords
        F15=File-level comments   F17=Subset       F24=More keys
```

File-Level Comments

Before creating the format, we will create file-level comments with function key F15.
These comments will be placed in the member before the first record.

Press F15 and enter the following comments:

```
*...1....+....2....+....3....+....4....+....5....+....6


A**********************************************************************
A*   APPENDIX C SCREEN 1      YOURNAME            DATE
A**********************************************************************
```

The editor works much the same way SEU works. Press F3 to exit and save your
comments.

File-Level Keywords

File-level keywords can be added or modified by pressing function key F14. SDA will
put all file-level keywords before the first record. File-level keywords are in effect for
all formats in the display file. When you press F14, SDA displays the Select File Keywords screen shown in Figure C.5 (page 242). For this demonstration, we will add
the file-level keywords CF03(03) and Print.

To add or edit an indicator keyword, type **Y** beside Indicator keywords on the
Select File Keywords screen and press Enter. SDA will now display the Define Indicator Keywords screen shown in Figure C.6 (page 242).

Figure C.5
Select File
Keywords Screen

```
                           Select File Keywords

      Member . . . :   APPENDIXC1

      Type choices, press Enter.

        General keywords
        Indicator keywords. . . . . . . .   Y
        Print keywords. . . . . . . . . .   _
        Help keywords . . . . . . . . . .   _
        Display sizes . . . . . . . . . .   _
        Alternate keywords  . . . . . . .   _
        DBCS conversion . . . . . . . . .   _
        Window Borders  . . . . . . . . .   _
        Menu-bar keywords . . . . . . . .   _




        F3=Exit    F4=Display Selected Keywords    F12=Cancel
```

Figure C.6
Define Indicator
Keywords Screen
with Command
Function 03
Defined

```
                           Define Indicator Keywords

      Member . . . :   APPENDIXC1

      Type keywords and parameters, press Enter.
        Conditioned keywords:        CFnn CAnn CLEAR PAGEDOWN/ROLLUP PAGEUP/ROLLDOWN
                                     HOME HELP HLPRTN
        Unconditioned keywords:      INDTXT VLDCMDKEY

      Keyword    Indicators/+ Resp Text
      CF03       __ __ __     03   F3=Exit


                                                                      Bottom

      F3=Exit    F12=Cancel
```

As shown in Figure C.6, you fill out the definition for command function 03 (CF03). The keyword to be defined is entered into the keyword column. The three indicators columns hold the conditioning indicators. They appear to the right of the A-spec and control when a keyword is active. Because we want CF03 active all the time, we will leave these blank. The RESP indicator, the indicator that the keyword turns on, should be 03. Finally, we can provide comments such as F3=Exit. Use the Enter key to exit this screen and save the changes (F3 exits without saving the changes). SDA will take this data and create the file-level keyword CF03.

```
*...1....+....2....+....3....+....4....+....5....+....6

A                                                     CF03(03 'F3=Exit')
```

To add or edit a print keyword, type **Y** beside Print keywords on the File Keywords screen and press Enter. SDA will now display the Define Print Keywords screen (Figure C.7). The print keyword lets the user use the Print or PrtScr keys to print a screen to a spool file.

```
                        Define Print Keywords
   Member . . . :   APPENDIXC1

   Type choices, press Enter.
                                        Keyword
      Enable keyword . . . . . . . . .  PRINT    Y            Y=Yes
         Indicators . . . . . . . . . .

      Program handles print:
         Response indicator . . . . . .                       01-99
         Text . . . . . . . . . . . .

   System handles print:
      Print file . . . . . . . . . .                         Name, *PGM
         Library . . . . . . . . . . .                        Name,
                                                                *LIBL, *CURLIB
      Leave print file open until
         display file is closed . . . .  OPENPRT               Y=Yes


   F3=Exit    F12=Cancel
```

Figure C.7
Define Print
Keywords Screen
with Enable
Keyword
Selected

To add the file-level keyword Print, type **Y** in the Enable Keyword field and then
press Enter (not F3, which fails to record the change). Press F3 to exit the Select File
Keywords field and select 1 to save and exit the File Keywords screen.

Adding a Record

To add a record format to the display file, type a **1** in the options column of the
Work with Display Records screen. SDA displays the Add New Record screen
(Figure C.8).

```
                        Add New Record
   File . . . . . . :   APPENDIXC          Member . . . . . . :   APPENDIXC1
      Library . . . . :   A300C1_BOK        Source type . . . :   DSPF

   Type choices, press Enter.

      New record . . . . . . . . . . . . . . . . .  TESTREC1    Name

      Type . . . . . . . . . . . . . . . . . . . .  RECORD      RECORD, USRDFN
                                                                 SFL,     SFLMSG
                                                                 WINDOW, WDWSFL
                                                                 PULDWN, PDNSFL
                                                                 MNUBAR



   F3=Exit     F5=Refresh     F12=Cancel
```

Figure C.8
Add New Record
Screen

On the Add New Record screen, enter the name of the record format (remember that RPG III/400 is limited to eight-character record names). Notice that the second field on that screen is used to define the type of record entered. A simple screen such as the screen that we are developing is of type RECORD.

When you press Enter, you will see the blank screen where you will paint your record. To add the user ID, move to the position row 2, column 10. The cursor position is displayed in the lower left corner of the screen (row 2, column 10 would be shown as 02-10). Type ***USER** and press Enter. The *USER should be replaced with 10 Us to represent the user ID's 10-character length.

Move to the position row 2, column 28 (02-28) and type **COMPUTERS ARE US INV SYS** and press Enter. Then press F20, which highlights blocks of text. Notice that it breaks this string into four separate strings at the blank spaces. We will find it more practical to keep this string together. Had we included single quotes before and after the string, it would have been treated as a single block. (It's not too late. Just type a single quote before and after the string and press Enter. The entire length of the string is now highlighted, indicating that it's a single string.)

Move to the position row 2, column 56 (02-56) and type ***DATE,** which inserts the keyword and format for the system date. These fields aren't very well centered, but you can move fields left one character for each < you type before the field. To move fields to the right, type the number of > symbols that represent the number of characters you want to move the field.

Place the cursor beneath C in "Computers," and then move it one space to the left. Type **WORK WITH INVENTORY LIST** at 03-20. Move to 07-13 and type **Locate Part Number:**.

Move one space after the colon (:) and type **+I(11)** to define an input field 11 characters long. Alpha fields use I (Input), O (Output), and B (Both). Numeric fields use 3 for Input, 6 for Output, and 9 for Both. The system has named the field FLD01 and would name the next field FLD02. To give the field a more meaningful name, press F4 and type over FLD01 the new name **SELPN**.

We would like to do to more with SELPN, and there are two ways to get to the field-level keywords for this field. On the Work with Fields screen, type a **1** next to the field that you want to work with; from the screen painter, type an asterisk (*) immediately in front of the field that you want to work with and Select Field Keywords appears.

I suspect that you can work out the COLOR keyword for yourself.

The Define Database Reference screen (Figure C.9, page 245) will let you change the structural definition of SELPN to be just like field INPN. This ensures that subsequent changes in the physical-file structure will automatically be incorporated into the display-file structure with a recompile of the DSPF.

The original screen (Figure C.1) has a double line near the bottom, which has been created by typing a series of equals signs ('='). Remember to put single quotes around the line, as follows:

```
'======================================================================='
```

and below the line add the text **F3 = Exit Subsystem**.

To change the color of text, you treat it just like a field. An * just before the text will bring you to the screen where you can select colors.

```
                    Define Database Reference
 Field . . . . . :    SELPN              Usage . . :  I
 Length . . . . :    11                  Row . . . :  7    Column . . . :  35

 Type choices, press Enter.
                                   Keyword
    Reference field . . . . . . . .   REFFLD    Y          Y=Yes
    Reference current DDS source . .  *SRC                 Y=Yes
    Field (if different) . . . . . .            INPN       Name
    Database file . . . . . . . . .             INVPF      Name
      Library . . . . . . . . . . .             *libl      Name, *LIBL, *CURLIB
      Record . . . . . . . . . . . .                       Name
    Override existing field definition:
      New field length . . . . . . .                       +nnnn, -nnnn, nnnn
      New decimal positions . . . .                        +n, -n, nn
      New keyboard shift . . . . . .                       N A X W I D M
                                                             J O E G

    Ignore previously specified:
      Validity check . . . . . . . .  DLTCHK               Y=Yes
      Editing . . . . . . . . . . .   DLTEDT               Y=Yes

 F3=Exit    F12=Cancel
```

Figure C.9
Define Database Reference Screen

You can "cut and paste" data from the screen by marking a rectangular block with a hyphen at the beginning and end (upper left and lower right) and then putting an equals sign at the position to which you want the upper left corner of the block moved.

You can delete a rectangular block by marking the upper left and lower right with double hyphens.

F1 provides additional Help.

You can exit your design screen by pressing F3 and selecting 1 to save the design.

You can exit the Work with Display Records screen by pressing F3.

Check over the Create Display File screen; you will want to be sure it has identified the correct library in which to create the display file. The Library field is in the middle of the screen. The upper section of the display-file screen defines where the source member is to be stored. The middle and the bottom of the display-file screen control the creation of the display-file object, including the object name and library.

Exercise C.1 Using SDA to Create a Simple Screen

Purpose
To demonstrate using SDA to create a simple format, edit the format, and compile the display file.

Instructions
Create the display file SDAC1. It should have a single record that is similar to the simple screen shown in Figure C.1.

1. Create the input screen to locate part number using SDA as described in the previous sections of this appendix.

Testing Screen Designs

The display file must be successfully compiled before it can be tested. Press F3 to Exit as far as the initial SDA screen and select option 3, Test display files. SDA will assume that you want to test the most recently designed screen. Enter the Record name or Press F4 and select the record name to be tested and press Enter.

The testing process has the following three steps:

1. We can prepare values for fields and indicators that are output from the program to the screen. In our current record, no fields are Output or Both, and our only indicator, 03, is used as an output from the screen. Therefore, the first step is blank except for the text "No output fields for this record." Press Enter.
2. This step displays our record as it will appear to the user. With our file and record rules, we could

   - Press Enter.
   - Press F3.
   - Type a Part Number and press Enter.
   - Type a Part Number and press F3.

   Try any of these and you will see that after pressing Enter or F3, the test system will advance to step 3.
3. This step displays the results that would be returned to your program.

   You can then press Enter to wrap around and repeat the test. Try all four possibilities. How would the results be different if the F3 definition were CA03 instead of CF03?

   Exit the test with F3 and go back to the design phase. Use F14 to change indicator 03 from CF to CA and return and test out your assumption. Which options produce different results? How are they different?

Adding a Window

Return to the Work With Display Records screen by exiting the test environment and selecting 1 to go into the design environment. SDA will assume that you want to continue working with the same member that you were most recently editing. This time we want to add a new format, WINDOW1, the window shown in Figure C.10.

Figure C.10
WINDOW1
Window

```
    CHANGE Inventory Values

   Part Number: A124
   Description: COMPUTER PENT
   Quantity on Hand:    215
   Unit Cost:     2100.16
   Warehouse Stored In:  FTW
   Warehouse Location:   219

   F12 = Cancel
```

Also, unlike our window in Chapter 2, we would like to use the actual fields from the data file. This would simplify the RPG code because this window will display whatever record is current from the data file. If you change the data on the window, all your program would have to do is an UPDATE. This saves several MOVE operations, but it also means that we get to experiment with picking fields directly from the file and placing them in the window.

The following steps are used to create a window:

1. On the Work with Display Records screen, select 1 to add a new record format.
2. On the Add New Records screen, enter the record name, WINDOW1, of the type, WINDOW.
3. Select General Keywords.
4. Use a Y to choose the Select parameters entry immediately below the Window parameters line.
5. Change the value of the Actual Line so that the window begins on 4.
6. Change the value of the Actual Position (the Column) to 5.
7. Change the value of the Window Lines to 12.
8. Change the value of the Window Position (Number of Columns in the window) to 60.
9. Press Enter twice to return to Select Windows Keywords.
10. Select Record Keywords. Add CA12(12) as an indicator keyword.
11. Press Enter until you return to the Work With Display Records screen.

WINDOW1 now exists but is blank. Select 12 to design WINDOW1. The window border is displayed on the design screen. Type your text in the window. Remember to use single quotes before and after strings and recall that F20 will show you the text in reverse video.

Now we're ready to add the database fields to the screen.

Press F10 to Select Database Files. The screen shown in Figure C.11 will be displayed. This screen lets you make the fields of one or more databases available for your design. Option 2 will make all of the fields of the database available for use in your screen design. These fields will be Input only. Options 3 and 4 also make all of the fields available but with usage levels of Output and Both, respectively. Use option 4 to select all fields as Both.

Figure C.11
Select Database Files Screen

Press Enter twice to return to the design screen. Now the field names appear at the bottom of the screen with a reference number. For example, 1: INPN indicates that the field INPN will be treated as field number 1. Go to where you want a field to be positioned and type **&RefNum**. Notice that the remaining fields' reference numbers will be renumbered immediately. So, if you were to place the field INPN with the command&1, the field INDESC would then have the reference number of 1. Locate the rest of the fields. You can place one or more fields on the display at a time by entering **&RefNum** on the screen wherever you want to add the field(s).

The Unit Cost field would look good with the edit code of J. Place your cursor immediately in front of that field and type an asterisk (*). Select Editing Keywords and type a **J** for the edit code.

Put the edit code of J on the Quantity on Hand field.

Exercise C.2 Using SDA to Create a Window

Purpose
To use SDA to create a window and to use a field reference file.

Instructions
Modify display file SDAC1. Add a window record format, WINDOW1, as shown in Figure C.10.

1. Modify the input screen of the window format WINDOW1 as shown in Figure C.10.

Creating a Subfile Record and a Subfile Control Record Using SDA

To demonstrate the design and creation of a subfile record format and its control record, we will step through the creation of the subfile record and subfile control record shown in Figure C.12.

Figure C.12
Computers Are US
Inventory List Screen

```
USERID                    COMPUTERS ARE US INV SYS              12/18/98
                          WORK WITH INVENTORY LISTS


PART NUMBER  DESCRIPTION                   QNTY       COST      EXTENDED

A123         Computer x486                  21    1,301.15    27,324.15
A124         Computer Pent                 215    2,100.16   451,534.40
A125         Printer - Laser                81      974.21    78,911.01
A213         Printer - Ink Jet              15      457.15     6,857.25
A214         Printer - Dot Matrix           21      251.14     5,273.94
A215         Scanner - Hand                 15      127.19     1,907.85
A216         Scanner - Flat Bed              5      421.15     2,105.75
A319         CD-ROM                          6      115.96       695.76


========================================================================
F3=Exit Subsystem
```

To create a subfile record and subfile control record in SDA,

1. Select option 1 (create record) from the SDA Work with Display Records screen.
2. Enter the record name and the type SFL on the Add New Record screen (Figure C.13).

```
                         Add New Record

 File . . . . . . :   QDDSSRC              Member . . . . . . :   SDADEMO1
   Library . . . . :     A300C1_TMP        Source type . . . :    DSPF

 Type choices, press Enter.

   New record . . . . . . . . . . . . . . . SFL1          Name

   Type . . . . . . . . . . . . . . . . . . SFL           RECORD, USRDFN
                                                            SFL,    SFLMSG
                                                          WINDOW, WDWSFL
                                                          PULDWN, PDNSFL
                                                          MNUBAR




 F3=Exit     F5=Refresh     F12=Cancel
```

Figure C.13
Add New Record
Screen

SDA will redisplay the Add New Record screen with an additional line for the name of the subfile control record (Figure C.14).

```
                         Add New Record

 File . . . . . . :   QDDSSRC              Member . . . . . . :   SDADEMO1
   Library . . . . :     A300C1_TMP        Source type . . . :    DSPF

 Type choices, press Enter.

   New record . . . . . . . . . . . . . . . SFL1          Name

   Type . . . . . . . . . . . . . . . . . . SFL           RECORD, USRDFN
                                                            SFL,    SFLMSG
                                                          WINDOW, WDWSFL
                                                          PULDWN, PDNSFL

 . . . . .   SFLCTL1         Name

 MNUBAR
   Subfile control record . . . . .

 F3=Exit     F5=Refresh     F12=Cancel
```

Figure C.14
Second View of
Add New Record
Screen with
Subfile Control
Record

3. Enter the name of the control record.

SDA will display the Select Subfile Keywords screen (Figure C.15). At the moment we don't need these options.

Figure C.15
Select Subfile
Keywords Screen

```
                            Select Subfile Keywords

    Subfile record . . . . . . . :   SFL1

    Type choices, press Enter

                                           Y=Yes
        General keywords  . . . . . . . . _
        Indicator keywords  . . . . . . . _


    TEXT keyword . . . . . . . . . . . . _




    F3=Exit    F4=Display Selected Keywords
```

4. Press Enter to advance to the next screen.

SDA will display the Select Subfile Control Keywords screen (Figure C.16).

Figure C.16
Select Subfile
Control
Keywords
Screen

```
                        Select Subfile Control Keywords

    Subfile control record . . . . . . . . . :   SFLCTL1

    Type choices, press Enter.


General keywords . . . . . . . . . . _
    Subfile display layout  . . . . . _
    Subfile messages  . . . . . . . . _

    Select record keywords  . . . . . _

    TEXT keyword  . . . . . . . . . . _




F3=Exit    F4=Display Selected Keywords    F12=Cancel
```

5. Type **Y** in the field for General Keywords on the Select Subfile Control Keywords screen. SDA will display the Define General Keywords screen (Figure C.17).

```
                    Define General Keywords

Subfile control record . . . . . . . . . :   SFLCTL1

Type choices, press Enter.              Keyword
   Related subfile record . . . . . .   SFLCTL      SFL1_____   Name
   Subfile cursor relative record . . . SFLCSRRRN   _____  Name
   Subfile mode . . . . . . . . . . .   SFLMODE     _____  Name



Y=Yes        Indicators/+
   Display subfile records  . . . . . . SFLDSP      Y           50
   Display control record . . . . . . . SFLDSPCTL   Y           50
   Initialize subfile fields  . . . . . SFLINZ      _
   Delete subfile area  . . . . . . . . SFLDLT      _
   Clear subfile records  . . . . . . . SFLCLR      _           N50
   Indicate more records  . . . . . . . SFLEND      Y           90
      SFLEND parameter  . . . . . . . . *MORE       Y
      SFLEND parameter  . . . . . . . . *SCRBAR     _           *MORE ...
   Record not active  . . . . . . . . . SFLRNA      _
                                                                More...
   F3=Exit   F12=Cancel

                                        Keyword   CFnn/CAnn   Indicators/+
   Subfile initially truncated  . . . . SFLDROP
   Subfile initially folded . . . . . . SFLFOLD
   Use instead of Enter key  . . . . .  SFLENTER
```

Figure C.17
Define General
Keywords Screen

As shown in Figure C.17, the Define General Keywords screen can be used to add the SFLCSRRN, SFLMODE, SFLDSP, SFLDSPCTL, SFLCLR, SFLEND, SFLDROP, and SFLFOLD keywords, which were introduced in Chapters 1 through 6 of this text. Only a few of these keywords will be needed at this time.

6. Enter the field names and indicators as shown in Figure C.17.

   Exit the Define General Keywords screen, returning to the Select Subfile Control Keywords screen (Figure C.16).

7. Type a **Y** in the field for the Subfile display layout screen. SDA will display the Define Display Layout screen (Figure C.18).

```
                    Define Display Layout

Subfile control record . . . . . . . . . :   SFLCTL1

Type values, press Enter.

                                        Keyword   Number
   Records in subfile . . . . . . . . . SFLSIZ      8
      Program-to-system field  . . . . .

   Records per display  . . . . . . . . SFLPAG      8

   Spaces between records . . . . . . . SFLLIN    ____



   F3=Exit   F12=Cancel
```

Figure C.18
Define Display
Layout Screen

8. Enter the correct values for the SFLSIZ and SFLPAG fields as described in Chapter 3.
9. Exit by pressing F3 until you reach the Work with Display Records screen, Figure C.19.

Figure C.19
Work with Display Records Screen with SFL1 and SFLCTL1 Records

```
                        Work with Display Records

File . . . . . . :    QDDSSRC              Member . . . . . . :   SDADEMO1
  Library . . . . :    A300C1_TMP          Source type . . . :    DSPF

Type options, press Enter.
  1=Add              2=Edit comments          3=Copy          4=Delete
  7=Rename           8=Select keywords       12=Design image

Opt  Order   Record         Type        Related Subfile   Date          DDS Error

        10   SFL1           SFL                            10/13/98
        20   SFLCTL1        SFLCTL      SFL1               10/13/98




                                                                        Bottom
F3=Exit                        F12=Cancel        F14=File-level keywords
F15=File-level comments        F17=Subset        F24=More keys
Record SFL1 added to member SDADEMO1.                                        +
```

10. Use Option 12 to work with the record SFLCTL1. SDA will display the paint screen for the control record for editing, and it will also display the subfile record (currently blank) to make alignment of the heading columns easy.
11. Fill in the heading information for the control record as shown in Figure C.20.

Figure C.20
Adding Text, User ID, and Date to the Control Record

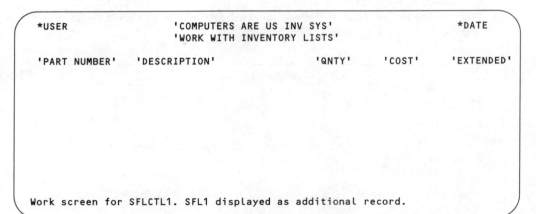

```
*USER                          'COMPUTERS ARE US INV SYS'                *DATE
                               'WORK WITH INVENTORY LISTS'

'PART NUMBER'  'DESCRIPTION'                        'QNTY'    'COST'    'EXTENDED'








Work screen for SFLCTL1. SFL1 displayed as additional record.
```

12. Press Enter to have SDA evaluate your entries and substitute the fields, such as user ID, for the *USER request.
13. Exit and save the changes to the record.
14. Select work with the record SFL1.

When you are working with the subfile record, SDA displays the headings on control record while you enter and edit the subfile record, which makes it easy to align the columns (Figure C.21).

```
 UUUUUUUUUU              COMPUTERS ARE US INV SYS              DD/DD/DD
                         WORK WITH INVENTORY LISTS


    PART NUMBER     DESCRIPTION               QNTY      COST      EXTENDED

      +O(11)         +O(25)                  +6(7 0)   +6(9 2)    +6(9 2)




 Work screen for SFL1. SFLCTL1 displayed as additional record.
```

Figure C.21
Work with the
Subfile Record
SFL1 Screen

15. Enter the Output field types and sizes as shown in Figure C.21 and press Enter. SDA evaluates your request, and because it's a subfile with eight records, shows the layout of the eight records as shown in Figure C.22.

```
 UUUUUUUUUU              COMPUTERS ARE US INV SYS              DD/DD/DD
                         WORK WITH INVENTORY LISTS

    PART NUMBER     DESCRIPTION               QNTY      COST      EXTENDED
    00000000000  00000000000000000000000000  6666666  666666666  666666666
    00000000000  00000000000000000000000000  6666666  666666666  666666666
    00000000000  00000000000000000000000000  6666666  666666666  666666666
    00000000000  00000000000000000000000000  6666666  666666666  666666666
    00000000000  00000000000000000000000000  6666666  666666666  666666666
    00000000000  00000000000000000000000000  6666666  666666666  666666666
    00000000000  00000000000000000000000000  6666666  666666666  666666666
    00000000000  00000000000000000000000000  6666666  666666666  666666666



 Work screen for SFL1. SFLCTL1 displayed as additional record.
```

Figure C.22
Work Screen for
SFL1 with Layout
for Eight Records

To adjust the alignment of subfile fields, use the < or > to the left or right of the fields. To adjust the alignment of the headings, you must exit the Work screen for the subfile record and work with the subfile control record. Then use < or > to adjust the headings to the left or right.

While in the Work with Subfile screen, you can rename the fields by pressing F4. You can change the edit codes, colors, and other features by typing an asterisk (*) immediately in front of the field to be changed.

Exercise C.3 Creating a Subfile Using SDA

Purpose
To demonstrate your capability to use SDA to create, edit, and test a subfile.

Instructions
Create the subfile shown in Figure C.12.

1. Follow the suggestions in the section on creating subfiles using SDA to create the subfile shown in Figure C.12.
2. Exit, save, and compile the display file. Enter the test mode and select to test the record SFLCTL1. Set indicator 50 on and indicator 90 off. Try the record with indicator 90 on. Try it with indicator 50 off.

Exiting, Compiling, and Saving the Design

Figure C.23 shows the Create Display File screen. Whenever you have made changes to the display, you will encounter the Save DDS — Create Display File screen as you exit the Work with Display Records screen.

The first section of this screen is used to determine whether and where the source is to be saved, as well as its name. The next section defines whether a display file is to be created, its name, and its library.

Figure C.23
Save DDS - Create
Display File Screen

```
                          Save DDS - Create Display File
       Type choices, press Enter.

             Save DDS source . . . . . . . . . . . .  Y          Y=Yes
               Source file . . . . . . . . . . . .    QDDSSRC     F4 for list
                 Library . . . . . . . . . . . . .    A300C1_TMP  Name, *LIBL
               Member . . . . . . . . . . . . . . .   SDADEMO1    F4 for list
               Text . . . . . . . . . . . . . . . .


             Create display file . . . . . . . . . .  Y          Y=Yes
               Prompt for parameters . . . . . . . .             Y=Yes
               Display file . . . . . . . . . . . .   SDADEMO1    F4 for list
                 Library . . . . . . . . . . . . .    RDTSRC      Name, *CURLIB
               Replace existing file . . . . . . . .             Y=Yes

             Submit create job in batch . . . . . .   Y          Y=Yes

             Specify additional
               save or create options . . . . . . .             Y=Yes

       F3=Exit   F4=Prompt   F12=Cancel
       Member SDADEMO1 already exists. Press Enter to replace.
```

Index

New Books in the Duke Press Library

BUILDING AS/400 CLIENT/SERVER APPLICATIONS
Put ODBC and Client Access APIs to Work
By Mike Otey

Mike Otey gives you the why, what, and how-to of AS/400 client/server computing, which matches the strengths of the AS/400 with the PC GUIs that users want. This book's clear and easy-to-understand style guides you through all the important aspects of AS/400 client/server applications. Mike covers APPC and TCP/IP communications, as well as the underlying architectures for each of the major AS/400 client/server APIs. CD with complete source code for several working applications included. 505 pages.

CONTROL LANGUAGE PROGRAMMING FOR THE AS/400, SECOND EDITION
By Bryan Meyers and Dan Riehl, NEWS/400 technical editors

This comprehensive CL programming textbook offers students up-to-the-minute knowledge of the skills they will need in today's MIS environment. Chapters progress methodically from CL basics to more complex processes and concepts, guiding students toward a professional grasp of CL programming techniques and style. In this second edition, the authors have updated the text to include discussion of the Integrated Language Environment (ILE) and the fundamental changes ILE introduces to the AS/400's execution model. 522 pages.

DATA WAREHOUSING AND THE AS/400
By Scott Steinacher

Data warehouses are designed specifically to support decision-making by giving you timely access to critical, relevant data. In this book, Scott Steinacher takes an in-depth look at data-warehousing components, concepts, and terminology. After laying this foundation, Scott presents a compelling case for implementing a data warehouse on the AS/400. Included on an accompanying CD are demos of AS/400 data-warehousing software from several independent software vendors. 342 pages.

DEVELOPING YOUR AS/400 INTERNET STRATEGY
By Alan Arnold

This book addresses the issues unique to deploying your AS/400 on the Internet. It includes procedures for configuring AS/400 TCP/IP and information about which client and server technologies the AS/400 supports natively. This enterprise-class tutorial evaluates the AS/400 as an Internet server and teaches you how to design, program, and manage your Web home page. 248 pages.

IMPLEMENTING AS/400 SECURITY, THIRD EDITION
By Wayne Madden and Carol Woodbury

Concise and practical, this third edition of *Implementing AS/400 Security* not only brings together in one place the fundamental AS/400 security tools and experience-based recommendations that you need, but also includes specifics on the latest security enhancements available in OS/400 V4R1 and V4R2. In addition, you will find updated chapters that cover security system values; user profiles; database security; output queue and spooled file security; using OS/400 security APIs; network security; thwarting hackers; and auditing, as well as completely new chapters that include discussions about Internet security and business contingency planning. 424 pages.

INSIDE THE AS/400, SECOND EDITION
Featuring the AS/400e series
By Frank G. Soltis

Learn from the architect of the AS/400 about the new generation of AS/400e systems and servers, and about the latest system features and capabilities introduced in Version 4 of OS/400. Dr. Frank Soltis demystifies the system, shedding light on how it came to be, how it can do the things it does, and what its future may hold. 402 pages.

1001 SECRETS FOR WINDOWS NT REGISTRY
By Tim Daniels

Without expert guidance, meddling with the registry can be disastrous. But for the accomplished user, *1001 Secrets for Windows NT Registry* is the definitive reference for system customization and optimization. Organized into sections that cover networking, applications, system management, hardware, and performance, the book also has an exhaustive index to help you quickly find the registry information you need. The accompanying CD is packed with innovative registry monitoring and performance utilities, plus an Internet link to our Registry Secrets home page (www.registrysecrets.com) for registry updates and many interactive services for registry "spelunkers." 321 pages.

THE ADMINISTRATOR'S GUIDE TO MICROSOFT SQL SERVER 6.5
By Kevin Cox and William Jones

This book guides database managers and administrators into a thorough understanding of the client/server aspects of the SQL Server 6.5 product, and includes many useful tips for managing security, troubleshooting, and improving performance. 469 pages.

INTERNET SECURITY WITH WINDOWS NT
By Mark Joseph Edwards

Security expert and *Windows NT Magazine* news editor Mark Edwards provides the quintessential guide to Internet and intranet security from the Windows NT platform. This comprehensive book covers network security basics as well as IIS and MPS, and includes specific advice about selecting NT tools and security devices. The accompanying CD-ROM includes security-related utilities, tools, and software packages. These tools, combined with the tips and techniques in the book, are powerful weapons in your security efforts. 520 pages.

THE MICROSOFT OUTLOOK E-MAIL AND FAX GUIDE
By Sue Mosher
Here's a book for Microsoft Outlook 97 end users and the administrators who support them. This easy to read volume will expand your knowledge of Outlook's e-mail functions and explain the real world tasks that you are likely to encounter. Sue Mosher explains the setup of individual e-mail services and components, e-mail options and when you might want to use them, and many time-saving techniques that take you beyond the basics. Users at all levels will learn from this comprehensive introduction to Microsoft's next generation of messaging software. 500 pages

RAPID REVIEW STUDY GUIDES
Series Editor: Mike Pastore
You know that becoming a Microsoft Certified Systems Engineer can be lucrative. Still, seeking the certification isn't a goal for the faint of heart. Our *Rapid Review Study Guides* give you pre- and post-assessments to measure your progress, exam preparation tips, an overview of exam material, vocabulary drills, hands-on activities, and sample quiz questions on CD and in the book. Current titles include

WINDOWS 95
WINDOWS NT 4.0 WORKSTATION
NETWORKING ESSENTIALS

TCP/IP FOR MICROSOFT WINDOWS NT 4.0
SYSTEM MANAGEMENT SERVER 1.2

Also Published by Duke Press

DATABASE DESIGN AND PROGRAMMING FOR DB2/400
By Paul Conte
This textbook is the most complete guide to DB2/400 design and programming available anywhere. The author shows you everything you need to know about physical and logical file DDS, SQL/400, and RPG IV and COBOL/400 database programming. Clear explanations illustrated by a wealth of examples demonstrate efficient database programming and error handling with both DDS and SQL/400. Each programming chapter includes a specific list of "Coding Suggestions" that will help you write faster and more maintainable code. In addition, the author provides an extensive section on practical database design for DB2/400. 772 pages.

AN INTRODUCTION TO AS/400 SYSTEM OPERATIONS
By Patrice Gapen and Heidi Rothenbuehler
Here's the textbook that covers what you need to know to become a successful AS/400 system operator. System operators typically help users resolve problems, manage printed reports, and perform regularly scheduled procedures. *Introduction to AS/400 System Operations* covers a broad range of topics, including system architecture; DB2/400 and Query; user interface and Operational Assistant; managing jobs and printed reports; backup and restore; system configuration and networks; performance; security; and Client Access (PC Support). 233 pages.

PROGRAMMING IN RPG IV, REVISED EDITION
By Judy Yaeger, Ph.D., a NEWS/400 technical editor
This textbook provides a strong foundation in the essentials of business programming, featuring the newest version of the RPG language: RPG IV. Focusing on real-world problems and down-to-earth solutions using the latest techniques and features of RPG, this book provides everything you need to know to write a well-designed RPG IV program, including information about subprocedures and using the RPG ILE source debugger. Each chapter includes examples as well as a section of thought-provoking questions, exercises, and programming assignments. Four appendices and a glossary support the topics presented throughout the book. An instructor's kit is available. 435 pages.

SUBFILE TECHNIQUE FOR RPG/400 PROGRAMMERS, SECOND EDITION
By Jonathan Yergin, CDP, and Wayne Madden
Here's the code you need for a complete library of shell subfile programs: RPG/400 code, DDS, CL, and sample data files. There's even an example for programming windows. You even get some "whiz bang" techniques that add punch to your applications. This book explains the code in simple, straightforward style and tells you when each technique should be used for best results. 326 pages, 3.5" PC diskette included.

FOR A COMPLETE CATALOG OR TO PLACE AN ORDER, CONTACT

Duke Press
Duke Communications International
221 E. 29th Street • Loveland, CO 80538-2727
(800) 621-1544 • (970) 663-4700 • Fax: (970) 203-2756

OR SHOP OUR WEB SITE: **www.dukepress.com**

We Want Your Response

Mail it

Fax it

Web It

Complete this form to join our network of computer professionals

We will gladly send you a free copy of

- ❏ *Windows NT Magazine*
- ❏ *Selling NT Solutions* magazine
- ❏ *NEWS/400* magazine
- ❏ *Controller Magazine*

Publisher of practical, hands-on technical books for Windows NT and AS/400 computer professionals. Providing help not hype.

Name _____

Title _____ Phone _____

Company _____

Address _____

City/State/Zip _____

E-mail _____

Where did you purchase this book?

❏ Trade show ❏ Computer store ❏ Internet ❏ Card deck ❏ Bookstore

❏ Magazine ❏ Direct mail catalog or brochure

What new applications do you expect to use during the next year?

_____

_____

How many times this month will you visit one of Duke Communication's Web sites (Duke Press, NEWS/400, Windows NT Magazine, Selling NT Solutions, Controller Magazine)? _____

Please share your reaction to *Essentials of Subfile Programming* _____

_____

_____

_____

❏ YES! You have my permission to quote my comments in your publications.
(initials) _____

[98SCXBOOK]

COPY THIS PAGE AND MAIL TO:
DUKE PRESS • 221 EAST 29TH STREET • LOVELAND, CO 80538
OR FAX TO (970) 667-2321
OR RESPOND VIA OUR WEB SITE AT www.dukepress.com